Help!
I'm a Parent!

Help!
I'm a Parent!

A collection of tips and information on being an affective parent in today's world.

JAN KNIGHT

iUniverse, Inc.
Bloomington

Help! I'm a Parent!
A collection of tips and information on being an affective parent in today's world.

iUniverse books may be ordered through booksellers or by contacting:

iUniverse
1663 Liberty Drive
Bloomington, IN 47403
www.iuniverse.com
1-800-Authors (1-800-288-4677)

ISBN: 978-1-4620-5739-9 (sc)
ISBN: 978-1-4620-5740-5 (ebk)

Printed in the United States of America

iUniverse rev. date: 10/13/2011

INTRODUCTION

When the owner of a local radio station asked me to be the hostess on a program and answer teens' questions, I told him that teens *think* they know all the answers, but their parents might need some practical advice. So we launched a program with the title *Parenting Teens*, and then I wrote the scripts and gave advice for several years until the owner was forced to move the station to a location too far from my home.

At that time, the editor/owner of the oldest newspaper in North Mississippi asked me if I would write an advice column for parents in his paper. I kept the same title and have been a columnist for that paper for over fifteen years.

During those years, I have had many requests for a book with a collection of my columns from parents and grandparents for their children, grandchildren, grown children, and for their friends. I had to retire from full-time counseling in order to have the time to organize a book. When I began reviewing in order to assemble this book, I found that I have enough material for several more books, but that will come later.

I pray that as you read this, you will find a chapter that will hold an answer to a problem you are facing, or that you will be able to use something in it to help a parent who is having some difficulty with a child or a marriage or other situation in their lives.

Jan Knight

DEDICATION

This book is dedicated to

My husband who has been a good example of a father
My best friend, Nancy, who kept encouraging me to get it done
My son, whose life experiences gave me so much "fodder" to use
Bill Bailey, who got me on at the paper and who has always encouraged me
My Lord, who was the reason I have completed this book
My readers, who have asked for this book for years now.

ABOUT THE AUTHOR

Jan is a product of the public school system, having attended school in Memphis, Tennessee, and Horn Lake High School in DeSoto County, Mississippi. Her formal education was received at Northwest Mississippi Community College, University of Memphis and University of Mississippi. She holds an undergraduate degree in English and a Masters in Counseling with additional college hours past the Masters level. She is a National Certified Counselor and a National Board Certified School Counselor. She has forty-two years in the field of Education; over twenty-four of which were spent as a secondary school counselor. For several years, she wrote the scripts and hosted a local weekly radio program. Additionally, she has written articles for professional publications; written Sunday School literature; conducted seminars and been the featured speaker on numerous programs on parenting, youth, and on educational topics. She authors a weekly column for the local paper DeSoto Times Today called "Help! I'm a Parent!" which has been running for over fifteen years. Jan has chaired or been a member of several committees for DeSoto County Schools and others including DeSoto County Extension Department, the Governor's Educational Advisory Council, and Desoto County Schools Crisis Management Board. She has also held officer positions in various professional educational organizations. She is the recipient of numerous community service awards and has received recognition for work within the educational and counseling fields. She is currently enjoying retirement but continues to be involved in education by chairing the Horn Lake High School Alumni Association Scholarship Committee. Through the publication of this book, she hopes to pass on some of the knowledge and insights she has gained from close to a half century of education, research, and working with children.

CONTENTS

FOREWORD

JAN KNIGHT'S BOOK, *Help! I'm a Parent!* comes straight from the trenches. She has been a teacher, guidance counselor, and parent. The wisdom she has gained along the way is indeed helpful for parents who face a mind-boggling array of contradictory messages about how to parent. Parents today are often confused, and children lose when that happens.

Knight's selection of columns that she wrote for a newspaper in DeSoto County, Mississippi, will leave no one confused. Her ideas about successful parenting are clear and on target. The reader gets a straight-shooting dose of common sense advice and practical solutions. High-sounding psycho-babble is not included. To truly love your child, you must be the parent, not a friend, as Jan makes clear in her writings.

She is a passionate advocate for the child, who, she believes, deserves to have a parent who can discipline in love and who can encourage when the child has given up on himself. She gives parents permission to take control in their homes and empowers them to be involved in their children's lives. Her advice addresses the world in which chaos and turmoil are the norm in many homes. She teaches firm consistent, loving, responsible parenting.

Reading one column, you might think: "Okay, she's convinced me that violent movies are bad for my children, but how do I stop their viewing of them?" At the end of the column, Knight answers that question in no uncertain terms, "Take control of the remote, of what movies are rented, of anything that could damage your child's mind".

This is the kind of specific, direct advice that makes this book so compelling. In a column on parental denial, she writes that "according to many parents . . . , the child must be in trouble because of something the teacher did, or the principal did, or another student did". She points out how damaging this approach can be. Then she poses the question: "Do I have a solution?" The question is rhetorical. She answers, "Yes. Don't be in Parent Denial: Don't make excuses for your child. Don't deny that he just might be guilty or to blame for what has occurred. Don't allow him to sass you or refuse to do his chores . . . . Don't buy him everything he wants or make material things too important in your family. In other words, be a responsible parent who sees the faults of your child clearly, and who wants your child to have consequences for his actions. Only then will he grow into a responsible adult who will also be a good parent someday."

She doesn't blink. At last, we have a book that speaks in no uncertain terms about the tough, but rewarding job of parenting.

The columns reprinted in the book cover a wide range of topics, including, but not limited to the following:

ADHD Meds, bullying, domestic abuse, drugging parents, abusive parents, out-of-control kids, children with bad attitudes, not letting TV 'parent' your children, not demanding *entitlement* for your kids, keeping promises, encouraging determination and persistence, setting a good example, making rules, establishing self-esteem, teaching kids to get up after being knocked down, dealing with bratty behavior, not allowing kids to argue with you, teaching kids to reach for their dreams, teaching responsibility through chores, and being a good dad.

Jan's practical, no-nonsense advice is a lifeline to parents drowning in mixed messages about how to parent their own children. She is an astute observer of parents' and children's behavior, and couples this with current research studies and other information in books and news articles. It's a winning combination.

As a parent, you may have felt at times that children should come with a how-to book. Now you have one: "Help! I'm a Parent!"

Bill Bailey is past editor and publisher of the DeSoto Times newspaper in Hernando, MS.

CHAPTER ONE

HELP! I MAY BE A PARENT FAILURE!

A TERRIBLE TIME TO BE A CHILD

MEMPHIS, TENNESSEE, WAS touting its latest crime statistics on TV: murders were down; robberies were down; homicides were down—it all sounded so much better than what was usually heard every night of every week. Then a reporter covered an incident outside a school: a car parked at the curb was investigated, and not only were ingredients to make meth found there, but also there was evidence that three batches of the drug had been made recently inside the car. In addition, a five-year-old little girl was found in the back seat. She had to be sent to a facility to be decontaminated before she could be taken to the Child Services Department to be put with a family and other children.

Then two other sad facts were mentioned by the reporter: that more and more children were having to be taken from their parents because of meth manufacturing and that domestic violence was on the rise. In other words, the crimes that affect children the most were becoming more of a problem than those that most affect adults. The innocent ones, the ones who have no choice, are being put in danger principally by their own parents.

When I was a counselor, this type of crime was so difficult for me to handle. One girl came in and was so angry. Her father and brother were making meth in the bathtub of their home. Not only were she and her mother breathing the volatile, damaging odors, but she was denied the tub to take a bath and she was afraid that the ingredients would explode and her entire family would be killed. What a terrible thing to do to a young lady who just wanted to graduate from school and go on with her life.

All areas of the country are seeing little children being led away or carried away from a home or a motel room or a car where they have been exposed to this danger, and the parents, who always look pitiful because of what the drug has done to them, seem oblivious to what they have done to their precious little ones.

The departments in all cities and counties which try to protect children from what their parents do to them, including child abuse, are having difficulty finding enough places to house them because the need is rising so rapidly. For many crimes the parents commit, the children cannot go back into the danger and so must be housed for longer periods. However, it is never just housing that is needed. When children are removed from their parents, they are traumatized because their security, even if it is

2

dangerous for them, is taken away. They also don't understand that their own parents would allow them to be in a situation that could kill them, cause them harm that could lead to death, or want to do something that causes them to be the least important thing in the life of the parent—the drug is the most important.

This also is true of parents who deal in street drugs. There is always the possibility of the home being invaded, of the parent being killed, of the house being sprayed with bullets, and so on. For a parent to put his or her children in that kind of danger shows a totally selfish mindset and probably an addiction that should be addressed for the sake of the children as well as that of the parent. Not only that, but if the child sees drug trafficking going on in the home, he accepts that as normal; he sees the money; and he usually goes into that same life of crime when he is able. Is that what his parents wanted for him?

Domestic abuse is another reason children can be in danger because it not only damages the other person, but it damages the life of the child who observes it. A boy child, by the age of six, will accept that type of lifestyle and will become an abuser of his spouse. The girl child begins to accept that the wife should be made to feel inferior and possibly beaten when the man chooses and will seek out a partner who follows that pattern. Is that what both of these parents or partners wanted for their children?

Children are not only in danger because of what the parents do physically, but also because of what the children are seeing. Their minds are photographing everything—the good, the horrific, the sad.

Parents have an obligation to protect their children and to be good examples of what adults should be. If they are not, then they deserve to lose their children and let someone else raise them.

ADHD MEDS—RIGHT FOR YOUR CHILD?

"**H**IS MATH HOMEWORK is two days late. It's in his backpack which was left on the bus again. It feels like everyone is giving up on him. I need a way to help him, but all I have is tears". (Laura, Kyle's mom)

The above is the beginning of an ad for Concerta which has been prescribed for Attention Deficit Hyperactive Disorder for around nine years and has appeared in many major publications. This column will discuss the use of meds for children—the good and the bad.

First, the above comment by the mother could have been mine when my son was about seven or eight years old, and the teacher had decided that he might be at least HD (hyperactive) and maybe even AD (attention deficit) as well. What I learned with my own and with a young relative is that some very bright children do have a tendency to be impulsive as well as forgetful because they haven't learned to control the speed with which their brains function, so they appear ADHD. They also become bored quickly and, because they can learn quickly, they see no logic in doing busy work which is what they consider homework to be, especially if they understood the concept the first time without the practice. We found homework in the backpack, in his desk, in his locker, under his bed—everywhere but turned in to the teacher where it belonged, yet he made straight A's and knew the material. To combat the situation, we simply required him to do the homework because the teacher had told him to do it and a failure to do it showed a lack of respect and direct disobedience. He later finished college with a Master's degree in Botany with very little effort.

On the other hand, I have worked with kids whose brains simply could not slow down enough to read, to spell, to do math or even to carry on a logical conversation. I have sat with boys who, as they talked, were so jittery that I had to touch them to calm them down. I have seen the frustration, not only of the child but also of the parent who didn't know what else to do. I have even recommended medication if all other avenues have been exhausted. However, let me say again—*only after all the other avenues have been exhausted.*

Finally, the ad I found for Concerta in FAMILY FUN MAGAZINE and another for prescription Vynase downright scary: "Concerta should not be taken by patients who have: allergies to methyphenidate or other ingredients in it (how would a parent know this?), have significant anxiety, tension or agitation (most children do at one time or another), esophagus, stomach, or intestinal narrowing (how would a parent already know this unless a problem had presented itself?) . . . Abuse of methylphenidate may lead to dependence (isn't that an encouraging thought?)" It goes on to say that the parent should tell the doctor if the child has had heart problems or defects or high blood pressure or there are family members with such, or if they have shown signs of depression, abnormal thoughts or visions (few children or teens tell their parents if they have these), bipolar disorder or seizures. Then the other scary part: "Contact (the doctor) immediately if you or your child (you?) develops abnormal thinking or hallucinations, abnormal or extreme moods and/or excessive activity, (or if) aggressive behavior or hostility worsens." The doctor may "interrupt Concerta treatment if the child is not growing or gaining weight as expected."

Now, the parents I know who are giving their children an ADHD med have done their homework. One mother has requested a change in meds twice, once because there was no appreciable change in the child's ability to concentrate and she was failing the grade. The other time was because the child had stopped eating and was too listless.

Bottom line: If your child does appear unable to concentrate; his grades are far below his ability; he has excessive inability to control his impulses; he is way too easily angered and unable to control violent outbursts; and he is overly frustrated with his inability to learn, then do several things before you see a doctor. First, have him tested for IQ ability—don't expect more than he can actually do. Second, look up diets that control his intake of carbohydrates, supplements, processed foods, and more. He should be eating fresh foods as much as possible, avoiding chips, sodas, processed meats, etc. Third, coach him on impulse control, focusing, work ethic, and respect for others. Fourth, if all else fails, take him to a doctor with documentation to explain why you think he may be a candidate for meds. Then be vigilant for any side effects.

Finally, don't allow any person (even a teacher) to diagnose your child without excessive documentation and don't hasten to give him a pill to "fix" the problem. DO everything else before this final step—do what's best for your individual child.

BULLIES: SOCIAL MISFITS IN SOCIETY

I WAS DELIGHTED TO find new information on bullying in the book
HEAR OUR CRY: BOYS IN CRISIS by Paul D. Slocumb, Ed.D.
(Aha! Process, Inc. Rev. ed., 2007).

"Where does the bully learn to be a bully? The first and most influential
teacher is the family." That is a profound statement and one we must all
face who have had children who have bullied others. Let's look at common
traits of bullies and then at the families which perpetuate a bully.

Bullies have common characteristics that lead to their bullying behavior:

1. They have a need to dominate others. In later life, they will be
   "controlling", whether it is their families or the people who work
   for them who have to be controlled. The bully has to be the one
   who "calls the shots" and those who do not comply with their
   demands will have to be bullied.

2. They are devoid of true empathy; in other words, their main concern
   is for themselves and their needs, and they are not concerned
   about the needs of others, and even as adults, they cannot seem to
   recognize the needs of their own family members. As children they
   do not care that they hurt others' feelings; in fact, they often gloat
   over the fact that they were able to get someone else to cry or to be
   left out of an activity or the crowd at the lunch table.

3. They are disgustingly narcissistic. In other words, they think
   they can be the only ones who are right, worthy, or funny, etc.
   They cannot see anything beyond their immediate needs and the
   attaining of personal satisfaction no matter who gets in the way or
   gets hurt.

4. They do not see their victims as people—only as prey who can be
   insulted, threatened, belittled, or physically hurt. Their inability
   to see or care what they do to others will ultimately make them
   dangerous as adults because of their sociopathic nature.

5. They never take responsibility for their actions, but always
   blame someone else—even the victim for being in their way, for
   being different, for being smarter—any irrational reason they
   can make up.

6. They are "attention seeking" (also a trait of narcissists). They are the ones who "stand out" in the room and even seem larger than they are. If they do not get the attention one way, they will find a way to get it in another.

What kind of family could create such a repugnant person? Principally, it is the family that has no rules—no boundaries. Whatever the child/bully wants, he gets. The family is quick to take up for him, to blame other children for what he does, to defend his actions with school administration or the police, to refuse to make him pay consequences for his behavior, to even believe that he is anything but a wonderful child. They allow him to decide when he will go to bed, what he will eat and when, and even whether he will go to school or not. Their family life is usually full of chaos and manipulation and the children are not sure whether they are actually loved or just tolerated.

How do parents help their children avoid being victims of bullies? First, teach him to be his own person, and this lesson can begin in the early years. Bullies collect followers who will do their bidding at any time. Children who do not follow may be ridiculed at times, but at least they will not be a part of bullying. In high school, bullies are more or less ignored and are seen for what they are. Often they become one of the most unpopular persons on campus while the kid who thinks and acts independently and decidedly is respected.

Secondly, teach your child the lessons in this column—what a bully is, what his home life is probably like, what to do to avoid one.

Thirdly, teach him to be *comfortable in his own skin* and to avoid trying too hard to be accepted. Don't allow him to make lower grades, to act differently, to change his personality or his appearance just to be accepted by a bully. The strength he will gain by being true to himself will be an asset in high school and in college and in the work world.

Fourth, make sure your home is a sanctuary. Allow him to talk about what happens at school without running to his rescue all of the time. Help him think of ways to handle conflicts and relationships rather than just playing the blame game. Let him know that he has value and worth and will be able to use his abilities sooner than later.

Bullies are social misfits. Do not allow your child to be one or to be the victim of one.

BULLYING—HANDLED AT SCHOOL AND AT HOME

I AM SO PLEASED that most states in our country have passed policies and procedures to handle one of the scourges of school campuses—bullying. I was fortunate to work in a school where all I had to do was to take a child to the office to report a bullying incident, and it was handled immediately and efficiently. The principal even went further than telling the bully that he had better not do it again—he told him (or often her) that if any of his buddies bullied the victim, he would have to answer for it. It worked.

There are many parents who are making plans to home school their children rather than send them to a middle school where bullying often reaches its peak. Rather than have their child made to feel inferior by other students, the parents will keep them away from mistreatment by peers.

However, I have seen too much bullying in the high school setting as well—among the girls as well as the boys. Granted, it is more prevalent among the immature ninth and tenth graders who haven't grown up enough to leave other people alone, but it is there, and it is sometimes carried over from the middle school.

Let me explain the bully. He appears to have it together and seems very sure of himself. However, it is from low self-esteem that the meanness presents itself and if he can put another person down and have others agree with him, then he thinks it elevates him in the eyes of his "followers." The truth is his followers are there because they know that if they are not with him, then he will pick on them or put them down too. Their purpose is self-preservation—another sure sign of immaturity on their part as well.

One day on the *Dr. Phil* show, he was interviewing an adult lady who had been bullied in school. Even in the present she is hurt by the memory of what was said to her, especially the repeated phrase, "You're too ugly to live." In actuality, she was a very attractive woman who had, in her young adulthood, been a model. However, the pain she still felt was evident as Dr. Phil talked to her. She was home schooling her daughters rather than send them to school to possibly receive the type of abuse she had endured.

Dr. Phil had contacted the "main bully" and asked her if she remembered bullying this individual. She barely remembered the person, let alone the incidents of bullying, and she apologized for the pain she had caused.

There are two truths apparent in this situation: the first is that bullying really is painful and can cause personal conflict even into adulthood. The second is the bully is too often so self-absorbed that he doesn't know the hurt he is causing and it goes right out of his mind when he goes on with his life.

Does a bully become a spouse-abuser or a child-abuser? I have not seen any research that might bring me to that conclusion, but I doubt if he is a kind spouse or parent because he is unaffected by the way he can hurt other people.

Dr. Phil said that bullying victims who allow what is being said to affect them so severely have several traits:

1. Their self-worth is low already;
2. They believe the toxic message that is being said to or about them;
3. They are not willing to test what is being said against what is real;
4. They are unwilling to generate a reality that is true.

Then he gave the reality-test questions: 1. Is it true? (He asked the victim on his show, "Are you too ugly to live?" She responded, with tears, "No I'm not!"); 2. Does what is being said help me? Does it prolong my life? 4. Does it give me self-worth?

Parents, you must be open to what is being said to your child at school (or at church, or wherever). If you determine that your child is being bullied, tell him to go to the counselor or to the teacher and let him/her know. Tell him to give specifics about what is being said or done to make him feel threatened. A principal cannot do anything to protect your child if he is unaware of the problem. Let your child handle the situation rather than running to the school yourself. Your child must learn to work through situations on his own.

Then, when the two of you are together, ask him some of the questions in the test above. If he really is short, tell him that height doesn't make him a good or bad person, and that he has talents and gifts the bully can't even see. Give him something he can take with him that will make him strong enough to hear the abusive words but refuse to believe or internalize them. Tell him that the bully has problems of his own that he can't handle and that is the reason why he picks on other people.

It will take these new policies and the school officials and you as parents to lessen bullying. At least it is a beginning.

BULLYING IS A SERIOUS ISSUE AND CAN HAVE SERIOUS CONSEQUENCES

BECAUSE IT HAS been proven that several teen suicides in our nation were attributable to bullying at school, there is, again, a renewed interest in this most disgusting of school-age activates. In fact, there is now a program in Austin, Texas, called TALK TO ME which addresses this situation for all grades.

Even Dr. Phil used most of a program to talk to parents whose teenagers killed themselves after being bullied for a length of time in school. I copied down some thoughts he presented.

First, he gave some indications we should look for that a child is being bullied: withdrawal from events that he has taken part in before, finding ways to stay home, acting shameful even when there is not a reason, showing fear when he has not shown it before. Also, if you see bruises that seemingly have no cause and that he doesn't want to discuss, and if you keep noticing his personal items coming home damaged or if some of them are missing entirely and he doesn't know what happened to them, you need to investigate and to try to get him to tell you what is going on.

Another indication includes diminished social contacts, even from friends he at one time enjoyed, and, last but not least, depression. I have written many times about depression and its symptoms, but here are a few you can readily see. In boys, depression often presents as anger, in girls it presents as crying. Look for a change in eating and sleeping habits, in disinterest in things that were once of interest and in a sad, lonely countenance and possibly a lack of personal hygiene.

Dr. Phil says, and I agree, that if some of these indications appear and your child replies that "Nothing is wrong" when you ask him about it, then you have an obligation to investigate. Look for notes he has written or that have been written to him. Find messages on his phone or on his computer to see if there are bullying tactics being used on him there. The notes he will have written will let you know if he has decided that he has become hopeless in an effort to stop the abuse and wishes that he could end it all or *go away* from it all. Get help for him immediately if you find anything to indicate this hopelessness to keep him from possible suicide.

If you can't find out what is going on in this way, find some of his former friends and ask if they have seen some changes in him and why. If they have become part of the bullying, they will probably be hesitant to talk about it, but eventually you may find one who is concerned about his former friend and will help you. If this proves useless, go to the school. In one part of the *Dr. Phil Show*, it became evident that one of the principals of a school was being held accountable for not stopping the bullying after he was made aware of it and the child hanged himself. Often, if the counselor is good, she will take an active role in monitoring the situation and in being an advocate for your child. She can also roll play with your child and help him to become better equipped to handle himself socially and stop the abuse himself.

I have talked to few people who have not been bullied in some way during their years in school: from being put in a garbage can by older, bigger boys, to having their pants pulled down in the restroom, to being "shouldered" in the halls, to being followed in the halls and discussed by several bullies. Bullies never act alone—they have a need for an audience made up of cowards who are afraid that if they don't go along, they will be bullied. So the one being bullied feels that the whole school is against him and that he is bereft of friends.

The good news is that I have taught in schools in which the administration does not tolerate bullying of any kind and will put a quick end to it once it is proved. Another good remedy is that some states have now made it illegal to bully another student. Pictures of students who now have a record because it was proven that they had bullied were flashed on TV. Some of them had been convicted of stalking, of violation of civil rights and a few of statutory rape. If your state has no law against stalking, it may be that you need to ask your Legislators to include various types of bullying in new legislation, including electronic bullying as on Face Book, on cell phones, and other means.

One person on the *Dr. Phil Show* suggested that bullying was a parental problem.—that if parents would teach their children how to treat others with dignity and respect, bullying would not be such a nasty part of the school scene. I agree.

CHILDREN OF ABUSIVE PARENTS
DOOMED TO REPEAT?

O NE WEEK I watched two movies in which parental abuse played a part in the plot. The first movie was based on a true story in which a son finds out that his mother was his dad's mistress when he and his sister were born. However, the psychological damage was caused by his dad's refusal to acknowledge the son that was born by his actual wife while they were married and his ultimate abandonment of both of them. The son was also disgusted with his parents' obsession with material things and their constant fighting over money and the company they had formed. All of that chaos and the chaos in his mind eventually drove him to leave home for good.

In the second movie, the mother is a spoiled alcoholic who goes into rages during which she screams, beats the kids and even leaves them for days. The oldest daughter, as an adult, is afraid of a relationship and especially of having children because she is worried that she will treat her future children as she was treated.

In real life I know of a mother who was verbally critical and disparaging of her daughter who then did become a screamer and often a verbally abusive parent.

Are those who were abused or bitterly disappointed by their parents doomed to be that kind of parent? Only if they haven't taken care of some very serious psychological issues they probably have. The young man in the first movie was told by many other people as he traveled to Alaska that he must learn to love something other than nature and freedom. They told him that people, including his errant parents, were worthy of being loved, and that his refusal to give of himself to others would keep him from being truly happy.

The daughter in the second movie had to face memories of the abuse and her feelings of inadequacy and self-doubt. Ultimately, as good movies do, it ended with the mother asking for her forgiveness and her not only forgiving her but also looking forward to having a wedding and possibly children in the future.

However, in real-life situations, too often the victims of parental abuse do not recognize that they may eventually perpetuate what was done to them. They don't realize that the suppressed memories could come flooding back and cause unwanted, damaging reactions to innocent children and even to a spouse.

One of the wisest sayings I heard from more than one teenager in my years as a counselor was "I have watched my parents, so I know how *not* to be one." Excellent advice which could work well, but only if the person pays constant attention to his or her reactions in dealing with children.

The other alternative is a good therapist who could help the victim work through the anger and disappointment and the self-worth issues.

The adult victim of abuse experiences anger because she realizes that other children had relatively normal, loving parents and close families. She agonizes over the wasted years and deals with profound disappointment. If she does not seek help, she becomes bitter in the ensuing years, and the results could not only be abuse of those she loves the most but also a depression that she doesn't understand and doesn't know how to handle.

The self-worth issues are there because she is not sure what she did or didn't do to bring on the abuse or how she could have been different so the parent would not been *forced* to punish her. Unless she can come to the conclusion herself that she did not cause the abuse, she may need a counselor in order to realize that the abuse was a character or psychological flaw in the parent—not in the abused child. She may also have to ask some questions about the childhood the parent had—*that* may hold a clue.

No parent wants to willingly hurt or psychologically damage a child born to them, but issues in life and in childhood can cause a person to do things they wouldn't ordinarily do.

No matter what your age or whether you have no children or several, if you were ever abused as a child either verbally or physically, or abandoned, or denied a normal childhood, do not wait to seek help in handling the issues that may still plague you.

CORRECTING NEGATIVE ATTITUDES/BUILDING POSITIVE ATTITUDES

T HE GRANDFATHER WAS quite frustrated, I could tell: "His problem is not ability—he has plenty of that, and he comes from a good, stable home. His problem is his rotten attitude". A father told me, "I need to straighten out his attitude or we are going to really clash soon". The principal of the school told the parents, "He has such a poor attitude that he won't even try to stay out of trouble or do what the teacher asks of him."

Attitude: It can either be a severe handicap to reaching success in any endeavor or it can be the reason a person with nominal abilities reaches heights he ordinarily couldn't reach.

Here are some negative attitudes you may be seeing in someone in your family:

1. The *"You can't tell me what to do"* attitude: This attitude can be found in young children as well as in adults and all in between. It is one of the most difficult to correct because the person appears to have a perpetual *chip on his shoulder*, and anything you say seems to make it worse. Along with this attitude is the appearance of arrogance and a know-it-all persona that makes this person unlikable and unpopular—sometimes with his own parents.

2. The *"I can't"* attitude: This one can be corrected in children, but it is difficult to handle in an older teen or adult. Some kids seem to be born with this attitude and refuse to try new things or to challenge themselves in many ways. They appear to be afraid of failing, so they just don't try. This is particularly frustrating in a subject that the child or teen decides is *too hard* (like math or English grammar), so they give up at the least bit of frustration in working a problem or completing a homework assignment.

3. The *"Nobody likes me (I'm going to eat worms)"* attitude: This one is often born at school where there has been rejection and hurt. Then, the harder the person tries to make friends, the more he is pushed away and hurt over again. A parent's first reaction is to become defensive and to lash out at the other kids. This only compounds the situation since the other kids will turn their backs on the *mother's kid* and the hurt child feels even more hopeless and forlorn.

14

Now let's look at some of the solutions to the above attitudes:

1. The *"You can't tell me what to do"* attitude has to be nipped at the first indication. Children, because of their age and maturity, cannot be allowed to tell their parents that they will not do what has been required. Even the cute little *"No"* that we hear from our toddlers should be corrected early. If a parent allows the child to refuse to do something, and you don't correct the attitude, you will then or later have a surely, disobedient teenager on your hands. If that happens, you will spend time at school trying to straighten out the trouble he is in for refusing to do what a teacher or an administrator has told him to do. If he *cops* that same attitude toward the law, you won't be able to afford the bail to get him out of jail.

    The solution is never to allow it to begin. Correct it early and often. Don't let the child get away with refusing to do what is asked of him even when he is a growing teen and trying to *spread his wings*.

2. The *"I can't" attitude* is corrected by the parent when it first begins. We told our son that those words were not allowed in our home, so he would have to find a way to do *whatever* rather than take the easy way out by saying he couldn't. I heard a dad tell his son to remember the handicapped gentleman who had spoken at their church service and to forget saying "I can't" when he didn't have a good reason.

    When it comes to schoolwork, it is true that many of us are better at one type of subject than others. However, unless one side of the brain has been damaged, all of us are capable of doing math as well as English as well as science. It may take more effort for one child to do math than another, but he may be stronger in science; therefore, don't let him say he can't do one subject or another. Require him to do his best in all of them.

3. Most of us have had the *"Nobody likes me"* attitude at one time or another.

    The parent lifts that attitude by reminding the child of his positive qualities and of the friends he has at church or in his sport or any other place where he is active. Remind him too that he must be true to who he is and not try to please everyone else (impossible anyway). The self-esteem you will perpetuate will make your child able to face the other many times in life when he feels that he is alone and friendless.

One's attitude can truly be a handicap in life or it can be one of the greatest assets he has. Parents owe it to their children to help them develop good, positive attitudes.

DRUG DANGERS IN THE MEDICINE CABINET

WHILE I WAS in Destin, Florida, on vacation one summer, I read an article in the *Northwest Florida Daily News* entitled "Add the Medicine Cabinet to Drug Dangers for Teens". It began with the story of the mother of a 16-year-old soccer player who had died as the result of taking 20 Coricidin pills to get high. It was only the second time she had experimented with drugs according to her friends. Her mother was speaking about her death in the hope that she could prevent another teen from doing the same thing resulting in another parent's anguish.

I also found it sad that the hospital staff and her family kept asking her friends if she had done anything that might have caused her to be so sick and they said nothing. Finally, after the girl had lapsed into a coma, one of her friends asked a nurse if taking Coricidin could have caused the incident. By then her liver was destroyed and she never regained consciousness. If the girl had just admitted what she had taken or if her friend had said something sooner, her life could have been saved.

"Partnership for a Drug-Free America" research shows that as many as one in five teens say they have taken a prescription drug without having a prescription for it, and as many as one in ten has done so in the past year. That includes everything from amphetamines commonly prescribed for attention-deficit-disorder, such as Ritalin and Adderall, to painkillers like Vicodin and OxyContin."

In Orange County, California, a commissioned report found an alarming number of deaths among teens from overdosing on over-the-counter and prescription drugs from 2005 to 2007. During that time period, forty-two people from the ages of twelve to twenty-five had died from that type of overdose. We must not think that this is a problem just in Florida and in California. It is happening all over the nation.

Several years ago, a student brought his friend into the principal's office at my school. The friend was disoriented, incoherent, had slurred speech, and could not stay awake. We called his dad and told him that we were having him transported to the hospital. He had taken a large number of Coricidin pills for the high, and the hospital told us that we probably saved his life by sending him when we did. At the funeral of the girl in the story above, the family had left the casket open so that the other teens could see how the drugs had caused her to swell from 125 pounds to 170, trying desperately to make an impression on them that death and bodily destruction can be caused by seemingly harmless medicines that can be bought anywhere.

"One roadblock in combating over-the-counter and prescription drug abuse is that many parents do not see it is a problem, and kids and parents alike do not realize these drugs can be as dangerous as their illegal counterparts." (*Northwest Florida Daily News*) So, now that you have read this, what is a solution?

First, you should inventory your medicine cabinet and remove any medicines that could be a potential danger to your children. If you or a family member becomes ill, go to the drug store at that time and buy what you need, but do not keep a cabinet full of OTC's (Over-the Counter drugs) that could give your child an opportunity to experiment with something that could do irreparable harm.

Second, become educated and knowledgeable about the dangers of over-the-counter and prescription drugs. Do not let your lack of awareness become a problem for your child.

Third, talk to your child about the danger of experimenting with anything that could cause harm to his brain, his body, his life. One of the ads that has been running for a long time now says that one of the best deterrents for youth is "a parent". Research shows that they actually do listen to you even if they act disinterested, bored, or even hostile. At least you love him enough to make the attempt to reach him—that effort and concern is not lost on him. Your talking to him could mean the difference between his trying to get high from drugs or not—it is worth the effort.

HANDLING THE OUT-OF-CONTROL CHILD

Is YOUR CHILD out of control? I used to ask that of the parents of teenagers; however, there are so many elementary and pre-adolescent children who are causing havoc at home and in the schools and communities, that it is a fair question of parents of all-age-kids.

A lot of the problem in many homes has to do with a struggle for power—and too often the parent is losing, which means everyone loses. Parents may let children get away with too much because they threaten: to run away, to do harm to themselves, to embarrass the parent. The child may deliberately become truant and/or allow his grades to suffer because he knows that education is important to you. He may try to manipulate you by saying, "You never let me do anything!" or "You don't love me or you would let me . . . ." or they may curse and whine and complain or use threatening body language.

If he is allowed to *bully* you in this way, he is in control of the situation and that will lead to a devastating end. Some of the struggle for power may occur because of the friends he is seeing who are in control of their homes and, consequently, have no curfew, no parental rules, no constraints on their behavior. Your child sees this activity as *freedom*, and pushes against you and what you have taught up to this time.

He may be *trying his wings*, which is a normal part of growing up. However, there is never a time when he should be allowed to be rude, disrespectful or threatening in any way during this time of attempting to achieve maturity.

There are some things that parents do wrong in handling a control situation: lecturing or preaching (the child, if he has the upper hand, will either ignore you or say "Whatever" and refuse to acknowledge your efforts), nagging, and going on and on (he will simply *tune you out;* after all, he's heard all of this before), name calling or labeling (there is never a reason to belittle your child or to call him names that will stay with him into perpetuity), asking "What is wrong with you?" (if he knew, he would try to do better unless he is trying to gain power over you), ignoring or withdrawing favor (he is still your child—don't ever forget that), using the worn-out phrase, "When I was your age . . ." (they don't think you were ever young or their age).

So, if all these things are all the wrong things to do and say, what are some methods of regaining control of your child and of your home?

First, never discipline when you are mad. Leave the room or go into the yard and cool down before you say or do anything you may regret later.

Second, if you are married to his other parent, always maintain a *united front*. He must never think he can *play* you against each other and get his way.

Third, (this is a hard one) never take what he is doing or saying personally. It is not always *YOU*. He may be trying to see where his parameters are and how far he can go before you *haul him back in*. Don't disappoint him. There must be a limit on his freedom because he is still immature and will make juvenile decisions. Let him know where his choices end and yours take over.

Fourth, make sure he knows what the consequences are if he goes beyond the limits you have set. He breaks curfew? Set it earlier the next time. He needs money (again)? Give less each time until he has exhausted his resource. He talks back? Take the phone or car away. He fails a class? Take everything away until mid-term or until he brings the grade up. He will only try once to break your rules if you are consistent and fair and firm. He must know, for his sake, that you love him enough to require good behavior, respect, good faith in all he does, and more mature decisions as he grows older.

Finally, give him the opportunity to help make better decisions. After he has been disciplined and his behavior has improved, ask him if he has figured out why he acted as he did earlier. Allow him to analyze his own behavior and to tell you why it won't happen again. As he matures, he should have a better idea of how to act more like a growing, more sensible person. Give him that chance. If he can't seem to improve, then his maturation process is not happening and he will eventually have to "pay" for his mistakes.

HEALTHY FOOD/CONFIDENT CHILDREN

I HAD THE OPPORTUNITY to observe the results of poor eating habits in children and realized how much this problem needs to be addressed (as if every magazine on the stands hasn't covered it already). While in Florida on vacation, I watched the dynamics between four pre-adolescent boys in the swimming pool. Two of them were thin (about average for their age), active, busy—just being boys and playing hard. The other two were heavier, but there was a distinction: one was active, confident, and popular with the two smaller boys; the other was way over the weight he should have been, was awkward in the water as well as on the side, looked uncomfortable all the time, and had very little confidence in himself. Even his feet were fat; his walk was a shuffle; and his eyes were little slits since his face was so fat.

I took notice because the first three had isolated the obese one and were being sarcastic and generally unkind to him. They would often do the same things together, but he was always on the outside looking in and was very unhappy though he tried very hard not to show it. One time his mother came in the pool with him as moral support (always a bad idea), and the other boys totally ignored him after that. Another time when he went to his mother's table, she pulled his bathing suit up and kissed him (a doubly bad idea in front of other pre-adolescent boys).

It should be a type of child neglect to allow a child to get so obese that he (or she) has to suffer socially, psychologically and even spiritually (whom do you blame if you don't take responsibility for your own choices? "God made me this way"?)

Paradoxically, I talked to a parent whose child refuses to eat anything except fries, mac and cheese, sandwiches (sometimes), chips, and other non-food groups (and not very much of that). The dad was worried that he should eat something before he takes his ADD med. When I told him that research I did while in college showed that processed foods (all of the ones he would eat) contributed to ADD and to ADHD, he was astonished and even more concerned than he was before.

I know a parent whose son began to show symptoms of extreme Autism when he was almost two years old. An older doctor asked her to try something before they put him on a drug—to change his diet to all non-processed, all-natural foods. She began to see a change in behavior

21

when she found more ways to fix foods that were good for him including cookies that contained fruit and vegetables, natural milk, and other food that would improve rather than worsen his condition. Incidentally, that same method is being implemented with more frequency today with positive results on this condition.

The bottom line is that the way you prepare your child's meals and what you prepare can make all the difference in his body size, his ability to learn, his self-control, his self-esteem, his self-confidence—just about all aspects of his life. The first way to do that is to serve vegetables, and if your child has not grown up with these important foods, you may have to train him to eat them (chips taste better because of the salt and all the other "junk" in them). Fruit should be a part of your child's diet, and summer is the best time to buy and provide them. Meat can be served sparingly and with as little ground beef as possible (way too many processes, hormones, fats, etc.). Chicken is better but not if you have to fry it to make the child eat it. Bread should be a treat rather than a necessity at every meal, and never white bread—only whole grain. Farmers' Markets are going to continue to be a big thing and you will not have to look far to find locally-grown produce to prepare. Never cooked except from a can? You can find anything on the internet. If your mom cooked her veggies with bacon grease, there are supplements that give the same flavor but no fat content.

If you will try to cook and serve this way and maybe let your child help pick out the food and/or even help prepare it, you may discover a different, more agreeable, more self-assured child when school begins next year. There will also be a more confident cook in the kitchen who will benefit by being healthier, slimmer, and proud of her efforts to do what is best for her children.

HORROR MOVIES, ACTION MOVIES, REALITY TV

I HAVE OFTEN WONDERED what effect violent movies have on children and teens. I do know that violent horror movies have caused lasting and debilitating phobias (the paralyzing fear of clowns as the result of watching *It,* the fear of spiders, of birds, of loud noises, of masks, etc.). I also know of an intelligent young man who became suicidal after years of watching horror movies and had to go into treatment for more than a year. Teens have brought up the movie *Carrie* in relation to the over-use of blood and how sickening it was to watch it.

There is also new evidence relating to action movies. Michael Gurian, who wrote *A Fine Young Man: What Parents, Mentors and Educators Can Do to Shape Adolescent Boys* (Tarcher Putman, 1999) says "images create an imprint on the brain of both adults and adolescents. The difference is the degree to which the brain has to be bombarded in order to be brainwashed. If a boy (whose brain is still developing) is exposed to sex, violence, and degrading social interactions, he has a new and distorted sense of what reality is".

"In action films, images move faster than the brain can process them", so the brain becomes over-stimulated and the result can be a chemical reaction that can cause an addiction to that type of stimulation. The rapid pace of the action films produces fixated-eye movements that in turn result in a visual consciousness, putting the mind into a state of relaxation that leaves it off guard." Gurian also says that our society, especially the youth, have become addicted to that type of stimulant if they watch action movies often which then can lead to depression, mental disorders (as schizophrenia and bi-polarism) and brain disorders like ADD and ADHD. It can also lead to violence. Many of the mass killers of recent years have been *hyped up* on violent video games and violent, bloody movies as they made plans and prepared to take the lives of as many people as they could.

Action movies also require no thought—just emotion, and often that emotion is aggravated by violent acts. Too many kids today watch movies that are rated R for violence and then the parents are amazed that they behave badly and get in trouble at school. What the parent needs to ask is "What were the last movies you watched? How many people were killed? How many women were abused? What did you think about what you were watching?" (making the foolish assumption that they were thinking).

Another concern relating to this steady diet of violent movie viewing is the devaluation of the human life. Too many lives are being taken, even those of tiny children, and because of that, kids and young adults today are not concerned with the taking of life or of the pain they cause the families and friends of those they kill or injure.

Gurian also weighs in on reality TV: "The popularity of reality television and shows sometimes described as 'train wreck TV' is one more indicator of a society that is fixated on stretching things to their outer limits. Adolescents are receiving messages daily about how to manipulate people and events in order to win. Messages about relationships are being communicated in a sick, disreputable way. The more popular shows rely on people's fascination with name calling, back-stabbing, hostility, exclusion, and attacking another person's weak spots.

On the other hand, we have stopped asking our kids questions, have stopped monitoring what they are watching, have stopped seeming to care what they are learning about life from the viewpoint of Hollywood. What we must face, then, is that we will continue to see a more violent society as these who have been continually fed violence become adults. We will continue to see more and more learning disabilities from over-stimulated brains. We will become more alienated from our kids who find our distaste for the blood and gore of movies and the bickering and yelling on reality shows silly and unacceptable.

Take control of the remote, of what movies are rented, of anything that you find damaging to the mind of your child. As the parent it is up to you to protect your child from the dangers presented by this type of media.

HOW TO RAISE A DELINQUENT

THE FOLLOWING LIST was prepared by the police department of Houston, Texas, and run by Ann Landers in 1959. I found it reprinted in April 1997. I find that the rules are timeless and that parents of all generations should pay heed to them. Included are some personal comments of mine.

Twelve Rules for Raising Delinquent Children

1. "Begin in infancy to give the child everything he wants. In this way, he will grow up to believe the world owes him a living." In addition, run to the school or the police station and refuse to believe that he could possibly be guilty, so he will grow up to believe that he can do no wrong and will never have to pay for anything he does to other people.

2. "When he picks up bad words, laugh at him. This will make him think he is cute. It will also encourage him to pick up 'cuter' phrases that will blow off the top of your head later." Also, allow him to call you names, his siblings names, and God names. He will grow up not knowing how to respect anyone in his life.

3. "Never give him any spiritual training. Wait till he is 21, and let him 'decide for himself'." I once heard that very few prisoners had ever been take to church by their parents. What can you lose by taking them? You can certainly gain a lot.

4. "Avoid use of the word 'wrong'. It may develop a guilt complex. This will condition him to believe, later, when he is arrested for stealing a car, that society is against him and he is being persecuted." Also avoid the word "NO"; he may get his feelings hurt and then may never learn that his rights end where another's begins.

5. "Pick up everything he leaves lying around—books, shoes, and clothing. Do everything for him so he will be experienced in throwing all responsibility onto others." Yes, well said.

6. "Let him read any printed matter he can get his hands on. Be careful that the silverware and drinking glasses are sterilized, but let his mind feast on garbage." This includes some internet content, movies, TV, and music.
7. "Quarrel frequently in the presence of your child. In this way, he will not be too shocked when the home is broken up later." This way you will insure that he will always be insecure, distrustful of others, unable to pick a suitable mate, and unhappy forever.
8. "Give a child all the spending money he wants. Never let him earn his way. Why should he have things as tough as you had them?" Then when he is unable to have all the things he wants, he will move back in with you and let you take care of him for the rest of his life. He will also be unhappy in marriage because he will be unable to sacrifice for the happiness of others, including your future grandchildren.
9. "Satisfy his every craving for food, drink, and comfort. See that every sensual desire is gratified. Denial may lead to harmful frustration." Then when he cannot find that perfect job, or wife, or house, or car, he can blame you.
10. "Take his part against neighbors, teachers and policemen. They are all prejudiced against your child." Make a special point to make the situation a racial, gender, or ethnic issue so he can learn to hide behind those excuses when he is older.
11. "When he gets into real trouble, apologize for yourself by saying, 'I never could do anything with him'." Teachers and police officers *love* to hear that from parents—it leaves the parenting up to them where it does not belong!
12. "Prepare for a life of grief. You will be apt to have it." You will also deserve it if you have not had the courage and fortitude to be a good parent.

It is never too late to begin to be a firm, consistent, loving parent, and loving your child means that you are not at all guilty of what this listing has described. Make the decision now to avoid raising a delinquent and both you and your child will be happy in life.

KIDS WHO DREAD GOING HOME

S HE WAS A new counselor, so she hadn't figured it out yet. "Why are we seeing so many more children now?" she asked. (It was two weeks before Thanksgiving.) "Because it is just before the Holidays", she was told. "What does that mean?" "It means that most of the kids you are seeing, and the ones who need to come in and won't, dread being at home for any extended length of time. There is so much chaos and anger and turmoil where they live that they would rather be here at school where at least the classes are quiet; an adult acts as if she cares whether he exists or not; and he is responsible for just himself".

Does your child dread being at home during the Holidays or a Break? Is he like the girl who said, "We never know what it is going to be like at my house. He could be drunk or sober, raving or asleep, sarcastic or complimentary. We dread going home every day."

Is your child like the one who came to school wondering where he was going to live the next day? His parents were losing the house (dad didn't pay the house note because he can't seem to find a job he likes, so he keeps quitting, and finally the bills piled up so much that he couldn't pay them anymore). They will probably move from their comfortable, large, new home to an apartment. Thank goodness the family is going to rent where the two kids can remain in the schools where they have attended most of their lives.

Maybe your child is like the boy who says that there is so much screaming and name calling between his mother and step-father that he would rather be anywhere than there. He spends many nights at his friends' houses—whenever they will take him in. However, there have been nights when he has spent the night on a bench in the park. At least it is peaceful there after the other people have gone home.

Or maybe your child dreads coming home because his clothes always smell like "weed" since there is so much pot being smoked there. He usually eats a sandwich or cereal for supper because no one cares whether anyone eats or not—they are too mellow.

Sometimes kids wonder which parent will be there when they come home from school. It may be the mother this time who slams the door after an argument and speeds off in the car. Often it is the dad who grabs his coat and keys and says something like, "Fine, then, you see if you can pay the house bills by yourself!" as he angrily leaves the house.

What all of these examples (actual cases) illustrate is that too many times it is the child who is the most negatively affected by the actions of the parents. Parents get so wrapped up in their addictions, their anger, their pettiness, their selfishness that they forget (or they don't care) that there are children standing there who learn to hate coming home.

Home should be a safe place—a haven from the cruel world, a place of belonging and love. Instead, for too many children, it is the very opposite, and those kids find refuge in the school building. There, they are with people who are not screaming at each other or at him; they are used to the normality of the bells that dismiss them from class and let them know when they must be in the next one; they find food already cooked in the cafeteria and they won't have to cook it themselves if they want to eat. Often they find a teacher or counselor who is willing to listen to them without criticism or sarcasm and who will encourage them to do their best despite their problems at home.

In fact, we try to help them see that education is a key to get out of the chaos at home. We teach them to separate their lives into two parts so that they can try to forget home and concentrate on what is being taught in the classroom. We help them see that their futures *can* be different from where they have to live at present—they *can* break the chain of a home that is not a good place to be.

Parents, you may never know, because they may not tell you, how much they dread coming home. What you must do is to make your home a safe, pleasant, caring place where they find comfort, peace, and love. Don't deny that for your child. Make some changes today if they are needed. You owe it to your child and to yourself.

LOVING YOUR CHILDREN TO DEATH

H E WAS A seventeen-year-old boy on the Dr. Phil Show—clean cut, nice looking, but with a haunted look in his eyes. He had been an addict for several years, had lied and stolen from his parents, and had no plans for the future. When Dr. Phil asked his mother if she still loved her son, her answer was "I love him to death". Later, as the psychologist probed the parents and the son, he found that the parents had given in to the son so often that they had actually contributed to his drug problem. Then Dr. Phil said something that has stayed with me since that program, "I hope someday that you won't have to be reminded that you 'loved your child to death'". He then asked if they all were willing for the son to be put into treatment, and all three of them agreed.

Are you "loving your children to death"? Do you give in when they beg? Are you allowing them too much freedom after school or at night without adult supervision, thus letting them make decisions that could jeopardize their safety?

Why are young people standing on the street becoming targets for drive-by shootings in major cities? Why aren't they at home doing homework or completing their chores? During dinner why aren't they sitting around the family table eating and discussing their day and any problems they had at school or work? At night why aren't they with their families rather than with friends or gang members getting into some kind of adult trouble? Sometimes parents love their children *to death* by allowing them to do what they want rather than what the parent wants them to do or thinks is best for them.

Then there are the parents who are so over-protective that they don't allow their children to experience life at all. I experienced this with a parent who hovered over her son at the pool and didn't let him experience the water even though he had on a life jacket. Later, when the kids were swinging on a rope swing, she was the only parent hovering close by in case he fell. How is this child going to learn to handle life on his own if he never has the opportunity to experience different aspects of it? If she keeps sending him the message that he can't *do life* without her, he will be sadly dependent on her for far too long. (This is one of the reasons some men never make good husbands, because they are too attached to their mothers who were *hoverers*).

29

Some parents love their children so much that they can't find it in themselves to discipline. They ignore the bad behavior; they speak weakly to the child, showing an unwillingness to be "tough" in a way that will cause the child to obey; they tell themselves that they will handle it when they get home then forget (but the child remembers and realizes once again that he has gotten away with something). They are poor parents because they are weaker than their own children. One English lady who talked to me about this problem said that when her mother got enough of something she was doing, she was made to *scrub the steps*. Do you have a chore that has become the discipline when your child pushes or defies you? I used to tell parents that their child could mow the grass even in the winter rather than act defiant toward or disobey the parent.

I realize that too many parents don't love their children enough. They are too busy having fun, living as if they were still single and not responsible for their children. However, sometimes parents err on the side of so much "love" that they damage their children. I put "love" in quotation marks because I use it carefully. "Loving a child to death" is actually a selfish issue—a desire to be loved by the child rather than loving him enough to help mold him and nurture him. We call it "love", but if we are hurting our children by loving them, then it cannot actually be love. Parents must be so unselfish that we are consistently looking out for the welfare of our children even if it means we must tell them "NO", if we must stay home because we had to "ground" our child because of his behavior, if we get counseling for them even if the neighbors find out, if we tell them they cannot have another cookie before supper.

Yes, it takes fortitude and insight to be a parent, and no, we are not given instructions when they get here. What we do have, if we are normal, is an automatic love for the child that looks beyond our selfish needs and looks at the precious life we have brought into the world—even if we are looking at him when he is fifteen and he has a surly look on his face.

We must love them, but not "love them to death"—there is a profound difference.

MOMMYISMS YOU MAY RECOGNIZE

I REMEMBERED SOME *MOMMYISMS* I used or experienced and wondered if a few of them will be familiar to you. They have what the mother was actually thinking after them:

"Get off that couch and get outside!
  I didn't birth you to be a mindless couch potato.
  I'm tired of moving your feet in order to vacuum.
  Your mind will become mush if you watch too much TV."

"Go to your room!!
  I have to count to 2,575 before I talk to you.
  I need time to think about what you've done and lower my
  blood pressure.
  On second thought, you have too many toys in there. Go
  the laundry room!"

"Don't scream unless you are bleeding.
  My heart drops every time you scream and it won't last long
  at this rate.
  This way of getting attention is nerve jangling and mine are
  jangled too much already."

"Don't tattle on your brother unless one of you is in mortal danger.
  I know every time he sneezes, sticks out his tongue or looks
  cross-eyed—enough already!
  I need ten minutes to regroup and remember why I wanted
  kids in the first place."

"Don't grab cookies, cereal, candy, or toys off the shelves and put
them in the basket.
  Last week I spent and extra $57.60 on items that were not
  and never have been on my grocery list.
  How did you get that in the basket from the middle of the
  aisles as little as you are?

Why do they put all that stuff at the checkout where kids can reach it? On second thought, never mind—I know the answer."

"Clean your room!
I know you had more than two pairs of jeans—they must be in the heap on the floor, and I'm afraid of what's in there.
I know there are some scary things growing in that room.
No wonder you sneeze all the time. The dust in your room could be used for industrial purposes.
What will your future spouse think of me as a mother if you are not trained to at least pick up your clothes and find your way to the laundry room? No, it's not in the kitchen."

"Wait till your daddy get home!
Maybe he can think more clearly at this hour of the day—I'm too weary.
A second threat may work—this one is shutting down for the duration.
It will give you time to think about what you has done. Wait, did I say "think"?"

"Get that look off your face!!!
—and let me watch you try to figure out which look it is.
Hold it right there and let's go to the mirror. No, don't get rid of the look—I want you to see it so you will know what to avoid in the future.
Where did he learn to do that? Does it come with being 13 (14,16,18, etc.)?"

"Don't use that tone of voice with me!
You're getting very close to crossing that invisible line that you really don't want to cross with me.
Do you want to begin dating at age twenty-four?
Does growing up give license to change tones with mothers? Answer: No.
I hadn't noticed how much his voice has changed in the past few months."

"Look at me when I'm talking to you!

He can find any speck on the wall to study when I am trying to make a point.

Am I that inefficient as a parent that he can pretend to ignore me? Not if he has to look at me!

I'm not getting through to him when I'm talking to the side of his head."

"You did what?!!

I heard you the first time, but I'm too shell shocked to absorb it.

Maybe after hearing it again I can think of a better parental response than fainting."

"Where did you get that?!

You traded your good jacket for it?

You dug it out of the neighbor's trash barrel?

You "picked it up" at the store? You can explain how you did that to the store manager and then we will handle it at home.

Did I skip the parenting lesson on stealing? Gosh, there are so many! Maybe I should make a list of all the lessons he needs. No, wait, I don't have time to make a list—I'm too busy trying to stay up with the parenting lessons I haven't faced yet."

"You're moving out?

You're not old enough!

Oh, you're already twenty-two?

My, how time flies."

PARENTAL DENIAL: ARE YOU GUILTY?

OFTEN WHEN I talk to teachers, I am amazed at their tenacity, their determination and their frustration. They are doggedly trying to instill knowledge in reluctant students (which has always been the case) while maintaining control of classroom behavior (which has always been done by effective teachers). What has made classroom control more difficult is that, by some state mandates, they are required to write up a behavior report before they can send a student to the office for an action that has made it impossible to teach the rest of the students. So, while they are writing a report, the rest of the class misses out on what she could have been teaching—virtually tying the hands of the teacher and giving control to the poorly behaved student.

In the past, a teacher simply had to send the disruptive student out of the room with a note or a discipline form to the principal so she could go on with the day's lesson. So why have policies become so extreme? One of the reasons is the parent denial we see so often in schools. According to the parents who have not developed a successful, adult method of parenting, the child must be in trouble because of something the teacher did, the principal did, or another student did. Consequently, the need for documentation has become routine in the school setting in order to justify sending an unruly student out of the classroom and in order to appease parents who are in denial that the child could do anything wrong.

Parental denial is insidious and causes a multitude of problems. First, even though the parent thinks he is helping his child when he defends him against any accusation, in reality, she is perpetuating her own inadequacy—the inability to take responsibility for her own actions in failing to properly discipline her child. Therefore, her child will become more and more adept at blaming the rest of society for his actions and will never "grow up" to assume positive character and integrity—for which the parent has herself to blame.

Second, parental denial causes problems for the parent. You will never be able to trust your child because he will do anything to avoid accepting personal responsibility for his actions. You will have to go to the school to get him, to jail to bond him out, to court to watch his trial, to divorce court to watch his family fall apart, back to court because he will not pay child support, and on and on. You have unwittingly created a societal monster. Congratulations.

Third, parent denial uses valuable time that could be used to educate children. Teachers should be in the classroom teaching—not filling out forms for disinterested, disruptive children. Principals should be encouraging successful students—not trying to discipline your child. Your inept parenting affects too many other people negatively.

Fourth, parental denial causes problems for law enforcement and judges because your child has not been successful at self-discipline since you have never been good at disciplining him. He is impulsive, foolish, and self-seeking. You have allowed him to get away with so much that he does not think he will ever have to pay for immature decisions. Hopefully, your inability to parent him correctly will not end up in his incarceration for many years or his untimely death.

Fifth, parental denial perpetuates parental denial. Your child will raise children very much like he was raised, and your grandchildren will have your life turned upside down when they begin to act like their parent. So you continue to suffer and society continues to have to take care of the discipline you did not give your own child. Others who suffer are his spouse and ultimately, his children and their children. You will have created a legacy that is negative, embarrassing, and costly.

I agree with Ronnie Agnew who writes editorials for the CLARION LEDGER (Jackson, MS): "If parents won't hold their children accountable, by what miracle are schools (and society) expected to?"

Do I have a solution? Yes. Don't be in parent denial. Do not make excuses for your child. Do not deny that he just might be guilty or to blame for what has occurred. Do not allow him to sass you or refuse to do his chores (yes, he needs chores consistently to help him learn to be responsible). Do not buy him everything he wants or make material things too important in your family.

In other words, be a responsible parent who sees the faults of your child clearly and who wants your child to have consequences for his actions. Only then will he grow into a responsible adult who will also be a good parent.

PARENTS ARE RESPONSIBLE FOR KIDS' ENTERTAINMENT

I OVERHEARD A YOUNG policeman talking to two older gentlemen at a McDonald's the week before the local loitering ordinance was passed in our area: "The parents bring kids of all ages and drop them off in front of the theater as late as 10:00 and just leave them. What are they thinking? We are not supposed to be babysitters, and yet there is no one watching these kids!" Already, in the evening, the "crowd" near the theater had become a problem for the businesses in the area as well as for the people trying to take their families to see a movie. The policeman I had overheard didn't look much older than the kids themselves, but he knew that the parents who were dropping their kids off were asking too much of local law enforcement to look after them and too much of their kids to stay out of trouble with that many other kids in the vicinity.

The problem is that even well-behaved kids from good families can become unruly when they are with such a large group of other teens and young adults. Psychologists know that there is a fine line between a large crowd and a *mob* when it comes to impulsive behavior. One of the adults who had had to walk through the crowd said that their language was disgusting and they were embarrassed to take their small children near there. Too many teens *show off* with filthy language, taking a joint, and other acting-out behaviors that are not usually part of their personalities when they are with other kids who are doing the same.

So, the question the young policeman asked is legitimate: "What are these parents thinking who take their kids and drop them off"? They are thinking that the kids will be safe because it is a public place and there are law officials there. However, are they aware of the number of kids who show up? Are they aware of what can happen in that large a group? Are they *dropping them off* because they have been coerced into doing it? Are they making the argument that "the kids don't have anything else to do" so why not?

First, we can learn from some large cities that being in a public place is not necessarily safe. Too many kids are killed or beaten up on the streets or at a ballgame to think that way.

In addition, policemen really do have more to do with their time and training than to take care of your child.

Secondly, those of you who are dropping them off, have you waited around to see what happens after your child is out of the car? Do you see whom he meets? Where he goes? Whether he actually sees a movie or just *hangs out* with all of the other kids? Your child is your responsibility—not the city's or the county's. If anything happens to him, you are as responsible as anyone else because you did not check up on him and know exactly what his plans were.

If you have not had the experience of being *carried up into a mob*, then you don't know better than to drop your child off anywhere. Large crowds can do a great deal of harm to other people and to things. It can happen to anyone.

If your child is able *talk you into* dropping him off, and you do not have enough sense to be concerned, what are you doing with kids in the first place?

If you are one of the parents who thinks kids should hang out in the parking lot because the city has not created a place for them to be entertained—what about your house? All you need is popcorn, drinks, a movie, a game of Kick the Can or Midnight Hide and Seek (dressed in all black and the porch is the only place that has a light for the *safe* place). Teenagers do need a place to "hang out" since they obviously do not go on dates any longer. There are churches that provide fun activities after home ballgames and probably other events that allow half-grown kids to "congregate". If your church does not provide anything like this, see if you can get something started for them.

Bottom line is—your child and his entertainment are your responsibility, not the community's. Find a way to make something positive happen since most local ordinances now prohibit loitering.

PARENTS CAN BE THE BEST/WORST THING FOR A CHILD

PARENTS CAN BE the best thing that can happen to a child or the worst thing. Let's look at some actual instances of the worst a parent can do to negatively impact a child.

A baby sitter asked me what she could do for the children who come to her house who have already endured their mother's wrath. They have been called names, screamed at, berated, and belittled. When they get to her house, the little girl goes off by herself and stays there until she is coaxed to come out for a snack. She comes with a sad little face and a hurt spirit. Her brother is angry, defiant, and wanting to lash out at whoever stands in his way—often a male's way of dealing with hurt and disappointment. The sitter just tries to *handle* them. She hates to discipline them because they are already resistant, so she just loves them—obviously the opposite of how they are treated by the parent.

She is a pretty girl, but the sadness in her face and the tears on her cheeks were a sign of hurt. She needed to tell someone, so she talked to me. Her dad was supposed to come from another state to take her out to eat and shop for her birthday. He arrived in town then called her and said he had turned around and was going back home. She begged him to come back and be with her. She even bargained—he didn't have to take her out, just spend time with her. He refused. She felt abandoned—again, hurt—again, guilty—again. ("Was it something I did?!") All I could do was sympathize and assure her that it was not her fault but that he had made a selfish decision; he was the one with the problem; and he is the one who should feel guilty. How sad that some parents, many of whom are divorced, forget how their decisions impact their precious children.

He was going to be recognized in a special way on a specific date, and he had made sure that his dad knew the day, time, and place way ahead of time. He came to me in the morning after his dad had told him that he had made reservations and would be out of state on that date. "He's the only parent who never comes to events I'm in!" He was hurt and angry and,

Help! I'm a Parent!

of course, feeling that he didn't deserve his dad's attendance (attention). It took me a while to try to convince him that he *was* deserving, but that his dad was selfish and immature if he couldn't be a more thoughtful, concerned parent. He was not totally convinced. It takes a lot to undo what a parent does to his child.

She couldn't keep from crying. Her mother had called her some vile names before school that she wouldn't repeat to me. "I'm not upset because she was mad—it was what she called me that hurt so bad!! Now I can't get what she said out of my head enough to concentrate on school!" I just let her talk and cry until she was spent, then we talked about how she should react when she got home and how she must not accept what she was called as who she is. Parents, your words do hurt, and they remain in your child's head long after your anger is over. They may even attempt to live up to what you have called them—"no good", "lazy", "stupid", and on and on.

Parents, you can cause so much damage to your vulnerable, precious children, no matter what age they are. Please guard your words, your actions, and your attitudes toward them. Above all, show them your love and give them your time—they need you, not your money or your empty promises—they need *you*.

PARENTS MUST KNOW
WHERE THEIR CHILDREN ARE

"**H**OW COULD SHE be pregnant? I thought we knew where she was all of the time!" (They were making out after school at his house when his parents were not at home and you thought she was staying for a school activity.)

"He's addicted to drugs?!! But he just goes to school, to work and then home!" (His *supplier* is a guy at work and he is using every night.)

"She has oral herpes?!! How in the world did she get that?!!" (She either kissed someone with it or she got it from doing oral sex with boys at her friend's house when she spends the night. Have you noticed how often she asks to *sleep over* lately?)

"Where is she getting these expensive clothes and shoes and purses and jewelry?!!" (As payment for oral sex or from the guys she is *servicing* after school and on weekends at parties.)

How can parents know what is happening to their child when he is away from home? How can you protect her from being *talked into* bad/immoral/dangerous behavior?

First, some of the best advice I heard many years ago from a child psychologist was "Spy, Spy, Spy." If she says she is going to a movie, see that she does by showing up to make sure she is actually there. (We would have three people who would be alive today if their parents had made sure that they were at the movies rather than in the pickup that crashed and killed them). If he says he is spending the night with a friend, call later and ask to talk to his friend or his friend's parent. If he happens not to be there, ask where he is and then go and find him. (We would have one live adult today if the parents had called to make sure that he was actually at the house where he was supposed to be rather than breaking into a house where he was shot to death by the owner). If the school calls the house and reports that he was not at school that day, don't believe him when he says that the teacher didn't see him. Instead, ask him enough questions to find out where he was and what he was doing when he was supposed to be in school all day. (We would have less people in jail if the parents had not believed them every time they made excuses about school).

Second, if school is over, and your child still hasn't come home, find out where he/she was. We had a call from a mother who was concerned that her child was being punished too often by having to stay after school and pick up paper at least three days a week. After investigating, we found that she had never been in trouble but was leaving every day with her boyfriend and then walking home from several blocks away.

Third, know your child's friends. If he disappears, or if the law comes to your house to ask questions, you must be ready with the first and last names of all of the kids he runs around with and even where they live. The life and future of your child may depend on how much you know.

Fourth, be sure there are responsible adults at any party your child attends. Notice I said, "Responsible". The chaperone should not be the older brother or sister who may have a pitiful reputation in the neighborhood. Nor should it be a parent who sees nothing wrong with giving alcohol to under-age teenagers. The responsibility of the safety of your child is yours—not someone else's.

Fifth, talk about and practice with your child on the ways to say "NO"—from the tactful way, the funny way, the assertive way, to the forceful way. Peer pressure is difficult to combat and we all know that peers can lead us to making stupid decisions. Practice will help.

Sixth, talk with your child. Note I said "child" because even ten and twelve year olds are getting into things that would shock their parents if they knew. Do not lecture, but make sure your child knows where you stand on moral issues and how their decisions can affect them in negative ways.

Seventh, talk to other parents. Being a parent is scary, isn't it? However, you are not the only one who is trying to do your very best to raise a child in today's world. Other parents are good sources of information and they are usually very willing to share it. Discuss it in your Sunday School class, in your dinner-party groups, at the ball games—in any setting in which other parents are present.

Finally, do your best. No one said we were going to be perfect when we first held that tiny little person in our arms. We are just asked to do our very unselfish best to be wise, discerning, careful, and loving. You will not regret it if you do everything you can to be the very best parent you can be. You are up to the challenge.

PARENTS MUST NOT DEMAND "ENTITLEMENT" FOR KIDS

I WAS TALKING TO an experienced teacher at an exclusive private school in my area and asked her how her year was going. Her complaint was that parents have begun to expect *entitlement* because they are paying a significant amount of tuition. They actually expect their children to receive good grades because of the expense of attending that school. This educator was frustrated over their demands despite little effort on the part of their children, over their *suggestions* concerning the curriculum, and over their subsequent undermining of discipline in her classroom.

"Entitlement" was also a word used in a book I read—*THE LAST LECTURE*, by Randy Pausch (Hyperion, 2007). He was concerned that when a student graduated from college with a degree in computer science that he fully expected to begin in a managerial position of the company that hired him. Many of those graduates were being left without jobs because of this attitude.

Entitlement is not a born trait—it comes as a result of being over-indulged as a child. In the book *The ULTIMATE GIFT* by Jim Stovall (Executive Books, 2000), the rich uncle has picked one nephew to give this ultimate gift; to the rest of his family he gave millions of dollars. He says to the nephew in a video tape after his death: "One of the great errors in my life was sheltering so many people, including you, from life's problems out of a misguided sense of concern for your well-being. I actually took away your ability to handle life's problems by removing them from your environment." The uncle says that most people learn about life through their mistakes and from facing struggles and problems. "Any challenge that does not defeat us ultimately strengthens us".

Parents who are overly protective and who refuse to allow their children to fail or to face difficulties are robbing them of their ability to solve their own life problems in the future. Too often, rather than helping them, the kids learn from your over-indulgence that they are not capable of making their own decisions, or of taking risks, or of trying new things.

They are crippled by their indecision and their fear of facing life without your continued guidance, so they are still at home when they should be going out in life on their own. They are incapable of handling hurt in a relationship because you have shielded them from any hurt in the past.

None of us is *entitled*. We all must learn the value of hard work and the reward of accomplishing something on our own, whether it is successfully studying and doing well on a big test, to completing a term paper, to interviewing for a first job, to being able to maintain a relationship, to handling our own checkbooks. We must learn, sometimes the hard way, how to handle adversity, how to yield to authority, how to make decisions and accept the results of those decisions, and so much more.

Every child, no matter what the age, wants someone to set boundaries, to have expectations, to direct but not lead so that they can learn to be autonomous when they have reached maturity. No child needs to have everything done for him, to have someone fight all of his battles, to ask a teacher to give him a good grade because of what is being paid for him to be educated.

If you are an over-indulgent, overly protective, "hovering" parent, back off. Allow your child to fight some of the battles and to see what it is like to succeed; give your child room to be himself; refrain from being too interfering at school; spend time directing from the home and give him the confidence that he is capable of dealing with life with his own set of skills, talents, and abilities. As you do this, you will have fulfilled what parenting is all about—giving birth to a child so that you can give him the love and the tools to eventually go out on his own and to be successful in handling life.

43

PROTECTIVE PARENTS

A S A SOCIETY, we have, since the 60's, moved from protecting our children to preparing our children. Rather than surrounding them with a close family unit, including grandparents who look out for the welfare of their grandchildren, we are divorcing, having children out of wedlock, taking care of our own needs before those of our offspring. We confess our sins to our children; let them watch TV and movies with vulgar language, violence, and sex. We also expect them to be "little adults" who can take care of themselves and not be affected by the *stuff* they see and hear and who can be left alone for periods at a time without adult supervision and remain out of trouble and feel secure and safe in an adult world. It seems that parents today, out of selfishness, are attempting to *prepare* their children for a world that is vulgar, ugly, and guilty.

One warm spring day, I watched a perfect example of *real* protective parents. The male and female wrens who were raising their tiny family in a nest on our front porch were making such a frantic noise that I stepped out to see what the problem was. What I saw was such a profound example of what loving parents would do that I was astounded. Those small birds were diving at a snake that was after their babies. As I watched, I realized that the baby birds were actually out of the nest, called out by their parents. They were hopping and half flying on the ground below the porch. The parents were trying to distract this threat to their children so those helpless little ones could get away.

Protection—from the enemy who would hurt this tiny family. Why aren't we afraid of those things that could negatively affect our family? Like a person who would deliberately cause a spouse to be unfaithful to the mother or father or our children, like taking a chance on getting hooked on gambling, like drinking so that we cannot give our full attention to the family, like going out in the evening and leaving the children at home unprotected, like not being fully aware of where your children are and what they are doing and with whom, like not knowing what is on the report card until the final four weeks of school.

But can you be too protective? The worst example of over-protective parents are those who refuse to recognize that their children can actually lie, that they can blame teachers for their lack of effort in a subject, that they really can skip school, and that they can act defiantly toward teachers and principals and Sunday School teachers. If you find yourself going to the school to protect your child, you may need to examine your own discipline at home and whether it is you or your child who runs your home.

While we are there, let me make an observation about home schooling. I do not mean the parents who are actually going to stay home and spend several hours each day in instruction, testing, etc., and who have a set time and a curriculum they faithfully follow to prepare the child for the work world or for college. I do mean the parents who pull children out for the following reasons:

1. Failure—often that is because of a lack of homework, a refusal to study for tests, and a desire to do as little as possible academically. If he won't work while he is being taught by a qualified teacher and with peer pressure urging him, why will he do it for a parent at home with dozens of distractions?

2. Can't get along at school—one of the reasons for going to school, whether public or private, is for the social adjustment—to learn to get along with all sorts of people of other races and cultures. Unless he lives in a bubble for the rest of his life, he will need this important lesson in social adaptation.

3. To avoid negative peer pressure—then what happens when he is 18 or 19? Can he learn in one year how to handle the pressure of his peers without some experience?

4. Because he wants to—who makes the decisions in your home—your children? Then Heaven help them!

Children are only children for such a short, precious time. That time should be full of playing, romping, learning, obeying. One of the most damaging objects we have in our homes that can rob children of their innocence and their childhood is the TV. It has, for too long, been used as a babysitter, a teacher, a giver of negative values, and the answer to lazy parenting. Please do what many young families have chosen to do—turn the thing off! One family I know is so busy being outside, playing, chasing fireflies, climbing trees, swinging from rope swings that they have little time to vegetate in front of the "tube". Then if they do watch it, the watching comes as a reward for putting up all of the toys or completing the chores, and usually the content watched is a made-for-children movie that has no negative impact on their minds of values.

Finally, some parents use TV as a way to "prepare" children for the real world of violence, divorce, sex, language, and all other awful things seen on it. Well, I don't know about you and your family, but there is little on that thing that bears even a remote resemblance to the world in which I live or anyone else in my area for that matter. Children should not have to be aware of that much ugliness while they are young. Give them time to grow up before they have to know so much.

During these years of childhood, your little ones, as well as the bigger ones, in your home need your protection, your love, your guidance, your care. You brought them into this world—now be good parents to them!

THE CASE AGAINST CURSING

THEY HAD TAKEN several cars full of kids, teens, and parents to the closest water park for a day of fun. When we asked them about it later, they had had a good time, but they had worked really hard to stay away from some older teens who had used really vile language and could not seem to have fun without using those kinds of words. It had made the park less appealing than it had been the other times they had gone.

For as long as I can remember, the consensus of opinion has been that a person who curses simply has a lack of education—he does not have enough vocabulary to speak without using inappropriate words. That still holds true even in the movie industry which seems to think that unless there is enough vulgar language in a movie, it may not be up for an Oscar—how sad.

Consequently, in today's society, vulgar language and cursing and using the Lord's name in vain are standard vocabulary, not only in the movie world, but also in the music your kids are hearing, on MTV and now on TV. They see nothing wrong with using the same language unless their parents forbid it.

There is still a discipline code in many school systems regarding profane language. If it is used in the hall or to another student, the student could very well end up in ALC (Alternative Learning Center) in our district. If it is used toward an adult, it is considered insubordination and the student is suspended for a certain amount of time.

But what if they are hearing it all of the time at home? Do they see anything wrong with using it? If they don't, your children will appear to be uneducated and ignorant to the public because they use the language they hear you use, and they could very well end up being punished for what they hear from your mouth or from the constant barrage of offensive language on your TV or from their Ipods or from the movies you rent.

I read a discussion on profanity in a book entitled *GOOD MORALS AND GENTLE MANNERS*, written in 1873; it still holds true today: "Profanity is one of the grossest forms of vice, for which there can not be the least apology or excuse. It is a perversion of language, and becomes a habit usually in youth among those who think it manly to be wicked and is practiced by those who have no command of elegant language and who suppose that to be earnest or emphatic they must be profane. No gentleman or lady uses profane language. The most worthless and vile, the refuse of mankind, the drunkard and the vagrant swear. Profanity never did any one the slightest good. No one is richer, wiser, happier, or more esteemed for it. It helps no man's education or manners; it never should be used in good society; it is disgusting to man and insulting to God." In polite society, none of that has changed.

Notice that the discourse above mentioned that cursing can become a habit in youth. That is where parents come in. We cannot allow our children to use profanity/vulgarities at home or they most certainly will use it in public. Every child will repeat a forbidden word just to see if it is recognized by a parent. If the word appears to be *cute,* and the parents laugh, then it has become OK to use it again. If your teen uses a word that shocks you and nothing is done, then he assumes that he has permission to use it again wherever.

Perverse language must be stopped at the onset. A child is told that he must not use that word again, and when he does (as he usually will), then the parent has an obligation to punish the disobedience and to remove the word from the child's vocabulary. If a teen or young-adult child uses profanity in your presence, your response should be immediate and unquestionable, and the person should understand that you will not tolerate that type of language in front of you.

I have even corrected men standing in the grocery line with me. A lady should never be subjected to inappropriate language from anyone, and when it happens, she should be offended and corrective. The last time I corrected it, the men were very apologetic and did not use those words again as along as we were in proximity of each other.

Parents, you have a tough task in trying to keep your children from using words that they hear in public, especially in so-called entertainment. However, if you do not do something about it, they will use it at times when they could get into serious trouble. They could also lose jobs, not get the job they want, not get the spouse they wanted, not be able to control words when they are angry or frustrated, and so on and on. Correct the words when they are used, and, hopefully, they will find other words to take their place that are positive and will lead to their success.

THE EMOTIONAL DEVASTATION
OF FREQUENT MOVING

EVERY YEAR, ALL over our particular county and in all parts of our nation, the schools are enrolling and withdrawing students in large numbers. One year in my school, I enrolled five seniors who had only one semester left and had to adjust to new peers, new teachers, new rules, new curriculum.

It is not an easy thing for children to be moved so often. There are two principle reasons why this is not a healthy thing for kids:

One is that it causes *educational gaps*. During the move or even after it, if the student misses a concept in a subject, as in algebra or English grammar, he may never be taught that concept again; therefore, it is lost to him. The consistent failure of many students can be attributed to the fact that their parents moved them often in the lower grades.

I once talked to a girl who had attended six different schools in the previous four years. She said that often she and her siblings would open the door of the house in which they were living at the time only to find all their belongings packed up and ready to be loaded into the car to be moved (again). She was failing her classes and her siblings were as well. Why? Not only because of the *pieces* of education they have missed during all of these moves, but also because of this second reason why frequent moving is devastating for a young person.

In the book *DEADLY EMOTIONS*, author Don Colbert, M.D. (Thomas Nelson, 2006) says that children often *stuff* (internalize) emotions they have because of some experiences, and one of those experiences was frequent moving. He states that "a child tends to perceive these circumstances as creating an environment that is unstable, insecure, fearful." He also says that the child "may feel anger that the parent or parents are not supplying all that he needs".

One girl who came to my office was worried that her mother was soon going to be evicted and would be moving to an apartment in another town. The daughter would not have a way back to our school and would have to transfer toward the end of her senior year. She was angry that her *circumstances* were as they were and that her mother could not provide a more stable atmosphere for her. Because of it, her grades were suffering;

she felt disjointed and out of place; she could not make plans for going to college because she did not even know where she would be living next year.

Why can't parents see that this "moving" thing is so difficult for their children? Well, you say, maybe it has to do with the economy. I admit that may have a lot to do with it. However, we as parents, owe it to our children to keep a roof over their heads (without having to move too often to do so), to feed them (even if it takes food stamps), and to love them. Seeing to their emotional needs by giving them more stability and security can be a way of showing love.

The book I mentioned presents the argument that the emotions we do not express become *trapped* and will find a way out somehow. Many children *act out* their frustrations and feelings of insecurity by behaving inappropriately. They are often sent to the principal's office because they react angrily to the least stimulus.

Others may become sick. They are more prone to colds, to asthma, to flu, and even to more debilitating and/or catastrophic illnesses. They will seldom tell their parents how they feel even if they can find the words to do so. As a result, they keep their feelings inside, and those feelings find a way out—a resolution—by hurting the child.

So, what is the solution? Stay where you are, especially during the school year. Do not let them move from parent to parent and lose credits and positions on the school campus. Don't pack up and move out, leaving them to stuff their emotions about the move and finding a way to express those emotions in negative ways.

Do everything you can to resolve your financial crisis without having to find another place to live away from a place your child has come to accept as his home.

Do whatever it takes without moving (again). Do it for your child.

THE FIRST TEACHERS AND CLASSROOMS
FOR EACH CHILD

THEY WERE IN Alternative Learning Class for cursing—three of them. They thought it was funny that the teacher was upset over their *language* and that the principal had punished them for something so minor. When some teachers were discussing it later, one veteran teacher said that she was not surprised that kids' language was becoming more vulgar. After all, they watch hours of movies on their TV's and the vulgarities in most movies today are becoming common-place words in the speech of children. Not only films, but also much of the music kids hear is packed with vulgar words and suggestiveness.

I watched another type of scenario in an office packed with older students. A young man got up out of a chair to offer it to one of the girls who was standing. She refused it. What I was seeing was a student who had obviously been raised to be a gentleman, but a young lady who had not learned to accept a gentlemen's graciousness.

Some students were sitting in a small group in the classroom for an assignment and one shy girl was refusing to take part. When the teacher began to watch them more closely, she realized that the girl would not look at the boys in the group. She pulled the girl outside and asked her what the problem was and found that she was being covertly called a vulgar term by the boys in the group out of earshot of the teacher. The teacher then made the boys apologize and took the girl out of the situation.

Do you have any idea what your children do when they are away from you? No, no one does. And, yes, our children are going to do things that are totally alien to the way we raised them. However, it is seldom the case that our children completely leave our instruction if we have taught them by example and in love.

I once heard a girl say, "Our family puts on a front. What you see is not what we are really like when we are in the house by ourselves." Do you hear what she is saying? Obviously, the example being set in that home is not what she would want her friends to see. I know that the way her dad acts toward his wife and daughter is not healthy for their self-esteem, and what his son is seeing will not cause him to treat women well as he gets older.

The home is the first schoolroom; the parents are the first teachers. Too many children today are learning how to treat others from TV, movies and music, not from a set of caring parents. The morals and mores of today's younger generation is warped if they are following the example of stars, celebrities, sports figures, musicians, and, sadly, politicians.

So, what are we to do? Put our kids in a room and refuse to let them out until they are grown? If we did, how would they know how to discern what is false, how to refuse to take part in what it morally wrong, how to choose friends who are trying to make good choices, in other words, how to live in this kind of world?

So, what we must do is lead by (good) example, and we must care enough about our kids to teach them what is right and wrong and then expect them to choose the right thing to do. We must turn off offensive media and so-called "entertainment"; we must teach manners and how to use them in public; we must respect both genders and give each room to be moral and strong; we must give our children reasons to respect themselves so that they will not think they must work so hard to be accepted by everyone else; we must give our kids reason to hope for a bright future rather than constantly complain about the world and its problems; we must be good parents/teachers in our *classrooms* and send them out from our homes as confident, positive, responsible adults.

Remember that parenting takes an enormous amount of effort, love, understanding, discipline, instruction, and time. Do not cheat your child of a valuable education from you, and be the kind of adult example that you will someday want him/her to be.

WHO IS PARENTING YOUR CHILDREN? YOU OR TV?

THE AUTHOR OF *HEAR OUR CRY: Boys in Crisis*, Paul D. Slocumb (Aha! Process, Inc, 2004) says that in the past, children learned to find their identity by the stories they heard from their family about the people who came before them. They were a part of a large extended family including frequent contact with the grandparents and often with great-grandparents. They were taught morals, values, accepted behavior, dangers, and such by the many family members who came and went in their lives. They knew the sting of death, the joy of birth, the praise of work well done, and the consequences of poor choices from those who loved them most.

In today's society, the 21st-Century family is made up of many of the following: single parents, step-parents, step-brothers and sisters, half-brothers and sisters, and *the media*. Michael Gurian, author of A FINE YOUNG MAN (Tarcher Putman, 1999), defines a family member as someone who is a regular part of our lives and the lives of our children: "Today a major new member of that family is the media. Young people become more familiar with some celebrities than they do with family members. Grandmother may be seen once a year; some TV personalities are visited daily. The stories told via the media have become an integral part of the process leading to self-identify.

"Machines have become the medium for most of the stories children hear, absorb, tell, and emulate. Drummed into young minds time and time again through the media are messages about one's identity; how to deal with a crisis; how to handle money (consumerism); instant gratification; and meanings of integrity, honesty, morality, and codes of conduct. A picture is frequently more powerful than a thousand words, especially if no one else is talking or no one is at home."

Now, why are we surprised that teen pregnancy is on the rise again? The media is saturated with movie stars, musicians, and other celebrities who jump from one bed to another and who are having children without the benefit of marriage. Why are we surprised that our children and young people are killing each other, even in mass numbers? Violence in the media has become commonplace and acceptable. "By the age of 16, the average American kid will have seen 200,000 acts of violence on TV, one-sixth of those will be acts of murder." (Gurian) Why are we surprised that the economy is in trouble? Uncontrolled spending is the norm, and kids are not being taught how to save or to be frugal in any part of their lives.

"The average U.S. household has its television turned on 47 hours a week. The average number of minutes per week that parents spend in meaningful conversation with their children is 3.5. In other words, the TV potentially has the child's attention about 800 times more that that child's parents!"

The new *suggestion* that families should eat at least two or three dinner meals together each week is falling on deaf ears even though we're seeing that kids who spend that time with their parents are less likely to do drugs, to have sex, to drink, or to join gangs. Over fifty percent of American households have a TV on while they are eating dinner.

Think children are not saturated with the media? "By the time a child is 18, he/she will have spent 22,000 hours watching TV—double the time he/she will have spent in classroom instruction and more than any other activity except sleeping." (Gurian)

So, the questions are "Who is raising your kids? Who is teaching them the values your family wants to live by? How will they know when to stop when sex is offered, and will they see anything wrong with having sex anytime, anyplace?" After all, it is done on TV.

Have you abdicated your role as parent to the square or rectangle *monster* in your house? For the sake of your children and the sake of society, I hope not.

TURN THAT THING OFF! and get a life that will benefit you, your children, your neighborhood, and the world. Be creative in doing things with your kids. Talk to them and then take the time to listen when they talk. Love them enough to want to spend time with them. Do not let TV and the rest of the media control your family.

CHAPTER TWO

HELP! I WANT TO BE A REALLY GOOD PARENT!

BEGIN VERY EARLY ON PARENTING SKILLS

PARENTING IS A challenge, no matter what the age of the child, from knowing when to begin cereal as part of the infant's diet to how to motivate the unmotivated adolescent.

I once asked the Peer Counseling group with whom I worked what observations they had made while working with the students who were in the Alternative Learning Class—a class that separates students who have broken a school rule or policy from the general population. Here are some insights based on the experience of these high school juniors and seniors. My added comments are based on parental needs.

When I asked them what they saw as a re-occurring problem among the students we saw each week, they observed the following:

1. Lack of motivation: They said they could not explain it, but most of these students had no goals, no plans, no hope for the future. In fact, the Peer Counselors were a bit defensive because they could not seem to help the ALC students grasp the importance of making plans for life after high school. I reminded them that if they could figure out how to motivate the unmotivated, they could package it and make a fortune. When I asked them why they (the peer counselors) were motivated, to a person, they replied that it was because their parents cared about them and wanted them to do well in life. Then, when we stopped talking, one of them said, "So THAT'S why these kids are not motivated—their parents have not taken an active part in their present and are unconcerned about their futures." However, I reminded them that some kids become this way even with good parenting, so what would be the answer to that? All of them agreed that the ALC students' choice of friends is probably what has stolen their motivation. We even had a seventeen-year-old boy who was several years behind his class to tell us that he didn't make plans for his future because he wanted to spend all his time playing and was not interested in growing up to take on adult responsibility.

2. Lack of sleep: More than a few times students are in ALC because of excessive tardies. In talking to them, we find that they are either working late or staying out late and are too tired to get up early enough to be on time to school, or their parents don't get them up, or the parents don't get up themselves. One sophomore girl, who works at one of our local fast-food restaurants until 11:30 every night, was there because of tardies. In addition, her normally good grades were now failing. When we asked her why, she admitted she was sleep-deprived and tired. When asked why she had to work, she admitted that it was for her own benefit but that her parents spend a lot of nights at the casinos. A Peer Counselor asked, "Do they win?" Her answer was, "Sometimes, but I would rather have them at home." Several articles have been written lately about the difficulty parents are having in getting children to bed. Believe me, this is not a recent parenting problem—it has gone on for generations. However, for the sake of the child, a parent must be firm and decisive and have a set time and routine for the "going-to-bed ritual". Your child needs sleep in order to function at school both academically and socially. Be sure he gets it.

3. Lack of parental involvement: Most of the students we see in ALC say they really do not get along with their parents, that there is little input by their parents in their present lives, and that they seldom talk about anything. Even though I have mentioned this earlier, let me add a few things the Peer Counselors said. All but one said that their contact with their parents is a crucial part of their decision making and their security. The only one who does not have this input does have it from an older sibling. Parents, there is never a time in your child's life, as long as he is in your home, that he doesn't need you. Oh sure, as a teenager he may *say* he doesn't, and he may act like you are an unnecessary impediment he has to endure, but, truth is, according to these successful, enterprising teens, parents are wanted and needed even to older high school kids. Never abdicate your role as the parent—you created that role when you created your child, and, until he goes out on his own, you must be involved in that life you made.

4. Laziness: The Peer Counselors were adamant about this one. They said that too many of these kids were being given everything without having to work for it, and, therefore, they had no concept of responsibility to themselves or to others. Each Peer Counselor that year worked in addition to going to school and maintaining excellent grades. They were saving for college, paying for insurance, learning how to work in public, being subject to a boss and work responsibilities, and they were proud of all they are accomplishing. Are your children doing something they are proud of? Are they learning from their experiences? Are you helping them grow up by giving them chores to do and making sure they carry them out well so they can accomplish even that small task? Giving your kids everything they want is not a loving gesture—it is a selfish one. You are trying to buy their affection, even their loyalty. It doesn't matter what the other children are getting, as the parent in your home, if your giving will create a problem for your children in later life and will prevent their taking on responsibilities, then you are hurting rather than helping your child.

Finally, one of the PC's made this remark: "If parents are having trouble with their kids, they have to begin really early, when the kid is very small, to be involved, to take care of the child, to let the kid know he is loved and valued by the parent." Not bad advice from a high school senior! Parents, are you listening?

ENCOURAGING DETERMINATION AND PERSISTANCE

I LOVE TO READ stories about people who have overcome a difficulty and have triumphed in life, especially if it is a problem that faces young people and children and parents. Numerous times we are told what to do by educators, doctors, politicians, and friends who give glib solutions to what we are facing. However, too many of those solutions are only temporary and cannot be used for years into the future.

I read an interview about a man named Tommy Spaulding who was on a book tour to sign and tell about his (already) New York Times bestseller, *It's Not Just Who You Know* (Crown Business, 2010). Mr. Spaulding is dyslexic, but he became a top sales executive for IBM and then became president of Up With People. By the time he had published his book, he had left his latest high-paying job and travel opportunities in order to found a non-profit leadership organization which seeks to help young people reach their potential despite any obstacles they may have. He particularly wants to teach them to reach for success instead of allowing themselves to become insecure or to feel sorry for themselves if they have seemingly insurmountable difficulties.

He said," I used to think dyslexia was a scar, but now I see it as a gift because it caused me to overcompensate in other areas to make people see that they were wrong about me. I wasn't a good student, so I went out of my way to excel in other ways. I didn't give up and I tried harder because I wanted to prove to the world that I wasn't stupid."

Mr. Spaulding did what a friend of mine did who also had dyslexia—he worked harder. Some of the things Spaulding did in order to achieve were that he went to summer school classes during high school in order to boost his grade-point average; he conducted "marathon study sessions" in college; and he maintained an optimistic (opposite of "poor me") attitude despite being turned down by more than thirty-six law schools. In other words, he didn't rely on pills, on extra tutoring (offered in colleges for educationally handicapped students), on pity, on government handouts, or any other aid. What he did rely on was his own work ethic and his determination to succeed. The college marathon study sessions have been used by all of us at one time or another—they are a meeting of students who are all studying for a test. Using the skills of each other to learn the information, they go into the test having heard the material more than once; they have been asked questions based on the material; they have studied more than one time; and they go into the test confident they can pass it. My brother held study sessions in calculus, physics and other mathematics at Mississippi State for his friends who were not catching on as quickly as he did.

Spaulding says that he used persistence and a can-do attitude to get a Rotary scholarship that paid for getting an MBA in graduate school. He had to convince the committee that he could overcome his less-than-good grades and achieve if they would give him the chance. He kept his word and more.

There was one other advantage Spaulding had in addition to his determination, tenacity, and persistence—he had the support of his family. They encouraged and praised him for each success he had. All children, whether they have an educational, physical, or other handicap can succeed if they have supportive parents. You have that opportunity as a parent—you won't be sorry if you give that support.

Kem Wilson, Jr., vice-president of Kemmons Wilson Companies, who had invited Spaulding to a speakers' event, said this of him, "He's a great example of the power of determination and drive . . . . By telling (his story), he's changing the world".

I also read an interview of Bill Gates who was always an outsider socially in high school. He said that since he didn't relate to his peers, he decided to relate to the teachers. He would ask each one what his ten favorite books were, then he would read every one. That way he had something about which to talk to them—a way to meet in the middle—and it worked. They encouraged him through school, and look at the success he has been!

Too many parents allow their children to use any excuse for not succeeding in school or in life. We handicap them if we allow them to cop out on life by giving them permission to feel sorry for themselves, for not doing their best, for not being persistent and determined to push themselves beyond what they think they can do.

Don't be that kind of parent. Expect the best; encourage the best of your child. The reward for both of you will be his best effort and his ultimate success in his chosen work. What a delight that will be!

MAKING PARENTING PROMISES TO KEEP

I SELDOM MAKE RESOLUTIONS because I find them so difficult to keep. However, I've found that if I make myself a promise, I keep it much better. So here are some parenting promises that could be adopted for the betterment of your skills as a parent:

I PROMISE TO BE UNSELFISH: Being selfish means that you are more concerned with your own wants than those of your family. It includes your drinking or drugging which "tells" your children that it is OK to do something that is possibly addictive and probably dangerous to their health and maybe even to their lives. It includes your foolish desire to be young again. No matter how young you married, once you bring children into your life, your principle objective should be to take care of their needs—all of them, from physical, to emotional, to psychological, to educational, and yes, to spiritual. It includes your being home with your children, not at a bar or at the casino or even too long at work. The most precious commodity you can give your children is YOURSELF. It also includes your sincere effort to be a good spouse so that you can be a good example of how to have a secure marriage for the sake of the children and how to build and maintain a relationship.

I PROMISE TO TAKE OUT MY FRUSTRATIONS SOMEWHERE OTHER THAN AT HOME: In times of economic difficulty, it is not an easy task to be upbeat when you are around your children. Yet, there is not a thing they can do to alleviate the situation (other than allowing your older children to work), so why give them the worry of your financial woes? Too many parents use their children as confidantes; then the children go to school carrying the burden of their own academic concerns as well as the family worries you have laid on their shoulders. There are adults with whom you can discuss your problems rather than using your children. This is also and especially true of any marital problems you may be having as well, and the yelling and screaming at each other only gives the children added burdens to carry all day long. It also makes them worry about home when they are away from it—they are concerned that they won't be able to stand the emotional pressure there; they worry that one of you will be gone when they get home; they worry about how all the chaos is affecting the younger children. Find somewhere else to express your frustrations rather than in front of the children, and if you and your spouse need to discuss something that is affecting your family, go somewhere away from the kids to handle it civilly then go back to them in agreement.

I PROMISE TO WATCH MY FINANCES MORE CAREFULLY: If economically lean years don't teach you anything else, it should teach you that nothing is certain; jobs can be lost; homes can go into foreclosure; credit card bills still must be paid; utilities can be cut off; and having to move is a possibility. Consequently, you have to be extra careful how you manage your money. If you can do something other than live from paycheck to paycheck, then do it. At the same time, teach your children how to manage money. After all, they will be paying for the national debt for most of their lives and their money will be even tighter than ours is now.

I PROMISE TO COOK HEALTHY FOOD: Too much evidence shows that fattening foods lead to obesity which leads to self-esteem issues and health problems, and that processed foods and sugars can exacerbate ADHD and autism. If you haven't already, learn to cook more nutritiously with more vegetables and fruits, less sweets and sodas. The health of your children as adults has a lot to do with how you feed them now.

If you keep these promises to yourself and for the sake of your children, then you and your children will be happier and healthier.

PARENTING LESSON FROM A MOCKINGBIRD

I HAD GONE TO read in a chair near the window that overlooks the lake at the local library and saw a mockingbird land on the concrete patio just outside the window. The bird was holding a worn in its mouth and was switching its tail and making a sound that shows that this particular bird is either irritated or wants something. I ignored it at first, but the second time it came to the same area and did the same things, again with a worm in its mouth, I watched until I saw what it was trying to do. Between the concrete base of a large pillar and the concrete window sill was a tiny bird with some of its feathers. As the parent bird made the sound, the little bird's mouth flew open. The difficult part was that the baby bird was so deep in the "well" between the concrete structures that the parent bird couldn't lean down far enough to deliver the meal. It would catch itself with wings flapping when it would lean too far and almost land in the well. Finally, as all good parents do, it improvised: it put one foot on the pillar base and one foot on the windowsill base and was able to lean farther down to feed that baby. Over and over again, that parent bird came with food for that little bird and made its noise; the mouth flew open; it leaned down with spraddled feet, fed the baby and flew off to do it again.

That demonstration of parental effort and determination reminded me of parents who will *bend over backward* to take care of the needs of their children. Notice I did not say "to take care of the wants of their children". There was the set of parents who lost a good income. The dad went to work in construction and applied for a second job at Lowe's; the mother found multiple ways to put hamburger meat into dishes, bought in volume, and stored cans of food on the porch, made her own pizza, and taught her children lessons on money management and *learning to do without* (without whining about it).

There is the single mother who refuses to take welfare checks. Instead, she works in the school cafeteria during the day and cleans hotel rooms in the afternoon. Her kids have learned to cook, so the meal is ready by the time she gets home; they do their homework without being coerced; and the oldest makes sure the younger ones have had their baths and set their clothes out for the next day. She has trained them well, and, rather than being sorry for themselves, the kids are self-confident, well-mannered, and self-reliant.

There is the family featured in a magazine one year who raise dairy cows and sell the milk. Because of the economic downturn, all of the hired hands have had to be laid off, and the family of girls has taken on the jobs of mucking the stalls, collecting the milk, feeding the cattle, while still helping with the house chores and maintaining their grades. Their parents make no apologies for having to make them work so much; instead, they have realized how much their daughters have matured and that they are not ashamed of the work they are doing in order to keep the farm and in order to honor the work ethic of their parents.

I am not so sure that *it takes a village*. I am sure that it takes at least one loving, determined parent to do what must be done for the children to live healthy, productive lives. I also know that children whose parents use all of their resources to give them what they want and to pamper them are not as strong in character, in life skills, in integrity, or in self-confidence.

Sometimes the circumstances in life become those priceless *teachable moments* when we have to improvise, to be creative, to work something out, and the beneficiaries of these efforts are our children.

The worst thing we can do is to whine (There is nothing so obnoxious as an adult who whines about his circumstances while he does nothing about it). Rather, we can find a job mowing grass, cleaning businesses, doing construction clean up, running materials across the city, whatever. There are jobs to be had. Granted, they may be less important than what you did in the past, but, if a paycheck is what you want, then it is worth it.

The best thing we can do is keep at it so we can feed our little ones, or we have to go out time and time again to do what we must to meet their basic needs. Good parents will find a way.

PARENTING TAKES ENERGY AND PATIENCE

SOMETIMES THE MOST dangerous thing for a child is his own parent. We have had too many examples for this not to be a concern: To be too little to know when there is danger and be left by your parent in a house that catches fire; to be left by your parent with teenagers who beat you and ultimately kill you; to be left by your mother with her boyfriend who tries to keep you from crying by hitting you and causes permanent damage; to be the child of a mother who wants to be young and enjoy freedom and who abandons the husband of many years and the children of that marriage to find *happiness* with another person; to be the daughter of a father who sees nothing wrong with molesting and even having sex with her—thus destroying her self-esteem, her sense of right and wrong and her ability to have a *normal* life without counseling.

For the rest of us, the question is, "Why did you ever have children in the first place unless you were going to spend the next many years taking care of them and looking out for their safety and welfare?" Too many kids are roaming the streets without the knowledge of their parents for this not to be a serious problem. Too many small children are being neglected; too many teens are raising themselves; too many girls are having children of their own in order to achieve *love* from either the boy or the child itself. The problem is that the *burden* of raising a child as it should be done takes time, emotion, effort, love, energy and patience and for too many young parents who did not plan the child, those attributes are totally missing.

I was with a grandmother who was asking her son about the brother of the new baby. It seems the brother was in the process of getting attention any way he could in order to make sure he was still loved despite this new addition in the family. The daddy had become tired of making assurances the night before, but he had finally convinced the child that he was still loved and cherished. The grandmother made the comment that she was glad her days of parenting small children were over and that the young generation was doing it because they had more energy and patience.

Energy. Parents must have it in order to successfully take good care of the little ones they have brought into the world—energy to chase little bodies that want to run and play, energy to dash into the street in order to snatch the little person from danger, energy to plan and execute teen get-to-gathers in order to let them have fun with adult supervision until they are old enough to be on their own, energy to wait up all hours until the car pulls into the driveway with the young driver or the rider, energy to make a *statement* with firm discipline when it is needed and to stand by what has been set into motion—energy to be a parent.

Then another attribute needed by parents is Patience. I do not mean the patience to let the kids do things until you have worn out the patience you have. I mean the patience to let them go only so far and then to *pull in the reins* before they reach the point where their inexperience could get them into trouble. I do not mean the patience to let the child in the grocery cart scream and cry because you have refused to let him have a treat while the rest of the patrons are losing *their* patience. I mean the patience to leave your cart, take the little spoiled brat to the car where you patiently discipline his behind until he knows how to behave in public. I do not mean the patience to let your child roam the neighborhood at all hours while the rest of the adults try not to run over them. I mean the patience to say "No, you have homework and chores to do, so you must stay home until the chores for which you are responsible are done".

Being a parent is a full-time job despite the fact that the majority of parents are working a full-time job in addition to parenting. However, since so many of us have parented successfully and worked outside the home too, know that it can be done. It just takes a lot of love, which means that you love the child even more than yourself and want the best for him or her. It takes a lot of energy. It takes an abundant amount of patience. If you are sadly lacking in any of those attributes, please do not have children—just love your nieces and nephews or volunteer at the library or teach a Sunday School class and let the people who have those attributes have the children.

PRIORITIES FOR THE STAGES OF OUR CHILDREN'S LIVES

EACH STAGE OF our lives is more successful if we have goals and established priorities. If we look at some of those stages in relation to the stages through which our children will go, we can decide if we are making progress.

In our adult lives, if we're parents, our main priority should be the psychological and physical well-being of our children. This includes providing for them financially; however, if making the money to provide for them becomes a priority for you, then you will probably neglect the psychological aspect of raising healthy children. There is nothing in good parenting that requires that your off-spring have the latest fashion, shoes, games, toys, or such. Rather, the requirement is that you are a present, available, caring parent whose primary concern in life is your child.

One night we were at a high school football game when an elementary child came up to my husband and complained that he thought he had broken his foot. The ankle was already swollen and the child could not put pressure on it. The adults around us went for an ice bag and we began to call the home and cell phone numbers for the parents. The little boy told us that we would not reach them because they were at the casino and could not hear the phone. Finally, an EMT had to administer aid to him without the consent of the parent. The only person with him was an embarrassed teenage brother who was unsure why there was such a fuss over a possible broken ankle.

Why was an elementary child at a ballgame without a parent? Why was he in the care of an adolescent? Because the priority of the parent was not the child!

Now let's look at various stages in the life of a child and discover some priorities as we go:

First, during the first few years of a child's life, the priority should be just being a child. Children should be allowed to run and play, to be read to, to have his questions answered, to be protected, to learn obedience, to learn how to get along with other children. In other words, the child has a successful childhood according to the care and attention he receives from his parents. There is no time during these years when a child does not need his parents—both of them.

Next, during the early school years, a child's priority should be to become an integral part of the educational world. So much of his future depends on how he perceives the process of learning and being educated. The parent has a responsibility to be enthusiastic, encouraging, and participatory if he wishes to have a successful student in the next twelve to sixteen years.

Then we have the very important years of fifth to seventh grades when so many children begin to be interested in other things besides school. Yes, there is a life outside the classroom, but if those outside activities interfere with his success in school, then the responsible parent will limit anything that would cause failure in academics. These activities could include but are not limited to watching television, playing video games, and playing sports. Yes, it is easier to get our own work done if the child is mesmerized in front of the TV, but we are actually neglecting our responsibility if we allow them to spend an inordinate amount of time there or if he is too tired to do school work because of the late night in a sport. Children this age have homework, tests to study for, projects to do, and reading assignments to complete. Parents who are correctly prioritizing are making sure these education tasks are complete each night.

Teenagers want to be socially acceptable, attractive, funny. They will do many unacceptable things in order to achieve what, to them, makes them all of those things: they will work too many hours to buy a car and pay for insurance, not realizing that they will be paying for a car and insurance for the rest of the their lives; they will take a chance on going to parties on the weekend and drinking or drugging, forgetting that their very lives could be in danger and their futures jeopardized; they will spend so much time on the phone or on internet or with their friends that they have no time for homework or studying, forgetting that many of those friends will go their own way in just a few years; they will have sex to keep a boy/girlfriend, forgetting that a baby will change their lives forever and that AIDS could end their lives prematurely.

Bottom line—it is the responsibility of the parents to steer their children into activities and lifestyles that will help them realize what areas of their lives are important and lasting and that will contribute to their future success.

It comes down to you—the parent.

If you could decide now that the first priority of your adult life after the birth of your child is the raising of that child in a home that is positive, affirming, caring and disciplined, then you will be assured that your reward will be in the future success and happiness of the precious children you brought into this world.

RAISING EMOTIONALLY HEALTHY CHILDREN

W E AS PARENTS want to raise children who are healthy—we feel successful if we can do that. However, physical health, as important as it is, cannot compare with the emotional well being of the children in our homes. How can we be assured that we are doing our best to lead our children into adulthood as emotionally secure, confident people? I have a few suggestions.

First, love your child unconditionally. Oh, yes, he is going to disappoint you at one time or another—he is, after all, human. However, your love for him should not be based on how successful he is in sports or in the classroom; rather it should be based on the fact that he is your child, born of your flesh, brought into your life by choice. One of the saddest counseling sessions I have done was with a young lady who was watching her family disintegrate—her dad and mom were arguing regularly and the mother would leave in the car and say she was not going to come back. The child said (while sobbing) that they never would have gotten married if they had not been expecting her. What a terrible thing to do to a child! Why did she have to know they conceived her before marriage? Do they not realize that this lovely daughter is actually blaming herself for this miserable marriage?

Second, remember that discipline is a form of showing love. Not abusive discipline, but rule setting with protective parameters and a list of consequences that will let your child know that he is being held in check because he is not mature enough yet to make decisions that will keep him out of harm's way. Then remember that consistency and fairness are extremely important to a child's sense of fair play, and he expects it from his parents as well as from peers and playmates.

Third, discuss your child's personal strengths and weaknesses so he can build on the strengths and improve the weaknesses. We all have them both, but if you ridicule your child's inability to do something—from catching a fly ball to understanding factoring, he will consider himself inadequate and will quit trying. You are always the most influential person in your child's life, even when he is a teenager. If you tell him you are proud of him for anything, he thinks he can move mountains. If you make fun of him, he is hurt, defensive, and will not wish to have your comments. Be very careful what you say and do so you will not wound the spirit of your child. Children who feel good about themselves and what they can accomplish are more successful as students and as citizens.

During most of the parent conferences in my office when we found that the child had changed from a caring student and child to a failing student who was no longer getting along at home, he was usually being influenced by peers who were doing the same. Yes, as parents you have the right and the responsibility to help him choose positive friends whether he likes it or not. His future depends on your guidance, not on the advice of his peers.

Be excited about education. Whether you graduated from high school or not or ever attended a day of college, your enthusiasm about what your child is learning and what he is doing in school will carry over to him and cause him to want to be more knowledgeable about many things.

Enjoy your children while they are home. All too soon they will want to be on their own and you will no longer have the opportunity to raise them. Read a lot. Go to seminars on parenting. Ask questions. No parent is perfect or does a perfect job, but we should be doing the best we can as long as we have our children at home with us.

RESPECT AND SELF-RESPECT ARE NECESSARY

ONE OF THE most important things parents can teach their children—whether they are five, fifteen, or twenty-five-is respect. Not just respect for the parent, which is the most important, but also respect for others, and, of significance, respect for themselves. During the months after the Columbine shootings, investigation revealed that the two boys who killed and wounded the other students and a teacher had little respect for their parents, for others, for themselves, or for life itself. Part of being a child and a teenager is their exclusivity. If another child is different, he can be isolated and/or treated cruelly by others, which seems to give the isolators a false sense of power. As adults we can remember a time when we were either isolated by others or did the isolating and we feel remorse about it if we have matured into full adulthood. It is the *sick* adult like the man who shot the children in the Jewish Center in California who carry that childish cruelty and lack of respect for others and their differences into adulthood.

Teaching respect begins at home. One of my least favorite TV ads in the past was one in which the mother is driving a van full of children who are screaming, throwing things, and acting generally hateful, and the mother is telling them in a tired, ineffective voice to be quiet, don't misbehave, etc. An elementary school teacher friend of mine said that this type of ineffective parent brings her kids to school and expects the teacher to be able to make them mind. A kindergarten teacher once told me that most of the children came out of the cars and off of the bus so out of control that it took her all morning to get their attention. At the high school level, if the student is not respectful toward his teachers, the parent may find himself coming to the school for conferences or to take him home. Respect is vital for your child to be a successful part of the school setting, and the respect must begin with you which will carry over to respect for others.

However, teaching respect cannot be a demanded reaction. Your screaming at the child: "You'd better show respect to me!" is not the way to teach it. Your life should be lived in front of your children in such a way that you *deserve* respect. Are you fair, ethical, honest, caring and concerned at home, or just at church or at work? If your child acts disrespectfully, do you stop right then and make it a *teachable moment*? Why is this necessary?

Because in school educators must require respect and obedience from your child so they can teach him and also so they can teach the rest of the kids in the classroom. During the second day of class, an elementary teacher finally said to a disruptive student: "Would it help if I called your mother and told her how you are acting?" The student had enough respect for his mother that he cleaned up his act and the teacher was able to teach everyone from that time on.

You would be surprised at some of the answers teachers receive when they call some parents regarding discipline: "I can't do anything with him at home either!" "You are the teacher, why are you calling me about this?" Why would they answer this way? Because they have not gained respect at home and they need someone else to blame, so they blame the school, the police—anyone but themselves.

Are you so prone to dislike others because of their color, religion, or economic class that you are teaching your child by example to be disrespectful of anyone who is not like him? If so, what is to keep your child from going into a Jewish Center and shooting small children?

And if your child does not respect you or other authority figures or the lives of others, he probably will not respect himself, which is a necessary thing to be happy and content in this life. It is part of what was missing in the lives of the young men at Columbine High School. Even though we are sometimes isolated from others during our lifetime, if we like and respect ourselves, we can live with that isolation—ask POW's and concentration-camp victims. Those who are missing self-respect may plan and execute a massacre and suicide to resolve their feelings of anger and resentment. Can you live with that?

If your child has not been taught respect for the property of others, will you be surprised if your child calls from jail because he has been caught shoplifting or burglarizing?

Now, if respect begins at home, then I agree with the legislators who say that the parents should be held responsible for the criminal actions of their kids. Oh, yes, I realize that our children can make really *dumb* decisions that are not indicative of how they were raised at home. I also know that if your child was taught self-respect and respect for others and for you, he will think twice if he thinks his actions are going to cause you to have to suffer or that you will make him suffer for what he has done.

Teach respect at home and give your child an advantage in school and in life.

RIDING TO SUCCESSFUL PARENTING

I HAVE COME TO realize that my years of breaking and training horses taught me a lot about parenting.

Lesson 1. Don't let the horse know you are afraid if you want to ride him.

In parenting, the child must have confidence that you are going to make good decisions on his behalf. Children who cannot trust their parents to do what is best for them are forever bereft of confidence. They are never sure whom to trust and often trust the wrong people.

Lesson 2. Once you have the bridle, don't let the horse have control of the bit. Too many parents let go of their children way too soon. They have the delusion that because he is their child that he can be trusted to make good choices despite his age and his maturity. Then when he makes a choice that is devastating, the parent wants to blame him rather that the fact that he was let go of prematurely. Parents have an obligation to hold on to the reins in order to have some control of children who would run wild with too much freedom, and all of them are capable of doing just that. Putting reins and a bit on a horse teaches him that there are ways to act that will allow him to be a pleasure to be around. Keeping the reins on a child, no matter his age, teaches him that there are ways he should behave so that he becomes a positive influence on society rather than a scourge and an embarrassment.

Lesson 3. If you get thrown, fall *loose*. This means as you sail through the air, relax your muscles and you will have less chance of getting hurt when you hit the ground. With children, parents will get *thrown* once in a while. He will make a decision that will seem like it is the end of the world for him and for you. However, take it from parents everywhere, you will live through those difficult times and will learn from your and his experiences. Don't ever think that you are the only one whose child has disappointed a parent. Take if from all of us, your kids are not different from ours. However, we learned from our mistakes and theirs, and we did not get hurt permanently.

Lesson 4. If the horse throws you, don't take it personally, just get back on, take control of the reins, and ride. Too many times we as parents take what our children do to embarrass themselves and us as a personal assault on our parenting skills when, in truth, it was their youth and immaturity that caused the choice and had nothing to do with whether we are good parents or not. When your child makes a poor choice that makes him look foolish, realize that it is his immaturity that has caused him to make the choice; then get back up, dust yourself off, and begin to parent again. Do not give up on him. Do not take what he did as a personal affront to you; rather, consider the source and go on.

Lesson 5. Once you have trained the horse, both of you will enjoy a wonderful relationship. I guess you have to have loved horses and riding as much I did to get this part, but I found great pleasure in riding a dependable but lively horse. I never wanted to break his spirit—I just wanted him to cooperate so I could enjoy being a part of a terrific relationship. As parents, we do not want to break the spirits of our children; we do want them to be loving, dependable, gracious people who contribute to society and who raise loving, dependable grandchildren. Parenting takes time and training and effort. We cannot expect our kids to raise themselves and be successful at it. Our careers are not as important as what we do with our children—the training they receive from us is more important that anything else we will do in life. Our effort at times seems to be beyond our ability to do, yet we make that effort so that our children will receive the benefit.

The result is a relationship that grows as our children grow. They surprise us as they mature into adults with the poise, the spirit, the maturity they show. They shock us with the words they use to train their own children because they sound so much like the words we used to train them. They reveal themselves as contributors to society and we are rewarded.

Parenting is one of the things we hope we do right because so much is *riding* on our success.

SPENDING TIME DOING
WHAT IS TRULY IMPORTANT

H E WAS A self-employed dad, working many hours to provide a certain level of comfort for his family, and he had just returned from a camping trip with his two elementary-aged children. What he had found on that trip was that he was working so hard to maintain their life-style that he was losing time with his kids as they grew up. As he put it, "Soon they will be teenagers and they won't care if I'm around or not. I need to spend less time at the office and more time with them".

Profound words—excellent philosophy. We only have our children for a short time before they are involved with other people, other activities, other lives. So the time we have them to ourselves is precious. It is also the time we have to teach them values, morals, manners, and so many things that the schools don't have time to teach and that society would teach an entirely different way.

So how can this dad and other parents like him spend less time at work and more time with their children? One way is to take them with you when you leave the house on errands rather than leaving them parked in front of the television. At the grocery store, you can teach percentages, good nutrition, getting the correct amount of change back, and much more. At the bank, they can begin to learn how to write checks, how to balance a checkbook, and how to save. In nature, they can learn how to read signs of changing weather, how to find their way out of the woods, and how to recognize dangerous snakes. The advantage is that you have the child with you and there is that *time* element you would not have if they had stayed at home.

Another way is to simply cut down on the non-necessities of living. One of the new societal mantras is *Spending is so old school.* Parents are finding that their kids don't have to have everything they ask for (excuse the preposition). They can have fun things and still not break your wallet, and you, in turn, can spend more time with them doing fun things that don't cost an arm and a leg. A few of us were discussing a family that had it all—the skis, the skidoos, the boats, the hunting licenses, the cabin—all of the expensive ways to have a good time. Now the parents are divorced; the kids are gone; and the importance of having those things disappeared long ago. What the kids actually needed was more time with their parents, but the expense of having fun was more valuable than the kids were.

Many parents today are finding ways to be wealthy that depends less on earning more cash and having more things than it does on being with family. As they discover that truth, they are finding that they have a lot more free time—what adults today want more of than anything else—time to take care of the truly important things in life.

Because of the economy, we have moved away from the mantra of spending more than we earn and from living paycheck to paycheck. Many average American households owe approximately $10,500 in credit cards and are tied down to a mortgage that is more than the value of the house. Personal bankruptcies and foreclosures are at all-time highs. In fact, the papers are now saying that the new houses being built do not have those lofty ceilings and wasted space—what they do have is room for the family to live and enjoy life more and rooms that require less heating and air conditioning.

Do you have dinner with your family at least three to four times a week? This main element of family life can prevent drug use, premarital sex, school dropouts, and so many other societal problems. Some families have even found that rather than getting up from the dinner table and rushing to the TV, that they are spending more time after the meal talking and sharing their day with each other. What a novel idea!

So, the bottom line is—not necessarily the bottom line. It comes down to spending less which means having to earn less which then means having more time to spend with the children. Relieving the pressure to buy more and more creates less stress, less headaches, less requirements to balance what will and will not be paid, and will create time to develop relationships that will go on into perpetuity.

Spending time doing what is truly important has nothing to do with money and things—it has everything to do with the people in your life and the time you spend with them. Take charge of this aspect of your life before you kids are so out of your life that you lose the joy of being with them.

THE MOST IMPORTANT SENTENCE IN PARENTING

I WAS READING SOME biographies one day and realized that some of the most successful people in our nation's history and in our individual lives were handicapped either physically or environmentally (like the homes in which they were raised). However, they were given a two-word sentence during their childhood or adolescence that allowed them to overcome odds and obtain victory—that small sentence made all the difference in their futures.

For instance, Helen Keller could neither see nor hear, yet she had a loving family who did everything they could to communicate with her and allow her to communicate with the world. In doing so, they allowed us a glimpse into that marvelous mind and philosophy. They gave her that sentence and did not let her wallow in self-pity and despair.

Another child was diagnosed *abnormal* by relatives and mentally ill by the school and so was taught at home by his mother. He spent an inordinate amount of time alone *tinkering* with inanimate objects but was encouraged to do this by his mother. His name was Thomas Edison.

One of our childhood friends was orphaned while he was in college. Yet he had always been told that he could do anything he wanted to do. He became a renowned orthopedic pediatric surgeon.

A teacher I know spent her later hears as a teen without the love of either parent, both had died; and another was raised by a single mother who worked in a school cafeteria to allow her children to eat and stay in school. Yet both of them finished college and have devoted their careers to teaching children and youth. They had the courage to fulfill their dreams because they had been told they could do it.

Why did these people, facing great odds, succeed? I believe it is because they were told during their upbringing, "You can", and they did. Those two words make up one of the most inspirational, motivational, loving sentences parents or guardians can give to the children in their care.

Can you remember a time in your life when your parent, teacher, coach, or someone else said "You can do it!" and you did not feel empowered to do whatever "it" was?

Why do parents ever ask that opposite, negative sentence? "<u>Can't</u> you do anything right?" or "Why <u>can't</u> you make better grades?" or "<u>Can't</u> you at least do one (chore) without being told?" Parents, have you ever heard of self-fulfilling prophesy? Psychologists tell us that we will live "up" to the words and comments made to us all of the time. What are your words conveying to your child or teenager in your home?

It may be difficult at first, but all of us can begin now to make our comments to our children sound more positive—"You <u>are</u> a good kid". "I'm glad you are <u>my</u> kid". "You <u>are</u> doing better every time (at playing ball, mowing the lawn, cleaning the kitchen, feeding the dog, finishing homework)." "You <u>can</u> do it!" (algebra, college anatomy, getting up on time, preparing for a test).

Oh, yes, it is easy to be negative as parents—it seems to come with the parenting *package* when our babies come into our lives, and most of us are masters at the negative sentence. It requires more thought and creativity and concern for the child to be positive, but WE <u>CAN</u> DO IT!

THE REAL WAY TO ESTABLISH SELF-ESTEEM IN YOUR CHILD.

ONE OF THE best comments about children's self-esteem I have read lately came from Randy Pausch's book THE LAST LECTURE, "There's a lot of talk these days about giving children self-esteem. It's not something you can give; it's something they have to build." Then he used an example of a football coach he had when he was a child and finished with this, "He knew there was really only one way to teach kids how to develop it (self-esteem): You give them something they can't do; work hard until they find they can do it, and you just keep repeating the process."

I agree entirely. When have you given your child a task that *pushed* him before he completed it? When our son was eleven, he was getting to the age that he was asking for *things* that we felt were unnecessary and not within our budget. So we told him that he could mow the grass for an elderly lady we knew and earn the money. His first day on the *job* was a disaster. He left gaps in the mown grass; he had a *wavy* line on the edged driveway; and the hill in the backyard was obviously too steep for him to reach. Rather than do the work for him, I followed him as he did it again—all of it, until the yard looked like it should. The elderly lady felt sorry for him as she watched him from her windows and offered him a snack when he finally completed the work. However, from that time on, his work was excellent, and he went on to earn quite a lot of money for yard work from individuals and from a company. His obvious pride in his work gave him the self-esteem he needed for other tasks down the road.

There are other ingredients that need to be mixed into the bag that ensures self-esteem in our children. Here are some of those:

Parental love. When Randy Pausch was writing his book as he also prepared for his death from cancer, he interviewed people who lost parents when they were children. "They told me they found it consoling to learn about how much their mothers and fathers loved them." Volumes of research have gone into finding how some children have self-esteem and some don't. Much of it has come down to this one thing: when a child feels he is loved and valued by his parents, he has confidence in his ability to face life's challenges.

Now I don't mean *smothered love* where you don't allow the child to be himself and to deal with life on his terms. I do mean that he never has a reason to doubt your love even when he disappoints you. He knows that you will make him face consequences for bad decisions but you are doing it out of love for him that transcends everything else. He knows that if he is alone and afraid, there is that parental love that will sustain him. Every child needs that kind of love from a parent.

Memories. When you are gone, what will your child remember that will give him solace? The family in which I was raised had dinner together most every night. Because dad worked on the railroad, he was not always there, but the kids and mom where at the table with hands washed and seated at the same time nightly. "Family day is a day to eat dinner with your children" according to a grocery ad. That same ad went on to say, "Join us in supporting this national effort to promote the family dinners and effective way to reduce substance abuse among children and teens". One day I talked to a mother about her son and his apparent disinterest in school work. When I asked if they discussed school at the dinner table each evening, her answer was encouraging. They do meet every night; they do discuss each person's day and what they learned at school or at work; they do have a good time with each other. Way to go! The kid will begin to see the value in school work—it just may not be at the top of his agenda right now.

Your child not only needs that time every day (not in front of the television), but he also needs other memories, Do you ever have picnics in a park? Do you go on short little day trips that get you away from the house and the neighborhood for a change? Do you do the yard together? Do you cook together? Bottom line is—do you do anything that will create memories and give your child a sense of family, which will then help build his self-esteem? If not, you have some planning to do. Do it soon for your child's sake, and ultimately, for yours as well

WHAT KIND OF EXAMPLE ARE YOU?

T HIS PAST MONDAY was my precious mother's funeral after several weeks of illness that could not be treated successfully. I wrote the following tribute to be read at the service. My question to all mothers (and fathers) is, "When your children are preparing for your funeral, what can they say about you that showed what a good example you were to them?"

"My mother was such a terrific example for her children in so many wonderful ways:

1. FAMILY: Above all we knew that she loved her family and she showed us that we were the first priority in her life. She took an active part in our lives when we were kids: If the rest of the neighborhood came over, she taught us how to play Kick the Can and we played until she served food in the kitchen. If there were no Cub Scout leader to be found, then she became one; if a Sunday School Teacher was needed, she taught; if there was no Youth Director in the church, she organized the Valentine banquets, the hay rides in the fall and wrote and directed the plays for Christmas. She was a great counselor to a daughter about what to do and not to do on a date, and she threw baseball with the sons since Dad was gone so much. Every holiday and birthday was cause for a celebration with decorations and food and family time.

   Her greatest earthly love was our dad, and it was normal to see them holding hands as they walked or holding each other in the kitchen as they cooked breakfast together.
   We learned to love others from Mom and Dad.

2. FINANCES: Mother was a brilliant mathematician and used that gift in maintaining our family's budget while dad was gone on the railroad. When our family needed help with that budget, she was not afraid to do whatever it took to bring money into the home by going to work. When the railroad put dad on the Extra Board, they bought a little store, and then when dad's work was more steady, she ran the store alone for several years.

She was an entrepreneur before I knew the definition of one and became a Realtor and the owner of her own company that was the second real estate company in our county and the first one in the north part of our state that was owned by a woman. "Strength and honor (were) her clothing." (Proverbs 31:20) She was well known in the community for her hard work, her integrity, and her fairness. Many times when she became aware that the potential purchase of a house was going to cause marital issues between a couple, she would counsel them to wait and talk more about buying rather than allow it to cause problems for them even if it meant the loss of a commission.

One of the greatest truths she and dad taught us was from Paul: "Whatsoever you have, therewith be content" (Philippians 4:11). We never had a lot of money, but we had a good life because they were our parents.

3. FUN: Mom loved to have a good time and it showed in her love of life and her fun times. She and dad loved to camp, to walk in the woods, to cut wood for the fireplace, to have bonfires—anything to have fun. Life was never boring as long as Mom was in charge of planning what we were going to do even if it was connected to work. However, she also believed in discipline, and we were not allowed to go with friends or to play unless we had completed our chores. She must have wanted us to be smart, because she was a believer in Proverbs 12:1 which says, "Whoever loves discipline loves knowledge, but he who hates reproof is stupid." We had a lot of occasions to love discipline and ample opportunity not to hate reproof!

4. FRIENDS: She was a loving and loyal friend. Some of the friends who were waiting for her when she got to Heaven were from when she was a teenager, and they were still friends when they went on before her. The friends she had at our church have almost been as affected by her death as we are. There are other friends who will miss her from other towns and other states and all over the nation. I have never known a group of friends who cared about each other more than those she and dad made as they grew older.

5. FELLOWSHIP: Mom loved her church and was a leader on committees, in Sunday School class, in the choir, and in other ways for over sixty years. Her children knew that if she missed church, it was because she physically couldn't get there. Even though we didn't always go where she went, we knew she was there, and that example of commitment and love for the people of her church and her love for the Lord were important life-lessons for us. We are examples of "Children who rise up and call her Blessed." (Proverbs 31:28)

Every child should have a Mother who is a great example of how to live and love. God allowed me to be born to one of those mothers, and I am so grateful to Him."

After having read this, I hope all mothers and fathers will consider the examples they are for their children. Will they be able to have positive memories of you and to share those with your grandchildren and with others as well? Begin now to establish that kind of legacy.

WHY I BELIEVE IN SPORTS AND OTHER
CHALLENGES FOR KIDS

W E WERE WALKING in a park one morning and there were little football players everywhere! I didn't know they made pads that small, but there they were in full pads, running plays in practice for dads and coaches. There were two other teams on the hill playing a game, and they were just a little bigger than the ones practicing.

Two scenarios were such fun to watch and were reminders of days when our son played ball. There was obviously a really good play happening on the hill, and half of the little fellas on the practice team had turned toward the cheering crowd. It is difficult to keep the attention of little people on something serious when the fun seems to be somewhere else. The other scene was when a white turkey left where she was and walked onto the practice field of the same players. The boys were trying not to be distracted, but it was hard when the turkey had her eyes on the nearest coach who had his back to her. I admire the players—they didn't crack a smile—but kept listening to the coach talk about plays until someone came and tackled the turkey and took her away.

Those who know me understand that I believe in kids playing on a sport team whether its football, basketball, soccer, volleyball, track or whatever else is available and the child can play with some measure of success. Not all players are going to be stars on the team, but if they learn the life lessons they can experience, then they have gained something valuable that possibly cannot be learned any other way.

Team sport teaches a child how to work toward a common goal with other players. It teaches discipline, stamina, sportsmanlike conduct, and how to win or lose gracefully. The value of a good coach is priceless if he or she can not only motivate the team members, but also can teach the players how to grow as a person and how to self-motivate so that the lessons learned can lead to a productive life in the future.

With the exception of one, my husband and I and our siblings (one had a vision problem) played one or more sports in high school. We don't want to relive that time or to show that we are still capable of dong what we could do then. However, we are thankful for the patience and endurance of our coaches, for the life lessons we learned from being part of a team, for the times we heard the crowd roar their approval, and even for the times we had to walk off the field or the court in defeat. We found out that the same challenges happen in life, that we must give our best to whatever we are doing, and that we can overcome the defeats because we learned to try again while playing in a team sport.

What of the kids who just don't have the interest or the skills to play a sport? I also believe in music, like the band or the chorus where there is teamwork, and the voices or instruments make separate sounds but the end result it lovely. I believe in theater where the hours of effort produce something that everyone else can enjoy. I believe in participating in clubs and activities where teamwork and leadership skills can be honed and improved. These activities can teach more about life than learning in the classroom

What I don't believe in is parking in front of the TV watching endless shows or movies or playing mindless games for hours on end. I don't believe in spending hours on the computer Twittering or Facebooking or other means of communicating electronically. Yes, I know that this is the new age and that kids are going to take part in each of these. My problem with it is that the child spends so much time with electronics that his body becomes mush; his brain is never challenged; he never has an opportunity to be a part of a team of his peers; and he never learns to challenge himself to work toward a common goal and to get along with other people who are not like him.

I do believe in challenges because life is a challenge, and those who never have been challenged or who have never challenged themselves to do something beyond what is comfortable or easy will probably fold at the least difficulty in life and throw up their hands in defeat.

I learned a valuable lesson at a Prayer Retreat during quiet time. I still held resentment toward a girl who had made my last year in high school miserable socially. During that time by myself, I realized that despite her actions toward me, I had succeeded in doing well in my various careers, and as a wife, as a daughter, as a mother. Then I had a new thought, I had not succeeded *despite* her—I had succeeded *because* of her. The difficult challenge she presented at that time made me want to go on and find success in a different arena, and I did.

Children must face challenges in life in order to grow and to later succeed because of how they learned to handle them. Give your child something that will make him grow and reach and strive, and require his best at it. He will realize later in life that he is a better person for having faced a challenge and overcome or won.

WHY PARENTS MAKE RULES FOR CHILDREN

I WAS READING THE last of one of my favorite novel series when a parenting truth jumped out at me. The main character in the Mitford Series, Father Tim, is having a serious talk with one of the children who had been abandoned by his mother and raised by his alcoholic father. He had caught the boy smoking and was reminding him that one of the rules he had to follow if he was going to live there was "No Smoking". The young man was protesting the various rules that had been set forth when he came, voluntarily, to live with Father Tim and his wife.

Father Tim said, "Here's the deal about rules. They are not meant to put you in a box: they are meant to give you freedom. Doesn't pool have rules? (The boy was a master at pool.) Can you ignore the rules and win the game? You have a secure roof over you head, three meals a day, a job you say you like, a paycheck, your own room, people who care about you. Does that mean anything to you?" (The boy was still angry after this little talk and left during the night, but he only went as far as the barn and came back to the house in the morning.)

Rules. Every parent should make them, and every child should obey them. They have many purposes, so let's look at a few of them:

1. Rules give parameters to children who are not capable of making good decisions all of the time. When most of us were growing up, we felt safe in the knowledge that our parents cared where we were, what we were doing, and when we would get home safely. Rules allowed us to do some things but not to do others because we knew what the consequences would be when we got home. There were limits, but they actually gave us the freedom to have fun without having to pay for it later.

2. Rules give the freedom that would hinder play because the child doesn't have to wonder whether he should take part in a certain activity or not. If your child follows your rules, he will, more than likely, come home at the appointed time (ours would fly in the driveway on his bike and later in his car right at the hour), and he

will not be followed by the law or a mad parent. He knows how to act with others, how to be polite and respectful, and how to excuse himself from something that would be harmful if he did it and broke your rule.

3. Rules give, especially to the teenager, an excuse to refuse to stay out late when he could get into trouble, to refuse to drink, to turn down the drug, to say "No" to sex, and so forth. He may not want to use you as an excuse (though your rules are a terrific reason not to engage in unlawful or immoral activities), but your rules are always in his thoughts as a deterrent to what his friends may be asking him to do.

If you have not yet made rules for your children, there is one thing that must be done first—the two parents must agree to uphold whatever rules you establish whether they are still living in the same house or not. If one parent makes the rules and the other refuses to help make them stick and help with handing out the consequences if the rules are broken, then the child receives mixed messages and will refuse to abide by any of your rules. If you haven't already, spend some time deciding on some specific rules that must be followed by your kids no matter what age they are.

To some things the automatic answer is "NO", like drinking, drugging, having sex, speeding, texting while driving, and so forth. Your child should know what the consequences are and that they will not be changed no matter what the argument is. These rules are protective and could keep your child from making a truly life-changing mistake.

Some parents make it a rule that the kids are not to use profanity, to make racial slurs, to disrespect adults, and so on. These rules can very well keep your child from getting into trouble with society and the law. Other parents have rules about a child's responsibilities and actions as a part of the family which, in turn, keep harmony in the home.

So, obviously, rules are given because the child is loved and protected. They are not given to keep him "in a box", but to, hopefully, assure that he will have a future and that the future will be good and successful. They may even help him become a good parent someday when he will use some of the rules you used with his own children. What a compliment!

WILL YOUR CHILD THINK OF YOU IN TIME
OF A CRISIS DECISION?

I WATCHED A SCENARIO that reminded me of parents and kids. A young calf and her mother were in a pasture, and there was a large black dog watching them from a hill not too far away. The calf was curious, and took several tentative steps toward the dog. The dog did not move. Before the calf took another several steps, she looked toward her mother and then took the steps. The cow continued to graze and was apparently oblivious to the events taking place. Again, the calf looked over at her mother and then took more steps toward the dog, which remained alert but unmoving. They were now just a few yards from each other. Finally, the cow picked up her head and began to walk away from the direction of the dog, followed obediently by the calf.

Wouldn't it be nice if, before our children took steps toward a bad decision, they stopped and contemplated what our reaction would be? If they would just linger a short time and wonder whether they should take part in something or not, they might not face the danger or the trouble or the consequences they might otherwise have to face.

So, how do we cause them to think of us before they make a decision?

First, we make sure that we have discussed what we expect in behavior when they are away from us and what they will face at home if they don't comply with what we expect. They should know beyond a doubt that we will stand by what we have discussed with them and that they can use us as an excuse with their friends if they need a way out of a difficult situation. It is also important that we cover, not only the rules we expect to be followed, but also the values we consider important to our family.

Second, we must be sure that we as the parents are standing together in this very serious situation. We must be on the same page when it comes to our expectations regarding the boundaries we have set for our children. Eventually, a child, especially a teenager, will challenge the parameters we have set, and, if we are not unified in our effort to keep our child safe, he can *worm* his way around us, even divide us, and maybe get hurt in the process. Not standing by each other also gives a child a feeling of insecurity and leaves him open to making choices that may get him into situations he would rather avoid. Presenting a united front lets him know that he has two people who genuinely love him and will stand for him when the going is no longer easy.

Third, be good models for your children. If you don't want him to smoke, then don't smoke. If you are worried that he might someday have a problem with drinking, then don't drink or have alcohol of any kind in the house. If you don't want him to do drugs, then don't do them or even condone it. If he is a teen and is looking for a model of a secure relationship as he begins to date, then be that example for him. Children learn how to treat others as they watch their parents at home. They will either learn how to verbally and/or physically abuse their partners, or they will learn how to be kind, gentle, loving, and giving with others. They should see respect and good communication modeled before them at all times.

Fourth, not only let your child know what is and is not expected of him, but also make yourself available to listen. Children are perpetually curious about how to relate to others as they grow and mature; and it is important that you actually listen as they ask questions, make comments, and let you in on their thoughts and happenings. If they notice that you only partially listen and that they have to fight to gain your attention, they will either find someone else who will listen or they will stop communicating altogether. Too often that other person will be another child who gives poor feedback or, for a teen, who may develop into a relationship that causes your child to become too dependent on the other person.

Fifth, the best impact can come from short conservations rather than *the big talk*. Do not wear your child out by going on and on about a subject. Allow time for questions and for feedback and make sure that your child has heard you rather than tuned you out.

Sixth, be available for fun. Invite other kids over, have fun parties, have teens over after the ball games. Be sure that you know the first and last names of the friends your child likes to be around. What you know could mean the difference between finding your child or teen some dark night or not.

Will your child think of you and your expectations before he makes a difficult choice? The answer lies in how you handle the six steps above.

CHAPTER THREE

HELP! I WANT TO BE A GOOD TEACHER FOR MY CHILDREN

GETTING UP AFTER WE'VE BEEN KNOCKED DOWN

L IFE SOMETIMES "KNOCKS you down—but it is how you get up and handle it that's important". (Kenny Chesney in an interview regarding his documentary "The Boys of Fall")

"Football emulates life", according to Chesney, and when I asked my husband if that were true, he came up with these comparisons: It teaches teamwork—how to play in harmony with the rest of the team and the rest of the positions that make up the team. He has always said that playing football made him a better employee and later a better manager in the work world. He's never said it, but being under a coach who cared about his players and knowing how he motivated them probably taught him how to motivate the people he managed when he went into the work world.

He also said that football teaches that it takes everyone working together to accomplish a goal, and that translates to the work world where everyone doing his job resolves into getting the product out and into the hands of the buying world. It also translates to the family—everyone should have a responsibility in maintaining the household so that it will run smoothly and the entire work load does not fall on one person.

Another truism from the world of football by my husband, Joe: "You have to sacrifice your own well being to help the team meet its goal." As a cheerleader in high school, I was close enough to the game to watch the players come off the field with dislocated shoulders (coach worked the bones back into place, put a tight brace on it and sent him back in), cleat-cut hands, broken bones, mud or lime in eyes, and much more. The boys would come out long enough to get something fixed and then run back in. There were no *babies* on the field. Life sometimes makes us hurt either physically or emotionally, and we succumb to the pain and give in or we can run out to be fixed—to the doctor or therapist—and then run back into the game of life and live fully.

"You can't just quit because you hurt—you have to keep going." My husband played many times with a broken hand, but it did not keep him from using those shoulders to block the opposing team so his team could reach the goal or prevent the opposing team from reaching theirs. Even now, when what he is doing looks impossible, he never gives up, but, using the math he loved to teach or other skills, he figures out how to get it done and finishes.

Because he played on the line, I learned to watch more than the quarterback and receivers. There is no way the team could accomplish their objective of getting to the goal in front of them without the blocking, tackling, and creating a hole that the offensive line did. Often in high school they are the unsung heroes, yet they get out there day after day in practice and in the games doing their jobs. On defense, they are the reason the other team is prevented from reaching their goal. Sometimes we think that our jobs are menial and unimportant; however, it takes all types of work to make a business or a home hum. In a school, one of the most important jobs is maintenance—as teachers we were so dependent on them to keep the building clean and everything running so that we could teach and work with the kids.

Chesney says, "Football taught me how hard you had to work to achieve something—knockin' heads and talkin' trash, slingin' mud and dirty grass" (words from the single "The Boys of Fall"). If a child gives up too quickly with his homework or his project, he must be taught to keep at it until it is finished—until he has achieved his goal. This is a lesson, not for the teacher to teach, but for the parent to instill in his child.

Chesney also learned something that is vital in all walks of life—focus. Too often we and our children, who have watched way too much TV, lose the ability to really focus on what we are dong—even our relationships and our parenting. We allow our minds to wander off to other things and eventually any and everything is more important than what is right before us. We must learn to focus as well as the boys do who are working to score or assist a score or prevent a score in a game.

Usually every team has a team leader or motivator who can rally the rest even when winning the game looks impossible. In the home, both parents (or the single parent) are the motivators, the encouragers (the cheerleaders). Sometimes a word of encouragement or praise is all a child needs to continue his work.

No one has a totally easy way in life or even in love, but, if we use football as an example, we learn to get up after we've been knocked down, put the pain aside, and put our best into whatever we are doing. The rewards will come if we work hard enough at it.

SELF-FAILURE VS. SELF-CONFIDENCE = SELF-TALK

O NE OF THE most difficult tasks we have as parents is raising self-confident children. As an educator, I have seen the results of the opposite—people I will call "self-failures". These kids come to the new school year *hoping* they can do better than last year, but I can tell from their answers, their faces, and their attitudes that they have little real confidence that they can improve.

What has happened to these kids who lack any assurance in themselves and who would rather fail than try? What can we do to help our children gain the self-confidence that is so necessary in a successful, peaceful life? The answers lie in self-talk—or how we *talk* to ourselves.

The *self-failure child* (my term) consistently tells himself "I can't do that"; "Nobody wants to play/be with me"; "This is too hard for me"; "I am a failure"; "Nothing I do is right". Where did these messages originate? God forbid if messages like this were first uttered by the child's parents! Remember, children have a tendency to believe and remember the negative messages we give more than the positive ones. So, let's assume the failure messages came from children in the neighborhood or on the playground or from siblings or even from insensitive relatives. What should be the role of the parent in this situation?

First, for Heaven's sake, don't rush on to the playground or the street or to school and confront the other child, call him names or call the kid's parents and rant over the insensitive brat they have raised. Have you every been guilty of doing just that, then within ten minutes the kids are back playing again and you have a nice coating of egg on your angry face?

Your duty as a parent is to restore the child's confidence by how much confidence YOU have in him. "Well, he doesn't know you like I do", "I happen to know you have nice red hair like your Daddy". "Well, he may have said that because someone has hurt his feelings and he is taking it out on you. So you can play inside for a while and let him cool off": He said WHAT? You tell him that the dog is in the back yard and I am in the kitchen if he wants to call us that again!" (Said as calmly as possible).

Not only must we dispel the negative talk others could give our child, but we also, as parents, must be *coaches* of positive self-talk.

The next time you watch the Olympics or most any individual sporting event or a basketball player shooting a free throw, pay attention to their faces and often their mouths. Most successful athletes have been coached to talk to themselves just before their event or shot—to repeat the words the coach has taught them. My track coach, W.S. Donald, told this short, skinny kid that she could run, and I believed it. As I set into the blocks for a race, I *talked* the language: "stay low, swing arms, dig, dig!" The relay hand-off had to be precise, the steps perfect, and I talked my way through every step—the same words Coach had used as he trained me.

Watch as Olympic gymnasts will even verbally talk to themselves as they prepare to take the bars, the mount, or the floor. They are giving themselves pep talks. It is said that the best tennis players and golfers talk to themselves just before they hit the ball.

So, how does that relate to our kids? The very best words we can give them are, "I can do this!" A 5th grade math teacher I know constantly tells his kids "You can do this!" And they can!

Here is a list of ways to *coach* your kids:

1. Don't let them include "can't" in their vocabulary—turn it to "can".
2. Remind them often that they are special and unique, with different talents, abilities and interests. It is fine not to be just like their peers.
3. When they do make a mistake, and they will, and lose some confidence, and they will, coach them to use it as a learning opportunity and to go and try it again.
4. Teach them that not everyone is going to like them. But that if they like themselves, they will draw others to them. They will think it is egotistical to like themselves, but even God says to love our neighbors as ourselves.
5. Teach them to praise themselves for doing well. As they succeed at things, they need to know that it is O.K. to say "Oooh, I did great!" (Silently, of course) This is an important part of the whole process and they will be able to do this part much easier if they have heard praise from you.

This *coaching* can start at any age—the younger the better—but our teenagers also need it desperately during their self-critical years.

The added bonus? Once they have learned to positive self-talk in their youth, they will carry it over into a successful adulthood. What a gift you will have given them! And when they are going through their own child-rearing years, they may even say to you, "Thanks, Mom/Dad/Coach".

TEACH YOUR CHILDREN WELL

I USUALLY DON'T QUOTE someone who is connected to celebrity because they are, as a rule, shallow and self-serving. However, I heard a short interview of Denise Jonas, the mother of the Jonas Brothers, that was exceptional. She was asked what she felt was the most important lesson she was teaching her sons, and her answer was this, "To me there is nothing more frustrating than being around a child who is annoying. We are teaching our kids proper manners."

The interviewer asked what methods she and her husband used to teach them, and she answered that they were always consistent with their discipline; they set certain boundaries that were not to be violated; and that they constantly reinforced good conduct until it became good behavior "because they are going to be adults a lot longer than they are children". She added that, even as the boys' popularity widened, they were required to have good manners and good behavior or they would answer to their parents.

How refreshing! How different from so many parents in today's society! However, there are positive exceptions:

I was listening to two young mothers discussing what they were trying to teach their sons now that they were in the pre-adolescent stage of maturity. One said that she was teaching her son to open doors for her, to order her food at restaurants, to pull her chair out for her, to wait for her to be seated, and other lessons in masculine manners that will serve him well as he matures. The other mother was excited about beginning to teach her son these concepts as well, and she added that she was helping to direct his temper as he learns appropriate ways to deal with other people. These moms are using their teaching time in very positive ways.

There are other things young people should know about how to conduct themselves in public. Many times there are teens who think that their conversations should be heard by everyone around them. Girls, especially, are guilty of talking and laughing so loudly that they literally disturb others who are anywhere near them. Mothers have the opportunity and the responsibility to teach them that they are not the only ones in a room, and that being obtrusively loud is very poor manners.

I find young men, very often, are delightfully aware of the needs of ladies who need assistance. I had the opportunity of taking my mother, who was ninety-two years old at the time, to several doctors' offices and often to a restaurant at least once a week. She used a rollator to get around. I very seldom had to hold the door for her—there were always boys or men who would wait for us so they could help in some way. Some parents somewhere are to be thanked for teaching their sons to be polite, considerate, and thoughtful.

In addition to behavior in public, there are also some things young people should know about manners. Does a child know which fork to use first? What is the large spoon at the top of the plate used for? Where and when do they move the napkin both before and after the meal? Where do they place their silverware to indicate they are finished with their meal? Do they know how to treat the wait staff with dignity and appreciation? Does your son know how to hold his arm so that a lady can place her hand on it at a formal affair? These are bits of information that could prevent embarrassment and could put your child in a good light for future employment or promotion. It is never too late to teach good manners.

Denise Jonas was right, our children will be young for too short a time, and we don't have forever to teach them how to conduct themselves properly and positively in public. They will be adults living in an adult world for so much longer—a world that is competitive, aggressive, and very difficult for the person who has no clue how to conduct himself in the business world or in any other life that he chooses. Take the time now to prepare your child for that future.

"Teach your children well."

Jan Knight

TEACHING KIDS TO REACH FOR THEIR DREAMS

IT WAS NEWSWORTHY that an NFL player was a special guest at our school, and it was newsworthy that we retired his high school football jersey, but the most impressive part of the day was the time he spent talking to the students.

Brandon Jackson played really great football at Horn Lake High School in northwest Mississippi; then he played terrific football for the University of Nebraska; and then he helped the Green Bay Packers win the Super Bowl in 2010. He has earned honors and a football card and a ring. It is how he got to the NFL that can inspire not only young football players, but also students of all ages.

Brandon used his own experience to convince his high-school audience that, if they had a dream—a vision—and then worked hard to fulfill it, they could reach it. He told them that he had always wanted to play Division I football and had always wanted to play pro football. To that end, he studied hard to keep his grades up; he took the ACT six times and brought his score from a 13 to a 23; he ran track to increase his speed as a running back; he lifted weights and was moved on the team from the lighter running backs to the heavier linemen. Finally, his best position was fullback, but he could still catch the ball like a receiver.

During those years in high school, as a principal pointed out, he never had a discipline referral—not even for tardies. He was well liked by his peers and the faculty; he was always polite and kind; he did what was asked of him in the classroom as well as on the field without complaint.

What a contrast from many other kids in school who refuse to turn in work; who complain about teacher methods; who go past deadlines to pay fees or turn in research papers or order their rings and then blame the ones who set the deadlines. They can't focus on the important part of school, the learning, but focus on *drama:* who likes who and why and who is *messin'* with who's boyfriend or girlfriend.

What is the difference? In the book *HEAR OUR CRY,* by Paul D. Slocumb, the author says it this way: "So why do some young people experiment with drugs, sex, and videos, while others do not? Scientists believe that a common denominator is MOTIVATION. Young people who are motivated to make something of their lives—those who have hope and are future-orientated—are less likely to experiment with things

100

that might divert them from their goal." In other words, they are like Brandon, they have a dream, a goal, and they work hard to reach it.

So what can parents do to help their children create a goal toward which they can work? We keep encouraging and teaching and telling them to reach higher and farther. We never make fun of their dreams, but give them insight about the goal they are striving toward. We make them feel important and wanted and useful and worthy—not like the mother who came to a parent conference in my office who never listened to the counselor or the teacher, but who talked on her cell phone the entire time. The student was actually embarrassed by her behavior and by her obvious lack of concern for him. How sad.

You teach them to listen to those who would lead them toward excellence. Here are the departing words of Mr. Ferguson, the principal of Horn Lake High School before he dismissed the assembly of students who had just heard Brandon: "Students, I want you to leave here today believing you too can live out your dream. You all have the potential to do extraordinary things in life. You must first Dream, then you must stay focused and pursue your dream with determination. You can not let negative influences drag you down to where you live beneath your potential. Please put some thought into what you have heard today. I hope you will begin to Dream Big Dreams and pursue them with all your heart. Don't live life with regrets."

Amen.

TEACHING RESPONSIBILITY THROUGH CHORES

O NE EVENING I met a delightful young mother who had three children and was two months from having the fourth. She had a degree in chemistry but was a stay-at-home mom who had a popular blog covering her own home-cleaning products made from items bought on the grocery shelf.

What fascinated me the most was her ability to manage her children as helpers in the home. Every morning, in addition to their *tidy* chore of straightening their rooms and beds, they have additional chores of *swishing* the potty and *swiping* the bathroom. The fact that they are doing it daily means that each area is getting clean. They are also responsible for taking their dishes to the kitchen where one child rinses and another puts the dishes in the dishwasher and another takes them out when they are complete.

Each of these six, seven and four year olds knows how to vacuum and only misses the far corners which the mother gets during the week. Their outside chores are to feed and water the goats and chickens and gather the eggs (This is in an upscale neighborhood).

Of course, my next question was "How do you convince your kids to do their chores?", and her answer was: "Because mommy said so".

My reason for giving children chores is to teach responsibility. Hers was so that all of the housework and the maintaining of the entire place were not solely on her shoulders. Amazingly, that is what the older generation and the farmers did. They gave the children, from young ages, things to do around the house and the farm so that they had help and did not have the entire responsibility themselves. Ultimately, the children grew up to be responsible adults who could take care of themselves and their property and who then began to teach their children to help.

Then came a generation which gave their children everything *except* responsibility and, as a result, we have children who feel they are *entitled* to all of the good things without doing anything to get them. So we have spoiled kids who seldom do anything around the house and expect their parent to do for them and expect the school to give them grades whether or not they work for them and expect their bosses to provide a salary for little or no effort.

One Christmas we were looking for an electronic gizmo at a large electronic store. When we walked in, we passed three employees who just stood there talking and laughing among themselves and never asked if they could help us. When we asked the man at the door (whose job it was to facilitate customer assistance) to find a salesperson for us, he couldn't find anyone to help us either (the first three had disappeared into the bowels of the store by then). So these three are making a living by standing in one place until they are needed and then they go off for a soft drink? Who raised these young people? (And, as my husband asked, "Why do they still have a job?")

So, how do you teach your children to be responsible and to have a good work ethic? You give them chores at an early age. You don't pay your children for doing them—it is part of being in the family and taking care of all that being in the family entails. They do it, not because they are doing you a favor, but because "Mommy said so." (They won't understand the concept of responsibility and work ethic until you have taught them.)

I know one mother who does some of the outside chores during very cold weather and snow because "the kids might catch cold." Yet, they spent hours in the snow one year building snowmen and forts without catching a sniffle. This mother is either a martyr (psychological need to be used so she can feel sorry for herself) or she is manipulated by her smarter children. I know from sending our son to feed the chickens in the cold that it doesn't hurt one bit; in fact, he never missed a day of school for being sick—he only missed one day in twelve years to take care of the broken arm which happened in the school gym. So much for hurting the darlings by sending them to do chores in the cold.

So, how many chores do your children have and how are they doing with that responsibility? It is never too late to solicit help from your children in the home or the yard, and the sooner you take care of teaching responsibility to them, the better off both of you will be.

TEACHING RESPONSIBILITY TO CHILDREN

D
URING THE FINAL week of school one year, several frustrated teachers said they had quite a few students fail their classes who were very capable of doing well in their subject. When I asked their opinion of what could be the problem, two of them, without knowing what the other had said, commented that it was because the kids were not responsible enough. The students had *hoped* something would happen and they would pass; they had *expected* the teacher to help them get a passing grade; they had been *surprised* that their grade was so low.

There is obviously something that high school students and their parents don't know—students are held responsible for their own grades. No one should give them a passing grade for being a good kid; no teacher should let them do nothing and pass a course.

One teacher had a good suggestion: Once summer comes around, parents have an opportunity to really concentrate on teaching their children responsibility. Here are some suggestions based on what parents in my office have mentioned:

1. Every child, from an early age to the day he leaves home, should have chores that are his responsibility only, and, like so many before him, he should not be able to leave home, or play, or get on the phone or watch TV, or get on the computer until those chores are done. Most adults today learned responsibility in this old-fashioned but effective way. If you have not tried this before now, and you have a teenager, he may balk at first, but when he wants to play ball with the guys down the street but his chores are not done and he has to finish them, he just may learn to complete those chores so he can again have his privileges.

2. For your child's sake, do not let him sleep late every morning during the summer. If your student has slept until 11:00 or 1:00 every day and has gone to bed after midnight, it takes him at least a month to adjust to being awake for his first or second-period class. All of us, adults and students as well, need to stay on a

consistent schedule in order for our bodies to work efficiently. So even if you are at work and your teenager or child is at home, be sure he is up and going at least by 8:00.

3. Limit TV and game time. Sitting before a TV tube or a monitor for hours at a time will starve his brain and numb his morals. It he won't read, let him meditate. If he will read (which is the most beneficial activity he can do), find a list of books appropriate to his age and get them from the library.

4. Limit internet time. Again, your child is in front of a tube, but with this thing you have no idea what he could be seeing or learning or with whom he could be talking. Every year young teenagers disappear after meeting with men they met on the internet. Please limit use of this technology to only when you are in the room and monitoring what is being done. This might seem excessive but just consider the largely amoral culture we live in today. There are predators seemingly everywhere.

5. Encourage him to get outside. It is refreshing to see kids on bicycles, kids playing ball in the front yard, kids sitting on the curb at dusk—kids playing again like they should. For too long they have been robbed of sunlight.

6. Decide now to carefully monitor his academic progress during the school year no matter how old he is. Every senior class in our country has students who did not get to walk at graduation because they realized too late they could not make a passing grade in a required class. Whose responsibility was it to stay on top of the situation? The senior, of course. But as the parent, you must also realize that every-age child needs nudging and encouraging and monitoring in his school effort.

Teach responsibility to your child beginning now and then be sure your child is truly being responsible both at home and in his schoolwork during the next school year for his sake and for your sanity. In fact, if he has a job, make him save a portion of his paycheck to be spent on Summer School. Then if he passes all of his classes, he can spend the money on something he has truly wanted—another way to teach responsibility!

TEACHING THE VALUE OF WORK

"**O**PPORTUNITY IS MISSED by most people because it is dressed in overalls and looks like work." (Thomas Edison) I have had the chance to experience both sides of *work* in the past few weeks. First, was the opposite of *work*. Some scumbag who obviously refuses to work broke into the home of an older couple I know while they were gone for a very short time. What they took was the result of years of work and effort; what else they took was the peace the couple had gained from knowing they were secure in their home. What a sorry way to treat hard-working people. Obviously the crooks have none of this: "Character is what emerges from all the little things you were too busy to do yesterday, but did anyway." (Mignon McLaughlin)

Second, I was able to watch little first graders work even though they probably were not aware that was what they were doing. They were helping a friend and I dig out two raised beds at a local elementary school and then refill them with layers of amendable material. They used child-sized shovels, hoes, rakes, and hands with eagerness and shining faces and squealed when they found earthworms to save and grubs to *smush*. They were a perfect example of this quote from Sidney Phillips: "Men are made stronger on realization that the helping hand they need is at the end of their own arm."

Conversely, there was one little boy who refused to do any of the assignments and who ended up throwing dirt in the faces of the others. He was marched back to his teacher quickly. "Hard work spotlights the character of people: Some turn up their sleeves, some turn up their noses, and some don't turn up at all." (Sam Ewing)

The third experience was not of my own choosing, but was such a delightful example: I watched dozens of nurses and aids take care of my mother for hours without showing exhaustion or frustration. Two of them were just days from delivering their own children; some were in our area because of Hurricane Katrina; some were Student Nurses completing their residency; all were so efficient, patient, and kind. They were such perfect examples of this quote from Martin Luther King, Jr.: "All labor that uplifts humanity has dignity and importance and should be undertaken with painstaking excellence."

Work of any kind completes a person: "I am a great believer in luck, and I find that the harder I work the more I have of it" (Thomas Jefferson); it gives satisfaction: "Far and away the best prize that life has to offer is the chance to work hard at work worth doing." (Theodore Roosevelt).

Those people who refuse to work should know how others think about them: "Even if you're on the right track, you'll get run over if you just sit there." (Will Rogers); "Nobody ever drowned in his own sweat." (Ann Landers); "The only thing that ever sat its way to success was a hen." (Sarah Brown); "Nothing will work unless you do." (Maya Angelou)

I realize that work is not that easy to find during difficult economic times. However, if nothing else, during the Spring, dig a few holes in your yard and grow a few vegetables; help a neighbor clean the leaves in his yard; offer to paint a house on your block for a small fee—just do something. Don't sit in the house watching TV or sitting in front of the computer—do something that makes you feel better when you have finished it at the end of the day or the end of the task.

By your example, teach your children what work looks like and how to complete it. Each child should have jobs at home for which he is directly responsible and which he must complete satisfactorily before he does something he wants to do that day. Even if you work, you can leave assignments on the fridge and then call by the time they were supposed to be finished and get a report. When you get home, if all is not done to your satisfaction, add something else to the work for the next day. Soon your child will find it easier to do the work assigned than to *shirk* it.

Teaching a good work ethic should be one of the main tasks of a parent—it will benefit that child for the rest of his life.

THE ANSWER TO A MAJOR PROBLEM IN SOCIETY

WHAT IS ONE of the principle problems in society today? We are all concerned and anxious about the way people, including teens and young adults, are shooting at each other, stealing, and living life dangerously, but we find ourselves also concerned about adults who have abandoned their responsibility as parents and leaders and who are setting poor examples for their children.

I sat in Sunday school class one Sunday where the lesson was on respect, and we concluded that the main problem in our communities is a general lack of respect for others.

If a person had respect for another's life, he would not want to carry a weapon to school or work or to set off pepper spray or to drive drunk or drive as if he were the only person on the road.

If a person had respect for other people, he would not want to take the belongings of other people. He would know how devastating it is to come out of the store and realize the car is gone; he would know how hurt a person feels when he comes home and finds his hard-earned goods gone—taken by someone who would rather steal than work.

If a person had respect for himself, he would want to be a person of character who would rather do anything than hurt another person or be dishonest. If he had respect for his life, he would not take a chance on his future by doing drugs, by drinking, by driving fast or taking chances on hurting or ending his own life or the lives of others.

If a person had respect for himself, he wouldn't say whatever is on his mind whether it offends others or not. Rather he would be careful with his words and his attitude so that he would not come off as rude and disrespectful.

Our society has a serious domestic abuse/violence problem and it stems from a lack of respect for the other person who is supposed to be a part of one's life and future.

So, why do we have so many disrespectful people in our society today? Because they were not taught respect at home. In fact, they have been allowed to be disrespectful to their parents, to their siblings, possibly even to their grandparents. Consequently, they get into trouble at school for talking back; they end up in handcuffs for disrespecting the police; they cannot get along at work because they refuse to show respect for the employer or for the customer.

From the very early years, children must be taught to respect others—from the first time they hit, or try to take a toy from another child, or say "No!" to an adult. Parents, if they are firm and consistent with their requirement to be respectful when the children are young, will find that they will have fewer problems when the kids are teens and young adults. In fact, there should be very few calls from the school or the police unless your child made a dumb mistake and then, if he has enough respect for you and for himself, he will not let it to happen again.

If you are struggling with disrespectful children—at whatever age—you should determine at this time that you will not permit disrespect toward yourself or any other person from now on. It may be difficult if you have not demanded it before now; however, for the sake of your child and his future, you must not allow disrespect to continue. His attitude will *trip him up* at school, at work, even in his personal attempt at success.

In talking to a boy recently, I could see why he has trouble holding onto a job. His disrespectful attitude toward adults and his "Everyone is wrong but me" opinion would make it difficult for a boss to tolerate him for very long. In talking to him, I realized that, as an only child, he had been *coddled* at home and had been allowed to be disrespectful toward his parents and anyone else in his life. I dread to see what his future will hold.

Then, of course, there are parents who have no respect for themselves or anyone else and are a poor example for their children. They come to the school or the jail demanding that their child be treated better than the others, that they should not be punished for misbehavior, that they should be given more chances to make up work they did not do, that their child "could not possibly be guilty", and on and on. Their kids watch the way they act; then they follow the example and often get into trouble.

As a parent, you owe it to your child to teach him to respect others as well as himself. There is too much at stake if you don't.

THE ONE WORD OUR CHILDREN NEED
TO BE TAUGHT

WHAT IS THE <u>one</u> word that would solve many of the problems in our homes, in our schools, in our nation, even in our world? What one word would guarantee that anger could be handled without the use of fists or guns, would stop rape and robbery, would help all of us in the work world, and would allow school teachers and principals to do their jobs without having to stop and discipline?

That one word is RESPECT. Rather than allowing your child to talk back to you—to even scream back at you, (It does happen in some homes.) why not demand that he treat you with respect? Scripture says "Honor thy father and mother and thy days may be long upon the earth." (Exodus 20:12) Do you really want your children to live, grow older, bring grandchildren into your life and die of old age? Then teach them to respect (honor) you.

Consequently, when your children are on the school campus, they will transfer the respect they have for you to the adults who teach in their classes and who administer the school and who sweep the halls. As a result, you will not ever have to worry about picking up your child at the police station for shoving or threatening or cursing his teacher or principal.

Because your child respects others, he is going to be able to get along with others successfully—even people with whom he disagrees. He will not feel like he must carry a weapon to school to defend his rights as opposed to the rights of others. In fact, he will respect human life to the extent that he would be horrified at the thought of taking another person's life

Because you have taught your child to respect the property of others, you will never have to explain to a storeowner or a homeowner or the police why your child stole or vandalized or otherwise showed a total disrespect (disregard) for another person's ownership.

Because your son respects young women, he will never force himself on a girl and you will not have a worry about a grandchild being born that you will never see, know, or hold.

Because you have taught your child to respect authority, he will be able to work for a boss even if he does not like that person or agree with everything on the job. In fact, if you have supported the school where you child has attended, he will have learned that even if he does not like the teacher, he can still respect him or her and work for a good grade. Then that respect will transfer to a successful work ethic.

Because you have covered respect so well while your child was in your home, he will respect the sanctity of marriage and the commitment made at the altar and will have a happy home life and raise happy children who will respect their grandparents in your later years.

Then you can sit back and tell yourself what a terrific job you did when you taught your child that one word that is so important to his life and future—RESPECT.

USING OUR OWN LIFE LESSONS
TO HELP OUR CHILDREN

WHAT LESSONS HAVE you learned from past trials, troubles or failures that you can use to help your child regroup and go on to other successes when he faces a painful experience?

I recently read a short piece by Jane Pauley of television reporting fame entitled "Success is Messy" with the subtitle "That big flop could turn out to be a big break". (*AARP The Magazine*, Nov./Dec. 2010, p. 66.) She recounted failing the cheerleader tryouts during her sophomore year in high school which turned out to be the "luckiest day of my life, because I was free to try something else". So she joined the speech team and within a month had won a first-place trophy for extemporaneous speaking. Without the time it would have taken for practice and for the games, she had the opportunity to pursue something that developed her talent which she later turned into a very successful career.

When I was not selected for *The Tiger* newspaper staff at the University of Memphis, I was told that my skills were more in creative writing than in organizing and stating dry facts. I was disappointed, and I could not see the value of my failure to make the staff at the time; however, they were right, and that truth has since worked to my advantage. I even taught several classes in creative writing in a high school and each year we produced a volume of student poetry, prose and art. Some of those students went on to use their talents in successful ways after high school, and I have also loved writing columns for parents for many years.

When the company for which my husband was working closed the doors and laid off everyone, we had to redo our budget; we cut out the one night a week we ate out; I learned to cook exclusively with ground beef as the meat; and we taught each other to play chess. It wasn't the last time his company left town or closed (he was in manufacturing), but we had faced it once and were able to weather the situations again. Not only that, but when a couple weathers a storm together and supports each other, it strengthens the marriage and gives them life lessons for helping their children later when they face similar situations.

As a result of our failures, we can find, as Pauley says, that "failure can be a step in the right direction". We must also be able to use the times of disappointment our children face as ways to encourage them to try again, try harder, or just to get up, brush themselves off, and get out there again.

Here is some advice you can give them to help them face those crucial times:

1. Look at the situation as objectively as possible. Sure enough, you may have failed organic chemistry because you probably will be better in sales than you would have been as a doctor.
2. Do not take it as a personal failure but as an opportunity to try something else and open more doors for your future.
3. Do not use it as a time for a pity party—an opportunity to beat yourself up and become defeated; what a waste of effort!
4. Do not assume the failure is an indictment of your character, your personality or your ability—it may just mean that you were going in the wrong direction. Now turn around and use your skills in another way.
5. Give yourself credit for taking the initiative to try again. I saw a former student the other day who reminded me that I *fussed at her* for missing so many days when she was in school. She could have graduated with honors if she had been there more often. However, she is finishing her Associates Degree in accounting and is pleased with her progress. I salute her for working at a job and for working at a degree and for the initiative she is showing now that she is older and more mature.

Our children cannot be successful in all aspects of school, of relationships, of social activities, of life itself, but you must <u>not</u> use his disappointments as a time to become angry, to become defensive, or to become protective. Those actions are counterproductive—they will cripple him rather than help him and will teach him to blame others for his subsequent failures. Rather, tell him to pick up where he left off and go on with his plans or, if the trial has taught him that he is headed for failure again, lead him to try something else and see if it is a good fit for him.

Teach him to use these times to reassess, to re-evaluate, to re-examine his plans and to recognize his response to the situation—whether it is negative or positive, and how it can benefit him in the future.

Life is a series of trials, disappointments, failed efforts and such as long as we live. If you *parent* well during these times in the life of your child, you will have given him invaluable tools that will help him throughout the other difficulties he will inevitably face as he matures and grows and develops into the fine adult you want him to be.

WAYS TO TEACH YOUR CHILDREN
PRACTICAL KNOWLEDGE

P ARENTS SIMPLY CANNOT depend on the educational system to totally teach their children all that they need to know, especially the practical uses of math and English, and I have written articles about using the dinner time as an opportunity to challenge children with topics like multiplication facts and history.

I found an idea in FAMILY FUN (April 2010) that is a terrific way to teach and enhance math skills: the mother allowed her child (could work alternately with multiple children) to keep the coin change if he could tell her exactly how much they were supposed to get back. I would add that the child must do the math in his head—not on a scrap of paper since subtraction is simple math learned in first grade. Not only will this prevent your child from being short-changed by a dishonest cashier, but it may keep him out of trouble due to short-changing someone where he works later.

Another method I thought of is that after your child learns to tell time and subtraction and addition, he can begin to figure for himself how much time he has left to play, to pick up his toys, to finish his homework, to eat. While he is eating breakfast, the parent can tell him that lunch is at 12:00 and ask how long that is from now. At the evening meal, he can be told that he will take his bath at 8:00 and ask him to figure how long he has until then. Getting ready for school in the morning is another opportunity to teach the importance of, not only how much time he has to dress, but also the importance of being somewhere on time and preventing the rest of the family from being late.

Shopping is a good time to teach percentages, if an item is 25% off, the child should be able to do the math in his head and come up with the reduced price (the cost would be ¾ of the original price). Even though it is a little more difficult, a 33% reduction is good practice, and 75% creates an excellent use of math (as well as a real bargain if you can find it). Figuring percentages is not always easy, but these are good practices for better math skills.

In all situations, if he has trouble doing the math in his head, give him time to figure it out, but do not let him guess or try to fool you into giving him the answer. Do not let him answer you by making a question out of it; rather make him be sure of his answer before he gives it to you.

In the kitchen, ask the child to cut a recipe in half or to double it. Working with these fractions can be a challenge but will come in handy in the future in class as well as while baking and cooking.

Once the child can work simple, practical math in his head, he will find it exasperating when the person working the cash register cannot figure out your change if you give him random coins. That is the time to teach tolerance and patience and to remind him how fortunate he is to have you as a parent because you took the time to teach him.

If you know the correct usage of nominative and objective-case pronouns, you should practice them in the verbal language you share with your child. The ACT is full of pronouns used incorrectly which must be changed, and if he simply picks the answer that *sounds right*, he may miss all of them because your family does not use them correctly. Certain pronouns must be used only as subjects and predicate nominatives; the others must be used only as direct objects, indirect objects and objects of the preposition. The students I tutored before an ACT test had to memorize the two types of pronouns so that they could *know* the correct usages. If this is not being covered thoroughly in your child's classroom, find the information and work with him on it.

The same is true of correct singular/plural subject and verb agreements. If he is not hearing it correctly at home, he will not do well on that part of the test and may even embarrass himself in the work world because he does not know how to use them well. Maybe you should attempt to improve your own usage in order to help him handle his with certainty.

These are all useful ways you can help your child in his everyday world both now and in the future and they do not require a degree—they just require your creativity, your patience and your willingness to be engaged in your child's education, especially the practical part of it. I'm not asking you to teach parallelism for the ACT, just teach the things he will face most every day of his life. TEACH YOU CHILDREN WELL.

CHAPTER FOUR

HELP! I'M FAILING DISCIPLINE 101!

APOLOGETIC DISCIPLINE MORE AKIN TO ABUSE

MORE AND MORE I am hearing about families in which there is sporadic, apologetic discipline, and the result is a child who insists on getting his own way with his parents, his playmates, and his teachers. Consequently, his presence is dreaded by his parents' friends; he is rejected and disliked by his peers; and he is a constant reason for parent/teacher conferences at school. Even total strangers are appalled by his verbal tirades toward his parents in the store: "Let go of the candy—you can't have any." (Screams) "I said you had to eat supper before you can have sweets." (Child) "I hate you! I want candy! Let go of me!" Meanwhile, the other store patrons are disgusted by the child, but more so by the weak parent who will allow a child to treat her this way.

Where did this pattern begin? In the early years when the child was seldom told "No" with authority because what he was doing was so *cute* and during the toddler years when the parents thought the child would not like him/her if he was swatted on the bottom for trying to force the cat to take a drink for the seventh time that day. Later, when the child is a teen, he will defy the parent at every turn and will not be afraid of any consequences for his choices. They are the *children* who are filling our jails today. "The world doesn't respond favorably to temper tantrums, whining or sulking. Once a child leaves home, the world is not going to tolerate his obnoxious manipulations." (Nora Profit Ross, *Home Life*, October 1992).

Here is a story by Ms. Ross that illustrates the danger of permissive discipline: "Donna, an energetic small-business owner and active member of her church, allowed a philosophy of permissiveness to destroy both her life and the lives of her children. She failed to teach them respect for authority or accountability for their actions. Donna's boys, Bryan and Joe, never obeyed their parents.

When they were toddlers, they screamed long enough to get exactly what they wanted in spite of Donna's repeated reply of "No." When they learned to talk, Donna made repeated excuses for their disrespectful demands. Her children often told her to "Shut up" or "Leave me alone."

Their teen years included bouts with teachers and the police. Drugs and crime followed. Through it all Donna offered excuses for their behavior. She always maintained the teachers had it in for them; the police had the wrong person; and that no one understood their sensitive natures.

Donna always found jobs for her boys who in turn didn't keep them. She supplied their living quarters and paid their bills and their fines and their bonds. They never grew up. Today Bryan is dead. He drove off a cliff only three months after his release from jail on drug charges. He was using at the time. Joe is serving 25 years to life in the state penitentiary. 'Of course he didn't do it,' says his mother."

Permissive parenting gives a child a false sense of reality and does not allow him a way to adjust to the real world. It gives a child and, later, the adult, a feeling of insecurity because no one cared enough to make him learn how to live successfully in the world. Society is beginning to recognize permissive parenting as a form of child abuse because it causes so much damage to the life of the child/adult.

If you have even an inkling that you are permissive in your parenting style, begin now, before it is too late for your child, to discipline with love, with firmness, with an eye to your child's future. Make him pay for the deliberate acts of defiance he shows; give him reasons to be respectful to you and to the other adults in his life. Give him rules and parameters and dare him to defy them. Children feel loved when their parents care enough to discipline them and to guide them. Love your children.

BEGIN NOW TO DISCIPLINE EFFECTIVELY

WHEN DO WE begin to be effective parents as a gift to ourselves and to our children and to society as a whole? Let's look at the results of the *lack* of parental discipline. Someone is the parent of the young men who are robbing, stealing, and carjacking in cities and towns all over our nation. The three young adults who killed a store owner one day in Memphis, Tennessee, have at least one parent. However, something must have interfered with their parenting skills to have raised children who are this calloused and cruel and selfish.

Don't we owe it to other people in our communities to raise our children well so we will not some day regret what we didn't do when we had the chance? Most adults who rob and cheat and steal and kill are selfish, self-centered people who were never taught to consider the needs of others or they were taught they deserve what other people have. Where did they learn this?

From infancy your child is selfish. He wants *his* needs taken care of; he wants the world to revolve around *him.* Your baby will become overly demanding if you do not establish a schedule that *he* must follow; you cannot allow him to dictate when he will eat, when he will sleep—or not. As he matures and begins to talk, his demands will become *more* demanding. He will be like the three-year-old who was being carried in his dad's arms at a large store when I was there. His cries and screams could be heard all over the huge warehouse as he demanded a toy his dad probably had hidden at home for Christmas. The dad was embarrassed, but not enough to take him out and administer a discipline that would stop the incident.

Sooner rather than later, if he is never effectively disciplined, the child will never develop *self*-discipline which is necessary as he goes on in education and in life. Eventually, because the school won't play as he wants them to or because they keep asking him to study or do homework which he won't do, you may have a dropout on your hands.

As an adult, will he finally be able to adjust to the demands and requirements of society? Probably not. Adjustment begins when a person is a child and his parents assume the vital role of loving disciplinarian. If they don't become effective parents, he may find it difficult to maintain a job, a marriage, and, sadly, he may take into his own parenting this permissive, weak way he was parented as a child.

When is it too late? When the child is an adult. When is it not too late? Any age while he is still under your roof, whether it is eight months or eighteen years. There must come a time when the child must see his life as just a portion of life itself, and his selfhood as one of many. When is a good time to begin to be a good parent who is not afraid to discipline the child in the home? Now.

If your child is not able to talk yet, your decision to be in control may take various incidents of crying until a schedule is established, but it is important.

If your child is able to talk but is quite young, a set of rules and requirements can be voiced, and the consequences laid out so he can understand. Then, be fair and consistent in meting out the punishment for failure to comply.

If your child is a teenager and you're beginning to make new rules and sticking by them as you have not done before, a conversation could be held, without argument or compromise, and the consequences made plain to that child. He needs to know that you mean business and that there is no room for negotiation if a behavior has been a problem for either of you in the past.

Begin now—next week may be too late for your son or daughter.

Jan Knight

BRATTY BEHAVIORS IN CHILDREN

Let's look at some bratty behaviors in children in today's society and how to *cure* their problem:

1. Answering parents the same way they would a peer or sibling. When a child answers a parent's question with an *attitudinal* "Yes" or "No", without being corrected, the adults around are aware of whose fault it is. Parents are to be answered with respect, and, if they are not, the offending child is to be taken to a private place and disciplined. If the behavior is not corrected in childhood, his answers when he reaches his teen years will have an added surliness that you will find very unpleasant. Screaming in public. I must admit that I hear this less than in the past. However, that screeching sound is unpleasant for the employees, the customers, and anyone else who is within earshot. One mother in line with me in a big-box store said that she solves the problem by leaving her basket where it is and leaving the store with the screaming child in tow. When they reach the car, the screeching turns to begging not to be disciplined, but she does handle the problem because she does not want to have to deal with that same behavior again (and leave her groceries again).

2. Insisting on getting his way. Children are, after all, children—not adults. One father was amazed that his son was furious over the fact that he could not have the same size off-road vehicle as his dad. When the dad tried to explain that he was bigger and stronger and could handle the large-size toy, the son became even angrier and told him how unfair he was. The dad realized that he was the cause of this unpleasant behavior in his son for allowing him to say whatever he wanted whenever he wanted without restraint. He commented that children should not be given the same authority as that of the parents.

3. Refusing to take part in family life and work. Children in the home should not have the authority to refuse to do chores or to do homework, or to get up when told to or not to get up from

122

the table until excused or to leave clothes, dishes and such lying around. The parent is the authority in the home—not the personal servant. Children raised by *servitude* parents are the ones who go into their teenage years with the feeling of entitlement—that they are *owed* by everyone else and are somewhat disconcerted that the rest of the world is not going to do what they want.

4. Being rude to others. Unless they are taught, children are quite capable of being cruel verbally and even physically. The old saying, "My rights end where the other person's begins" is a wise way of teaching children how they are to treat their peers and the adults who are over them. Calling another person a name or calling them "stupid" or making fun of them should never by tolerated by parents or they may find themselves involved in a law suit before the child reaches adulthood.

5. Being disrespectful to adults. If he is disrespectful to you, he will not know that he should not treat other adults in the same way. If you do not demand respect, you have caused him to be insolent and discourteous to the other adults in his life, and he is the one who will someday have to pay for that type of attitude and behavior.

Now, what is the solution to the *dissolution* of bratty behavior in children? It lies with parents who act like good parents—parents who are more interested in raising children well than being their *friend* or *having fun* with them. They are not your companions—they are your children. They need a parent who will guide them, not play with them all of the time. They need a parent who will discipline them, not one who is afraid they will not like you if you do. They need a parent who will be firm and consistent in requiring behavior that is acceptable, not one who changes from one incident to another. They need good examples of acceptable behavior, not parents who do things but tell their children not to do the same thing.

In other words, they need parents—good, consistent adults who are not afraid to discipline, to love, to require good, rather than bratty, behavior.

CHILDREN NEED DOUBLE JEOPARDY
WHEN CAUGHT TELLING A LIE

W E DO WANT to believe what our children tell us all of the time, don't we? In fact, it is important that we as parents should be able to trust what our children say because how else can we protect them?

However, the fact is that at one time or another in the years we are raising our children, you will have to deal with the fact that they will lie to you to keep from being punished for a bad choice, to protect their friends, or to keep you from preventing an activity they are doing that they know would not meet your approval.

What does lying do? It breaks down the all-important act of communication between parent and child. It destroys trust; it sets the wheels of worry and concern spinning for the vulnerable parent; and it requires extra parenting skills and patience for years to come.

So what is a parent to do when he catches his child in a lie? Well, first, you need to keep your cool. Our first tendency when confronted with the child's lie is to take it personally—after all, this is you child, and you have always thought that your child would never lie to you. You've even gone so far as to tell other people that he would never tell you a story. Ah! Rule #1 in raising children is: "Never say, 'My child would never . . . '".

O.K., so what do you do? I suggest that you institute Double Jeopardy. First, if you have had children long enough, you know what his answer will be when you ask why he lied to you. He will say it was to keep from getting into trouble! And you think that is such a stupid answer! But, if it has worked before—if he has lied and not suffered for a foolish act, then why not try it again to see if it will work? Problem is—it probably will work for a while until the parent finally begins to catch on. By then, the parent thinks that he cannot believe anything the child says.

So, you make a rule. "You are going to be punished for what you did; that is a reality, but if you lie about it, you will receive double punishment—one for the act, the other for the lie. You decide if you want to take that chance."

Then do it! He is going to gamble that if he tells you the truth, you are going to be so relieved that you will not punish him for the initial transgression. But you will never teach him not to lie to you if you don't punish him for the problems that were first and subsequent second.

Now, remember that children are masters of causing us to feel guilty. So his first question as he looks you in the eye is, "You don't trust me!" This is said with a look of incredulous hurt and disbelief. Your answer is, "I will believe you until I catch you lying to me." When you do find out he is lying, your answer is, "You're right, you lied to me before, so I find it hard to believe you now."

His next statement is a classic, "I've only lied to you once; how long are you going to keep bringing it up?" Your answer is, "I made the mistake of believing everything you said for a long time; it will take a while to begin to believe you again. I'll let you know when that time comes."

Children need to be taught that being able to believe what they say is for their safety and welfare. It is our responsibility to teach that concept to them—however difficult and trying it may be. The threat of Double Jeopardy will help.

GOOD PARENTS DON'T ALLOW KIDS
TO ARGUE WITH THEM

A H, THE PROVERBIAL parent/child contest: "Brian, get out of the pool". "Mom, wait!" Ten minutes later, "Brian, get out of the pool now!" (Notice the addition of the adverb.) "Mom, wait!" Ten minutes more, "Brian, I said to get out of the pool now!!" (Addition of three words with adverb and another exclamation point.) Brian begins to move oh so slowly toward the side of the pool, forgets his goggles, goes back to get them on the other side, slowly swims back, notices she's not watching, drops the goggles to the bottom of the pool, goes down to get them, comes up right beneath his mother who is looking at him sternly. "NOW!!!" We can certainly hear her, so we are sure he can. He reluctantly pulls himself up onto the side, gathers his goggles and follows her out of the pool area. Brian won the contest 6-1 and doesn't seem at all worried that he will be punished when they reach the condo for not obeying when he was told the first time and for continuing to manipulate his mom in front of an audience.

Why do parents allow these contests of will to occur over and over? Don't they realize that it will only accelerate as the child ages and becomes more stubborn, more resourceful? Haven't they already faced the frantic time when the child refuses or delays obedience and is in imminent danger? If not, it will happen some time or the other and the parent will rightfully blame herself or some other hapless person who happens to be the victim who didn't cause the incident but was unwillingly a part of it.

Why does the parent think it is necessary to argue with someone who can't drive yet? Arguing is not even sensible among adults and seldom results in a satisfactory ending. Arguing with a child diminishes an adult—his authority, his ability to parent, his patience. So why engage in it?

In too many instances, parent/child arguing began early in the child's life. It began because of several poor-parenting skills: it is too much trouble to force one's authority—much easier to just let the little darling irritate the people eating at the next table; it is impossible that someone as adorable as their child cannot be adored by everyone else, so when she screams at the top of her lungs in the grocery aisle, everyone will think she is cute; it is not possible that their child could do anything wrong, after all he is their child, so when the principal calls and tells them that he has been sent to jail in handcuffs, there must be a misunderstanding or it is probably someone else's child who is at fault for whatever.

Ineffective parents are blind, deaf and dumb to their own parenting mistakes and to their child's obnoxious behavior. They live in a perpetual state of denial. So who is the victim? The child, who, as he (or she) grows older, cannot understand when the world stopped revolving around him and why the rest of society can not see how perfectly wonderful he really is. He will parent the same way he was parented if he can find someone who will marry him and he will raise the same kind of argumentative, selfish, self-centered child who will always care more about himself than anyone else. I know of this kind of situation and found out recently that the son seldom sees his aging parents. "What goes around . . . ."

Good parents do not argue with their children or let them have their way if they have been told differently. They can see their children's faults and correct them with fairness and with authority. Good parents *parent* full time, not just when it is convenient. They cannot be outsmarted or outwitted by the children they brought into the world. They do not allow the child to argue with them because, as the parent, they are the ones who make the final decisions and the child is not allowed to usurp their authority. They do not allow bad behavior in public; they do not tolerate lying; they require respect; and they know that part of loving their child is giving discipline when it is needed.

Be one of the good parents—your child deserves it.

STRONG DISCIPLINE—SUCCESSFUL CHILDREN

D ID YOU KNOW that if you don't discipline your child and "cause" him/ her to be obedient, responsible, and caring, you could sacrifice his chances of being a good student and, consequently, a successful adult?

Some research I came across reached that conclusion. Marie Winn, in *Children Without Childhood*, wrote about several schools that followed the permissive educational philosophy of Sigmund Freud (in his early writings. He later changed his mind after he saw how the children acted as a result of his early teachings). We are seeing the same result today in children whose parents follow this permissive atmosphere of child-rearing in their homes.

How exactly do these parents correct their children that resembles those parents in the research? First, they seldom say "No" to aggressive, disobedient behavior or selfish tantrums. Rather, they attempt to *reason* with their offspring. How exactly does an adult parent reason with a two-year-old, a ten-year-old, or a fifteen-year-old? Have you tried it? It is a difficult, usually unsuccessful way of trying to disciple children.

Secondly, these parents think they owe their children an explanation for discipline. In a home, it should be the parents—the adults—who are the wiser, more experienced, more responsible persons than the other people—the children, who are in need of guidance, discipline, and love. They are so busy growing up and being children that they really don't have time for explanations, and **YOU DON'T OWE THEM ONE**.

Thirdly, these parents, rather than saying an empathetic "No", attempt to distract their children from bad behavior. I can imagine the creativity this must take. Children, by nature, from birth until they leave home, are trying to outsmart, outwit, and out maneuver their parents and teachers. It is your responsibility to set limits (boundaries) for your children and then to punish them when they challenge those limits. They are too immature to set their own limits or to make some of the decisions this type of parent wishes for them to make. In addition, this type of discipline takes away the childhood from the children.

So, what is the result of this type of parenting according to the research? First, these children refuse to tolerate the demands of adults—at home, at school, often on the job. So many child-psychology writers and speakers are facing the same questions from parents of every age child: "My child is out of control, won't mind, has tantrums, destroys things, and has no friends. What is wrong and what can I do?" The problem started when that child was born into a home where the parents didn't think they had a right to actually discipline their children; consequently, the child is in a constant state of conflict with the adults in his life.

Some of the possible problems and conflicts caused by a lack of firm discipline are as follows: refusal to follow a timetable (how long will you give him to pick up his toys?), anxious mealtimes, and even poor table manners (since it is hard to teach him anything). As these children mature, the research found that they are more prone to irritability, obsession, anxiety, and even depression.

On the other hand, children who had been disciplined with the emphatic word "No" and who were punished for bad behavior appeared to be happy, playful, and, surprisingly, more eager to learn than the other children. More eager to learn? You mean the way I raise and discipline my children will affect how successful they will be as students? Research says "Yes"!" If you have children at home, you are, at this time, determining the grades they will make and how successful they will be in life.

An awesome responsibility on parents, isn't it? Yes, indeed! And if you're not prepared to make that kind of sacrifice, then don't have children! If you already have children, forget your own selfish gratification and be willing to give to your children what they need most from you—love, time, and firm discipline.

UNDISCIPLINED CHILDREN—FRUSTRATED TEACHERS

H AS YOUR CHILD ever caused you to doubt your form of effective discipline because of his actions in public or in school? If your answer is "No," then you either don't have children or yours is a newborn. If you truly think that your child never fibs in order to make life easier on himself or if you think he will never embarrass you, then you have a problem with two areas of your parenting: either you are naïve and are actually afraid that you will find out that your child is not perfect and that your form of discipline is ineffective, or you are lazy.

Let me give you an example of a lazy parent. We were eating at a local restaurant seated near a young family with a two-year old. The first problem they had was telling him that he could not get his own food off the buffet table. The child's reaction was to run through the small restaurant crying and screaming while the parents got the food and sat down and waited for him to come back. The second thing the parents did to make the child unhappy was when the father told him that the place where he sat down was the mother's place. The child's answer was "This is MY place!" The parental response? "Well, uh, OK." When the child was finally, grudgingly, in a high chair, he pushed himself away from the table into the path of other, older people until he got his way and was removed from the chair. Then when he was told he could not get into the aisle, he screamed, cried, and generally disturbed the rest of the patrons. The parents' discipline? "We do not like the way you are acting." To a two-year-old? Did it work? Heavens no!

The moral of the story? It took too much effort to take the child out of the restaurant and *cause* him to behave in a civil way. The other reason this was not done is because discipline is probably never administered at home either. It is too much trouble. And the person who has control of the situation? The two-year-old! So what happens in four years when a teacher tells this child which desk he is to occupy in the classroom? She will have screaming, crying and non-compliance. The parent, then, is going to find himself going to the school for sessions until the child can be an integral part of the education scene. Who loses? The child. Who is frustrated and worn out? The teacher. Who could have avoided the problem? The parent if he had disciplined well in the child's earlier years.

This was particularly relevant when I spoke to several elementary teachers the first week of school. They were all exhausted and discouraged from trying to get undisciplined children to mind and behave and from the barrage of parents who believe everything their children were coming home saying, from "She picks on me" (refusal to do homework or to refrain from talking during instruction) to "She never gives homework" (a schedule of homework was on the board all week).

One teacher wrote "No homework" on the page where the weeks' grades were listed for the parent to see. Rather than assume that the message meant that the child had failed to do homework, the parent called the teacher and asked, in a derogatory tone, "What does 'No homework' mean?" When the teacher explained, the parent continued to attack the seasoned teacher in other areas—all of which had been relayed to the parent by the child. Why would a parent attack the teacher rather than to doubt the word of a child? Because the parent does not actually discipline at home, and he is not going to change now. What we have is a naïve, immature parent (no matter what the age) who wants to find fault with the adult rather than the child. Where did the support of teachers go?

One older parent told me, "I always believed the teacher before I believed my child." Why would she do that? Because one part of the equation is an adult professional educator who just wants to teach children and the other part is an immature child who is trying to get out of doing his work or to prevent the consequences of his bad behavior. Why would you punish the teacher? A parent's misguided loyalty to this child will prevent him from guiding the student successfully in all other aspects of life.

Most good educational systems want the teachers to give homework. When your child refuses to do it and knows you will back him up, he misses out on a very important part of his education. One educator was keeping a student in the room during recess so he could do the homework he had refused to do the night before. The parent sent a note to the teacher saying that snack and recess were more important than doing the homework. Now, what does this convey to the child? That the parent is more interested in having the child play than in learning or in obeying the teacher. Who loses? Both the child and the frustrated teacher and, someday, the parent.

Most parents have an interest in the very difficult task of raising children and assisting their success in school. However, there are many who, for whatever reason, neglect this very important aspect of parenting. Hopefully, these words will offer some awareness of a very real problem.

WHEN SOMEONE ELSE CORRECTS YOUR CHILD

ER MOTHER WAS ninety, using a walker, and they were in a local *big box* store. Two young boys were chasing each other, and the leader never checked up when he rounded the end cap to race down the next aisle, almost knocking the frail senior lady down, and kept running. The daughter caught the chaser by the collar as he rounded the corner to keep him from colliding with her mother and scolded him, not only for running, but also for endangering others in the store. He scowled at her and took off at a run again. Minutes later, he came back with his mother who was indignant that another adult had corrected her child and proceeded to defend him using profanity with a loud, obnoxious voice.

A father had taken his mother to watch the son/grandson play baseball, and they were having a good time until a restless toddler began to walk over their feet in the bleachers. Finally the exasperated grandmother, in her firm but gentle parenting voice, said "Let's get somewhere and stay. Ok, little fellow?" At which time, the heretofore oblivious mother turned around and proceeded to ask what right the older lady had to correct her son. The grandmother tried to explain that he was stepping on their feet, had spilled at least one of their drinks, and was in danger of falling off the bleachers. The mother of the child was furious, exclaiming that she was watching him all the time and that he was not in danger. She never apologized for the inconvenience and the annoyance the child had caused—she was just angry that someone had corrected her little darling.

Every night, it seems, we watch a TV reporter talk about another shooting, and then when the parent of the shooter is interviewed, she tells us what a wonderful boy he is and that he would not do anything like that. Has she spent most of her parenting years not allowing anyone else to correct her perfect child too?

In years past, children were raised around their grandparents, uncles, aunts, and cousins, and it was everyone's responsibility to correct the younger children, to keep them out of danger, and to even give them a job to do if they seemed bored or if there was just work to be done. In smaller towns, if a child needed correcting, anyone within range could reprimand him and the parents were grateful and apologetic. In school, children knew that if they were punished for a deed, they would *get it again* when they got home. Children found it more difficult then to get away with bad behavior and bad manners. They, therefore, grew up with more of a sense of right and wrong and of the way they were to treat others.

Now, parents go on the attack if someone says anything to correct their child and, consequently, they add to the problem. They become a bad example for the child because they react in such childish, inappropriate ways. They allow the child to be annoying to others without being corrected, so the child never learns to respect the space and the rights of other people.

Young parents need to relax a little. Not everyone is judging their parenting skills at every moment. They should learn to be less defensive and more willing to accept help when it is offered even if it is a reprimand of their child. They should learn to watch that their children are not running in stores, stepping on toes, endangering older people and pregnant ladies, spilling drinks, being in the way, or screaming in public.

I do not accept the notion that it takes a village to raise a child, but I think that we could all use a little help when it comes to raising children. Rather than being offended the next time someone asks your child to stop grabbing his shirt with sticky "popsicle" fingers, take the time to apologize for the actions of the child, get a rag and wipe the fingers (and the shirt), tell the child that he must stay with you, and keep his hands to himself. The stranger will appreciate that you have acknowledged his dilemma, that you have accepted that there is a problem, and that you have the situation in hand. Your child has learned from this teachable moment; you have responded appropriately; and the people around you will applaud your parenting skill.

WINNING THE "WHINING" WAR

Have your kids passed WHINING 101 and become masters at it, and you feel like you've flunked PARENTING 402? Then now is the time to make a change in some of the ways you handle your children and your life. It doesn't help that many commercials feature bratty kids who can sing and dance and take control of whatever so that they can convince the viewing audience that what they are selling or asking you to do is too vital to pass up. However, it is important to your stress level each day and even more important to the three-foot to six-foot-tall humans who live under your authority that you take a refresher course in PARENTING.

Whining is a form of disobedience; it is a manipulative tool used for two purposes: the first is the STALL. Child: If I get a "No", and I whine long enough, she may even forget that she wasn't going let me do what I wanted and I will get my way. The second purpose is called "Frustration Imposition". Child: If I whine and cry, they will be embarrassed and/or distracted and will give me what I want. If the parent yields to either of these tactics, he loses the battle, or Round One, and the child wins. Outsmarted again by a person who may not even be in the first grade.

One parent I observed has gotten in the habit of ending her affirmative statements like "Put up the books so we can leave the library." with "Okay?" So her two children naturally assume that the issues are negotiable or that she is asking for their permission; in any case, they usually whine and beg and usually win their case. Once she asked them to get out of the pool so they could leave and, anyway, they were turning blue. However, with her usual "Okay?" tacked on the end, the kids were almost purple before they finally agreed to drag their frozen carcasses up the pool stairs and into warm towels.

Another parent always gave a little apologetic laugh when she *demanded* that her child obey her. "Quit jumping on the furniture, heh, heh". The child never stopped jumping, so the parent left the room. Heck, even I would have been tempted to disobey if one of my parents had laughed every time they told me what to do or not to do. When a parent allows the child to disobey as this one did and to leave rather than make sure the child has understood the demand and has complied, the score is Round Three to the child; parent defeated and down for the count.

So, with all the hype about letting kids make decisions for themselves and how much that benefits them, what is a parent to do? Bottom line—letting children make their own decisions works only when you consider the level of maturity of each child. Having a philosophical discussion about the benefits of green tights with a pink dress rather than orange ones will lead to parent angst and child stress. Showing her what you want her to wear without negotiation means you may actually leave the house on time with both of you still in a good mood. Or, if the child is older and you want to allow him to decide on his clothes, lay out two sets and let him choose between those. Whatever, Parents, because of your age and experience and your love for the child, you must be the decision makers and "the final word". Period.

Twice in one short period, I had to endure whining/screaming children who had been kept up way past their bedtimes and were too tired. At that point, the parent simply should pick up the child and head for home and the child's bed. Sometimes we cause the problem ourselves if we push the child too far past his point of endurance.

Teenage whining is WHINING 1101. They sound a lot like older children, but the whining is so reminiscent of what they did as small children, you almost want to laugh. (Notice I said "almost".) No whining, whether it is from a small child or a teen, should be tolerated. Your *final word* should not be questioned. If you have not already set that standard before, do it now. Having an authority figure that is strong and certain is one of the most stable elements of a child's life. Don't disappoint yours. Win the battle on whining and you will win the war for the rest of your child-raising years (and maybe even when the child is older and you say, "No, you are forty years old. You may not move home with me—again.") Final note: Adult-child whining is the worst, but if you didn't put an end to it when the child was young, you may deserve this obnoxiousness forever . . .

CHAPTER FIVE

HELP! I WANT MY KIDS TO DO WELL IN SCHOOL!

DEBUNKING EXCUSES FOR FAILURE IN SCHOOL

"**S**UCCESSFUL PEOPLE HAVE learned to make themselves do the thing that has to be done when it has to be done, whether they like it or not." (Aldous Huxley)

This applies to a job, to a marriage, to school, to parenting, and to almost every aspect of life. Let me share with you some parenting excuses for why some children are not doing well in school:

1. "I believe she is hyper-active." My first response is "what grade is she in?" and "What does that have to do with her grades?" At some point in a person's life, if we are *hyper*, we learn to control our tendency to interrupt others, to stay focused on the situation at hand—even if it is on a conversation or a teacher's instruction, to maintain concentration, especially if it is on a textbook, and still to accomplish more than the average person because we have this *gift* of hyper-activity. If you think your child has more than the average energy, begin early to *train* him to stay focused, to remain calm, to slow down his energy, and to use his reserve energy to get a lot done. It may not be what your child *wants* to do, but if he can learn to "make himself do the thing that has to be done when it has to be done", he will be successful.

2. "He is like his father and will never be worth anything. He sleeps in class and has no desire to study." My response: "What does he lose when he is caught sleeping? The car? The phone? Why let him continue to sleep and fail when you have something he wants?" I realize that it is difficult to motivate certain students who have a good brain but who think it is too much trouble to use it. However, nagging is useless, threatening is futile, acting like the parental martyr is funny to them, and depending solely on the teacher is not fair. So, maybe you should read him the following quote: "The tragedy of life doesn't lie in not reaching your goal. The tragedy lies in having no goal to reach." (Benjamin Mays) Help him set a goal or set it yourself if he won't participate. Give him a deadline; then take away whatever is his favorite thing. He may decide that it is less trouble to do his work and stay awake

than riding the big yellow bus to school each day instead of being driven or being able to drive if he is old enough and has access to a car.

3. "She is becoming more social and her grades are slipping." My response: It is a fact of life that one can be social and still maintain good grades if the parental expectations are in place. Yes, it is true that somewhere in middle or early high school the hormones are working over-time, and the victim has a difficult time concentrating as he once could. However, it has been done for generations before, and it can be accomplished again. Expect it.

4. "If you just knew what our home life is like, you would understand why his grades are so poor." My response: An education is a *ticket* out of a bad situation. With it, one can make more money, have more confidence, refuse to continue the dysfuctionalism of the family in which he was raised, and have a better life. Why not encourage him to do that for himself rather than allow him to use your home as an *excuse* to fail?

5. "I just don't think she likes school." My response: So? "You are never a loser until you quit trying." (Mike Ditka). I know of very few students who are really crazy about spending eight hours a day, five days a week in a building where teachers are expecting you to pay attention, stay in your seat, remain quiet unless given permission, and keep your hands to your self. Most of them, no matter what age, would rather be outside or hanging with friends. However, "We are what we repeatedly do. Excellence then is not an act, but a habit." (Aristotle). That is why educators are there, to repeat information, require homework (repetition), give new information, give tests, and then do it all again the next day. We are giving kids the most valuable thing they will ever have—an education, a chance in life, an opportunity to be successful. Then we pray that they will do what Thomas Edison said: "If we did all the things we are capable of doing, we would literally astonish ourselves." We want them to astonish us and you as well as themselves.

"Opportunities are usually disguised as hard work, so most people don't recognize them." (Ann Landers) Don't let your child get lazy, make excuses, refuse to do homework, or repeatedly fail tests. You are the parent. You are the "enforcer". You are the encourager. Don't shirk your responsibility to your child/student.

EXPERIENCED STUDENTS GIVE ADVICE
TO LOWER CLASSMEN

USING THE EXPERIENCE of upperclassmen, I found some very wise advice for high school freshman that is also applicable to middle-school students and even to college freshman when I surveyed approximately 1,000 high school sophomores, juniors, and seniors asking: "What do you wish you had known your ninth-grade year that would have helped you to have a more successful year?" The responses were excellent.

The answer that was given the most was "I wish I had been more serious." In fact, some quotes that went along with that response were as follows: "Everything they (ninth graders) are doing right now will affect the outcome of following years." and "Freshman don't realize how their report cards can affect what college they can attend or whether they will graduate with honors," and "They need to know the consequences if they fail. I wish I had known how much it would affect me the next year." and "They need to know how serious high school is. It isn't a game."

The second most prevalent response was "I wish I had studied more/ harder." One quote they gave was, "Do all your work from the get-go." Then when I took some upper-class volunteers to the ninth-grade English classes to speak, they kept emphasizing the importance of doing homework and learning from it. One senior who has moved four times during his high school years has maintained a good average because he has a set time and a place to do his homework every night. No one has to ask him if he has done his work; the only thing they have to say is that it is time for bed because he will stay up as long as it takes to finish. Just this past week, a *second-year* freshman came in to ask me about the GED. When I asked him why he was considering leaving school, he said he was failing this year too!

The third answer that was given the most was "I wish I had paid better attention in class." A quote that emphasized that answer was, "They must stay focused on the teacher instead of on friends." When we went to classrooms, we reminded them that it takes will-power to give all of your attention to the instructor rather than thinking about the next time you will see your friends or what is being served for lunch. One junior boy told them that if they would really give the teacher their full attention, then studying for a test would just be a review because they could remember what was said in class. As an educator, one quote was particularly special to me—"They (teachers) are really here for our benefit."

The fourth response given the most importance was "I wish I had realized how different it is from middle school and how much harder it is." When we went to the classrooms, we reminded them that each level of their lives would be harder—from now until college and on into life. Freshmen have a tendency to bring their immaturity with them. If teachers can keep them from allowing that childish way of thinking to damage their grade-point average, then we will have accomplished what we wanted to do. One older student said it this way: "Learn it. Don't just try to get by—it only gets harder."

Another response that was given a good deal was about the seriousness of tardies and absences in high school. The upperclassmen gave two reasons for having an emphasis on school attendance: they cannot learn if they are at home by themselves or if they are late to classes, and they will find that the work world will not tolerate lateness or absence and still allow them to keep a job.

Another word of wisdom from the respondents on that survey was, "When you get to high school is when you really have to grow up." And another said, "Be responsible and be organized." Ah, the voice of experience!

Finally, a sage bit of advice that you as parents will find especially wise in relation to your children: "Don't hide your grades from your parents—you will get caught!"

FROM THE MOUTHS
OF THE EXPERTS—YOUR CHILDREN

O NE YEAR I asked most of the ninth-grade students who made the Honor Roll for the first semester at our school to answer some questions. The one I was most interested in was why they believe they consistently make good grades. I would like to share their answers with some comments.

"I have always worked hard and set goals before the year to make good grades." A ninth-grade student who set goals? I have found that the students who set goals, however farfetched at first and at whatever age, reach farther than those who have no goals or plans at all.

"I want to succeed in life." A student who wants to do something other than drive a car, watch T.V. and run with his friends? Yes, there are students out there who are looking at the future with hope and who know that their futures are determined by their own hard work and effort.

"I pay attention in school and do all of my homework." We consistently hear parents say that their students must not have any homework because they never bring a book home. It is close to impossible to complete all of the homework required during the time a student is in school. The student who does not take books home probably is not doing well in school because he is not practicing what he learned that day; he is not doing consistently well on tests; and he will not do well in college even if he decides to go.

Paying attention to the teacher is so very important. The teacher has completed four to six years of college, preparing to teach your children, but if your child will not listen to instruction, he will not benefit from the education the teacher has received or can give.

Does your child watch so much television that he can only pay attention for about twelve minutes at one sitting because that is the time allotted between commercials? Does he tune you out when you are trying to instruct him at home? If he is having trouble paying attention now, how will he be able to hear instruction when he has a job and must learn to handle a dangerous machine without endangering himself? Where is his self-discipline and when will he get it if not now?

"Study, study, study." Successful students know how to sit down and actually learn the material that will be on a test or the formulas required to work problems in math or science. It is difficult to teach another person how to study—it is an individual thing, but if your student never practices studying, how will he ever learn to do it?

"I read all the time so I know a lot and have a good vocabulary." There is little that can be learned on T.V. that will help a student pass the ACT, the SAT, or an Algebra test. But every student I have known who loves to read has done very well on standardized tests.

Finally, my favorites: "My parents encourage me." And "I like to please my parents and myself." You, the parent, are the most important element in the success of your child. Give encouragement, give praise, be a study partner, if needed. But never underestimate the value you can be in the life and success of your child.

GRADES SHOW DIFFERENCE
BETWEEN SUCCESS AND FAILURE

WHY ARE GRADES important to you as a parent? Because they could indicate the difference between the success and failure of your child in the future.

I have had several parents tell me that their child is mature enough to decide whether or not he wants to make good grades and to keep up with his homework on his own, even for young students in the elementary. Frankly, I have never known small children who were that mature.

On the other hand, some parents are so repetitive in their universal question: "Do you have homework?" that they no longer hear the real answer.

So what must you assume when your child has said each night that he doesn't have homework, but there are failing grades on his report card? I suggest that you contact the teachers as soon as possible and find out if your child is being assigned practice work or notes to study or pages to read. I would be very surprised if a child of any age never has homework or a reason to study several times a week.

One day I had two sets of parents in my office who had not gotten a report card until the second report period. When they did get it, the grades had dropped quite low and these were young ladies who had previously made very good grades. The first thing the parents did was contact me and set up an appointment with the teachers to see what was going on.

Notice they did not ask the child. They asked the people who are teaching and are with their children every day. In other words, you cannot always trust your child to tell you the total truth, especially when the grades begin to fall. For both of these girls the reason was a desire to avoid working on *academic stuff*. Many children spend far too much time watching T.V. or staying on the phone or the Internet or playing.

The most important responsibility a school-age child should have, whether he is in the first or twelfth grade, is preparing for the future by gaining as much education and knowledge as he can. And one of the most important responsibilities a parent of a school-age child has is to see to it that education is a priority in his child's life.

So, what should you do if your child has no desire to make good grades, do his homework, study for tests, or do his projects?

First, remember that you are still the parent: you have the right and even the responsibility to demand the best of your child, including his school effort.

Most teachers who have your child in each classroom also have approximately 149 more students than yours a day and as many as 30 per hour in high school and at least 25 students per class in elementary. The teacher cares about your student, but she also only has so much time and energy to devote to one person. This is your child we are talking about. You are the person who can still put pressure on him by grounding or some other discipline and by loving him into doing good work.

Keep up with when the report cards are coming out, keep up with his grades, and be consistent with the punishments you decide to administer because of poor performance. Don't give in to manipulation, and love your child enough to require his best.

When your child finally graduates, you can do as many of us have in the past, you can congratulate yourself that your child has succeeded thus far in life.

HOW TO HELP YOUR CHILD LEARN
WHAT HE IS TAUGHT

T HE MOST IMPORTANT part of your child's education is not necessarily his grades: rather it is what he knows when he goes into the world and has to use what he has learned; his grades are just an indication that he is retaining what is being taught.

How can you help your child learn what is being taught in school so he can retain it for years to come?

First, just as the teacher should be telling the student why the information he is teaching is important and why he should know it, you must emphasize that what he is learning today will be used again and again in his life. Try not to use the word "study" as you encourage him, but use the word "know". In other words, "I will *know* this material when I get up from here."

Check his notes to be sure he is taking them and check his homework to see if he did it by rote or whether he used it as a practice to know the material.

Never do as so many parents do and believe him when he says that he finished all of his homework in study hall unless he has been certified a genius and can do homework and study for tests for five to seven academic subjects in one hour. I have never met a student who can do it successfully.

Never let him cram one night for a big test. Even geniuses have trouble remembering volumes of material by going over it in one cram session and even then, they probably won't remember it long. Instead, require your child to go over the material for his classes every night for 20-30 minutes per class. Then when the night before a test comes, all he has to do is review the information; his retention will improve remarkably.

Be your child's study partner. Call out the information to him and let him say the answers aloud if he is an auditory learner or write them if he is a visual.

If he misses an answer, make a mark in his notes and suggest he go over the missed ones first the next night and review the rest.

Be an encourager. Never berate or belittle your child during the review time.

What if your child is freezing on a test; commonly called "test phobia?" If he has studied more than one night and feels confident he knows it, he can tell himself that there is nothing the teacher can ask that he can't answer. Then he can look around the room. Find one person who makes just a little better than he does and say silently: "If he or she can pass this test, I know I can!" This is called positive self-talk by psychologists, and I highly recommend it.

A final suggestion to parents—make sure your student is going to school. Some students won't miss because they want to be exempt from the final exams. But other students have to be made to go to school, and you as the parent are that "enforcer".

Be excited about what is happening at school, over what he is learning in each class, over his development in the academic world. If you see no need for an education, he will use you as an excuse for not going.

These are not easy years as your child attends school because of conflicts and concerns and worries and occasional failures. But other parents have made it, and you can too. Someday your child will parade across that stage and receive that diploma—and you will have succeeded in one of the most important areas of parenting.

LEARNING IS A LIFE-LONG JOURNEY

ONE OF THE most frustrating situations I encountered as a Senior Counselor was that of the student who had no direction, no plans for his future, and no idea how to determine what he should do with his life. Too many times the answer I received to my question, "What are you planning to do when you graduate?" was "I dunno, just drift in life, I guess. Let it happen, you know?" No, I didn't know. I would have found that *plan* very frightening and way too uncertain.

In the book *The Ultimate Gift* by Jim Stovall, the nephew who was given the *gift* by his uncle said this about his plans for his future, "I have never thought about what I wanted to do with my life. I guess I always felt just existing and drifting through day to day was enough". A twenty-year-old on the Dr. Phil Show answered the question about his plans this way: "I thought I would just let life happen and see how it goes". After Dr. Phil's eyebrows shot upward toward his bald hairline, he replied to the young man and his girlfriend, "You should be the one working on your life, not your parents or a boy/girlfriend—but you!"

This dilemma is not only difficult for counselors, but also for parents who would say to me, "I hate to see him waste his potential." What we both were seeing, and what Dr. Phil was seeing in the young man on his show, were very unhappy people who were afraid of the future because they seemed incapable of creating life-making decisions and then making them happen. Instead, many of them had become dependent on drugs and/or alcohol to *deaden* their unhappiness; they were, to the consternation of their parents, running with a crowd that also apparently had a *loser* attitude; they spent an inordinate amount of time doing nothing but watching television, playing internet games, twittering, partying—anything but actually building a life structure that would make them independent adults who could handle life successfully.

Often they either didn't begin college or they had already dropped out because, "I don't know what I want to be". They couldn't seem to hold a job because their supervisor either "doesn't understand" them or they had to be at work everyday, or they had to show up on time, or it's a "loser job". (What else do they expect?)

My answer to most of the seniors who were at loose ends about their futures was to start college anyway and take computer courses, English, history, some math. In other words, get some hours to show that they have potential and could prove to themselves that they could do the work. Eventually, a subject will ignite an interest that could be the threshold to a successful and satisfying future.

"Education is a lifelong journey whose destination expands as you travel". (Stovall). The author wrote one of the best definitions of "commencement": "(It is called that) because the process of learning begins—or commences—at that point. The schooling that went before simply provided the tools and the framework for the real lessons to come". Then he included this profound quote: "Life, when lived on your own terms, is the ultimate teacher". It can be a very hard teacher, especially for those who choose to "drift through life". It can also be a very exciting teacher for those who prepare for life by getting the most education they can get and then going out and using what they have learned. It is the desire, the hunger, for learning that will remain alive and precious in those who find that "learning is a lifelong journey".

How does a young person find what his/her chosen career should be? First, note the classes you enjoy most; then determine whether you want to use your hands or your brain or both; finally, look, as best you can at that young age, into your future and decide whether that is the occupation you still want to be doing at age fifty or more.

Young people determine their own futures, whether the parents pay for college or they make it on their own. It is up to them to make it by their own determination, their hard work, their plans, and their effort. Oh, yeah, and parental prayer helps.

Find a way to instill in your children a *thirst* for learning that will be with them for the rest of their life's journey. It will be one of the best things you give them.

LOOKING AT THE GENDER-ACADEMIC GAP

THERE HAS BEEN a lot of research on the Gender-Academic Gap in grades one through twelve. "They sit side by side and learn the same lessons, yet boys struggle with reading and writing, while girls avoid advanced math and physical science. The good news? By working together to teach more creatively, educators and parents can help raise grades and close the gender gap." (Peg Tyre, "Class Division". FAMILY CIRCLE, Sept. 2009).

It is true that between the girl/boy twins in our family the boy has little trouble grasping the concepts of all levels of math. The girl has more difficulty with higher maths, but has not found it too hard to grasp the others. They both read a multitude of novels and other materials, and neither has a problem with science. In addition, the elementary math teacher living in my house says that between the two genders, it was the girls who were the better math students. When I asked him why, he explained that the boys had too much on their minds—like sports and playing and such. When I asked if the problem, then, was a maturity difference, he said, "Probably".

However, research is still claiming that the principle difference is gender. The U.S. Department of Education conducted a survey and the results showed that 60% of female fourth-graders and 68% of males like science. However, by the seventh grade, only half as many girls still liked the subject. Then in high school, the gap widens and fewer than 17% of students in physics and advanced math are girls. (Tyre, pg. 92) "Educators are now realizing that beginning in elementary school they have to focus less on multiplication tables when she is supposed to have them in her head".

The answer for girls who have lost their confidence in doing math problems is for both teachers and parents to let them know that all students are capable of grasping math concepts—it just takes a little more work and effort on the part of some of them than it does others. Teachers must, as my husband did, encourage all students to do their work and to pay attention and to make an effort and that any of them can do math.

Parents should play math games with them like when they want to know what 40% of the price of a sale item is or what fraction can be converted to increase a recipe or what 4x9 is while riding in the car. They should teach them that "persistence, not talent, is the key" to success in math. (Tyre, p. 88). Parents must also keep a close eye on the progress of their students and when she is faltering in her math understanding, either hire a tutor or learn how to do it yourself so you can tutor her. Later, students who have taken to math well should be encouraged to take the more difficult courses.

Boys who are struggling with reading have to be engaged in it. There should be books available in the school library that interest him—probably more of blood and gore than the girls would want. They must also be allowed to be more active. One of the worst things that can be taken away from a boy is recess or gym or other ways to expend that extra energy they appear to have. If you school does not have such, make sure there is something after school in which he can run and exercise.

Dads have a lot to do with whether a boy likes to read or not. He should be read to by the dad as well as by the mother when he is too young to read himself. Rather than buy a new video game, buy a subscription to a magazine he may like—reading may come naturally if he is curious about the content. Rather than let him spend inordinate time on the computer or TV or playing internet games, require a set time to read, especially if he has a reading assignment at school.

As you can see, narrowing the gender gap in academics or giving a child the confidence to do well in a subject that is not his favorite has as much or more to do with the parents in the home as with the teacher in the classroom.

Don't just assume that because you had trouble with a subject in school that your child will as well. In fact, never tell a child, "Oh well, I wasn't good in math (etc.) either". Academic ability has more to do with overall ability and with effort than with genetics. Just remember that you have an obligation to be that helper and encourager at home to assure your child's success.

NOT MAKING THE GRADE

INSTEAD OF TRYING to analyze why our children do or don't do as well as we think they should, sometimes it is more effective just to ask them. One year, I surveyed the ninth-grade students in our school who made two or more F's on their semester report cards. They were quite honest in their answers, and I would like to share them with you with added comments. (By the way, there are high school students who are going to local print shops and attempting to change their grades. Maybe you should call the school to verify the grades on the report card you receive.)

1. "I did not try". Now, as parents, you are probably hearing "But I am trying!" and you feel guilty for putting so much pressure on this beleaguered, over-worked child, knowing all the time that if you don't put pressure on him, he will not do his best. When a student is not working to his potential in school, the responsibility becomes the parents' because the student is not able to make himself do what he doesn't want to do despite the consequences.
2. "I did not do my homework." "I didn't study enough." Amazingly, these kids know what it takes to make passing grades; they know that if they don't pass enough subjects they will be in that same grade next year, yet they lack the maturity to do what is required. Again, the parent must assume the responsibility. Many parents are making their children write the homework assignments down and the teacher signs the assignment for her class so the parent knows it is the actual homework. The student also needs to take all of the homework home, even the completed work, so the parent can check it off and know that it is done. Many parents require a Weekly Progress Report or whatever it is called in your district, which the student must pick up and hand to each teacher who will list the grades and effort for the week. Some schools have parental access to an internet link to look at the child's grades and teacher comments. For many parents if this report is not positive, the child sits in his room for the weekend until he can assure the parent that he will make a concerted effort to improve in all areas and can begin the process at that time. It takes parental effort, patience, and love, but you can force those grades to come up.

153

3. "I do not care". Now, when I see this answer, I have to refer back to the home. I have found that those students who truly don't care what kind of grades they make usually don't have a parent at home who is asking for the report card, monitoring the homework, or praising good grades when they are made. The student perceives this as the fact that the parent does not care—so he doesn't care either.

Parents, let me say it again—there is no more important job you have right now than parenting the children you have brought into this world. If you fail at this job, you have hurt your heritage, your grandchildren, and even society. Do not abdicate this responsibility.

Your children can see through you as if you are made of glass. They know whether you care about them or not. Please, for their sakes, care, and show it by being involved in their lives, in their schooling, and in their plans for the future.

PEOPLE LEARN BY SIGHT, HEARING OR DOING

A NEW TEACHER ONCE asked me to teach her class how to prepare daily for class and how to study for tests.

She had found that because she wasn't making use of study sheets, many of her students were failing her tests. Now, first let me say that I disapprove of handing out study sheets so students will know exactly what is going to be on a test. That simply lets the teacher know how well the student can cram and memorize the night before the test. It gives very little indication of exactly how much he knows the material.

What I taught that class that day can be used by parents, not only as they work with their children to improve their grades, but also so the students can get full use of the educational system to prepare for college classes, for technical training, even for getting instructions on the job so the boss won't yell at or fire your future working adult.

First I explained that we all learn in three ways, and most of us should make use of at least two of those three ways as we study and learn:

Some of us are visual learners—what we see is what we remember most. *Visuals* can remember where the material was on the board when the teacher wrote it down and can write it as they saw it; many can memorize whole sections and pages of notes and bring it to mind just as they would bring up information on a computer.

These students will study best by taking notes and then by reading them several times. So, when (or if) you as parents study with your children, you may want them to write the answers as you review and call out questions.

Another type of learning method is auditory. These *Oral* learners remember best what they hear. As the teacher is lecturing or going over the homework, this learner must listen intently. If he does, he will remember what was said and explained and will only have to review the material again for a test rather than actually study for it.

As parents study with this type of learner, calling out the questions and having the student give the answers orally is effective.

Then some learn best by doing, called *Kinesthetic* learners. That is why teachers require homework—so students can learn by actually working the problems themselves or identifying the parts of the sentence or putting the names of countries on maps. Many of these learners write their notes again. They should do problems or sentences as they study.

Most of us, as I said, learn by using two of the methods. That is why, as I taught this class, I made sure that every student was paying attention to me with his ears and his eyes.

If they both watch and listen to the teacher, their recall on tests can be actually doubled. If they also take notes or write problems immediately, they have tripled their ability to recall the material.

Work with your child enough to determine his best one or two methods of study so you can encourage that type of studying. If he is younger, you may want to help him study until he gets really good at using his type. As he gets older, he may be good at using his method himself.

The more we know about how to study and remember, the more confidence we have as we go into a test or a class.

POOR GRADES—UNHAPPY STUDENTS

DO YOU KNOW who the unhappiest students are on every high school campus? They are the ones who wasted their 9th grade or 10th grade year or both. They spend the first week or two of the next year trying to find enough classes to take so they can accumulate enough credits in order to catch the classmates they were with when they began high school. One of the most difficult counseling conferences I have had to conduct is the one where I had to show, mathematically and logically, when a student could finally be a junior or senior at the time the classmates would be.

Now, the problem was not that they didn't KNOW how many credits it took to go to the next grade. High school counselors go to the middle schools and talk to eighth-grade students about credits and effort and attendance in the final four grades. The parents are invited to attend orientations at most of the high schools so THEY can be fully aware of what is required of their children in high school. So, what IS the problem with so many students who are forced to repeat the first and maybe even the second year in high school?

First, and most important, (and with apologies to the dead horse we keep *beating*) is parental involvement. It is obvious when kids have someone at home who is encouraging, expecting the best, setting a time and place to do homework, restricting T.V., computer and phone use, and generally being a good parent. Second, if a student will not pay attention, wants to sleep or is disruptive, we have to suspect a learning disability, a sleep disorder or drug use. Thirdly, if the student has already begun to miss school the second week, we assume the parents are aware and don't mind, are not aware, or are too busy to care.

So, why is all of this important? Your child, in order to feel good about himself, must succeed in some area, and the most important area in his life is his education and getting ready for his future.

One part of my job as senior counselor was finding good employees for businesses in our area. My announcement over the intercom listed these requirements: at least a "B" average, good attendance, and good behavior. If a student was lacking in any of those areas, he need not come apply. Did you notice the grade requirement? The employers who called me made it clear that if the student couldn't make decent grades, he probably wouldn't be a good employee either.

The general manager of a local McDonald's refused to hire a student when he checked his school records and discovered that he had missed twelve days of school and was late thirty-seven times. The GM said that reliability, dependability, and professionalism (work ethic) were too important to hire someone who didn't care about when to get to school. Many employers are requiring that a student bring his high school transcript to the interview. If a student has not planned to attend college and, therefore, has the idea that his grades and attendance are not important, he may very well find himself looking longer and harder for a job. In addition, grades in English and math are important to many employers, especially algebra in even semi-skilled jobs. One employer told me that students who take a lab-based science do better with hands-on work.

Why are school performance and attendance important? Because your child's self-image, his future employment, and his future success could have a lot to do with his future happiness. One day in my office, a father told his son in my presence, "Please do well here (in school). Don't end up like me with a job you don't like, a body that is hurting all the time, and a dread to get up and go to work every day of your life—get an education!"

Who has the responsibility to get him up and to school and to check on his progress? The parent—yes, even up until the day he graduates! So much of his progress is up to you; don't disappoint your child.

PRAISING EDUCATORS
WHILE THEY ARE STILL HERE

W E HAVE A tendency to assume that our favorite teachers will live forever; that they may retire and then live happily on into perpetuity. However, as our school district learned one year, some good teachers die quickly and leave us devastated and confused.

Brenda Ballard was a good teacher. She had challenged children to do their best for many years; she had initiated some programs of her own; she knew her subject matter, and if she didn't, she was willing to go to sources and learn what she needed to know before she presented the concept to her students. She presented talks on gifted education. In other words, she was a consummate educator—one who loved the kids, loved to teach, and had a desire to have others do what was best for education in our district, our county, and our nation.

We began our teaching careers about the same time, but it was in the last years that we had become better acquainted through our profession. We especially loved to call our legislators and ask them to vote for better education in the state and to have them help us in ways they alone could. She was a strong advocate and used her command of the English language to get her point across to those who could do something about improving education for the children.

One of the things that endeared her to me was that she always took the time when we saw each other to compliment articles I had written. She could remember what was said and how it could possibly impact parenting for the readers. She was saving them for her own children, which is a compliment. I will miss those encouraging words.

So, since we now know that good teachers can suddenly be taken from us, let me ask: How long has it been since you contacted a teacher or other educator and told him or her how your life was influenced by what he or she did or said? Sometimes we have time to say "Good-bye", as Mitch Albon did as he sat beside the bed of his dying teacher, but too often we delay and tell ourselves that there is plenty of time—and too soon the time or the person is gone, and we have lost the opportunity.

One night I received an e-mail from a student who had been in one of my English classes. He was not giving compliments—he needed someone who would read his heart as he poured out his difficulties and heartaches.

I wrote back, encouraging him to do something positive for himself and for others in order to get his mind off what was burdening him so much. Now, why was that important to me? Because I was a person from his past—a teacher—and he gave me the gift of sharing what was bothering him. That was a compliment to an educator. We never forget our kids, no matter how long we teach, and we are concerned when they are hurting. We also rejoice with them in their joy, and we are more than devastated when we lose one in death.

One day I met a former student for lunch so she could interview me about my career. Another teacher who was with us had begun her career about the same time as I had. We had a great time remembering the plays we directed, the singing groups I led, the many students we had and their various gifts—the naturally funny ones, the musically talented ones, the very good students, and the ones who had strengths in other areas. We laughed and talked until the waitress was getting impatient to have her table vacated. Teachers, if they are called to the profession, enjoy all parts of their work—from the easy days to the more challenging ones. In addition, we remember our students as if they were in our classrooms yesterday. We may not always remember their names, but we usually can place their faces.

Never hesitate to speak to us—we are glad to see you and to know how you are doing in life. It is a gift you are giving back to us.

So, I challenge you to pick up the phone, find one on Facebook, write an old-fashioned letter, send a card—just don't let the time get away before you let one know how your life has been changed because that educator showed you attention, let you express yourself, encouraged you, used your talents, taught you so that you could later use what you learned in your career. Whatever, just don't wait too long to give a word of praise to an educator.

SCHOOL: WHAT TO EXPECT
AND HOW TO SPEAK "PARENTISH"

So, YOUR CHILD, or children, will begin school soon. As a former teacher and counselor, I can list a few things you should expect, no matter what grade he/she is in and how to speak a parenting language that will get good results.

What to expect:

1. Homework. This may not be totally true in the first or second grades, but from the third grade on, good teachers give homework—not because they are sadistic, but because it is proven that if a child leaves the schoolyard and then works on an assignment from what was taught that day, he *owns* the material. The best way for a person to learn is to use what he has been taught, whether it is a math problem, an English part of speech, a time in history or a science concept. So homework is crucial to education—to retaining what is being taught, then to being able to *drag it up* on a test or later in college or on the job. If the high school where your attend is on a block schedule, it is also important for students to review what was taught two days before so that they are ready for the class the next time it meets which will prepare them for a college schedule as well.

2. Discipline. If a child consistently disrupts the teacher and requires more attention than any of the other children, then he is *cheating* the other students in the classroom of their education. The teacher will only endure that behavior for a short time; then she will make the decision to discipline the student, usually by sending him to the office. That is a good choice—get him out of the way of hindering the learning of others and let him make the choice of whether he wants to return to the classroom to learn or not. If not, he may end up somewhere off campus for a length of time until he makes better decisions.

3. Expense. Labs, notebooks, novels, band fees, choir outfits—there are many expenses if your child chooses to take part in various activities and classes. Be ready to pay as soon as you learn about the expense. Don't embarrass your child by his having to defend you and why you haven't sent the money yet.

4. Frustration. Your child may come home elated from his first day to the last of school this year. However, most parents must expect some frustration in their children whether he is in the third or the twelfth grade. Be patient and let him talk about it when he is ready. If you push for answers, you may never find out what the dilemma is.

There are so many more, but I want to address the ability to speak "Parentish", as in a language like English. Here are a few examples: 1. Poor Parentish: "My child would never do what you say he did!" (If you have parented long, you know never to say, "My child would never . . . .") Correct Parentish: "We have raised our child to be kind, polite, and respectful; however, he obviously has not learned this particular aspect of that lesson. After tonight, he will understand the concept and you will not have to address this subject with him again".

Poor Parentish: "I don't know why you people have to give so much homework anyway!" Good Parentish: "I didn't know that you gave homework often and that he has not been turning anything in. After tonight, he will have it all done and will turn it in (rather than forget it in his locker as he claims). Will you please let me know if this does not happen?"

Poor Parentish: "I'm sure there is some good reason why he has missed ten days in the first three weeks of school!" Good Parentish: "I was not aware that he was missing school, but after we speak about this tonight, you will find his bright little face in his desk every day. Oh, he may have to stand tomorrow, but he will be able to sit after that."

Poor Parentish shows the child that he can get away with defying school rules and the teacher. His education will suffer because of it. Good Parentish shows the teachers and administrators that you support them, that you want your child to gain an education and really *know some stuff* when he graduates, and that you are aware that your child is not perfect. It also allows your child to face the fact that he is fighting a losing battle if he does not cooperate because he will have to defy you AND the school—and those are formidable odds.

Have a terrific school year every year, encourage your child to do his best, go to his activities, support the school and its teachers and administrators, and be proud next May that you and your child have had a good year.

STRATEGY FOR BETTER GRADES

How is your child doing in school this year or how did he do last year? If you are like some parents, you have been surprised, disappointed, and alarmed. Many have done what I have warned against—they considered their child old enough (in whatever grade) to be trusted to do his homework without being monitored. Then they realized that the grades they were seeing were the result of the student's refusal to do assignments or to turn in assigned work to the teacher or to prepare for tests or to complete projects. So, when <u>are</u> they mature enough to be trusted to do the work themselves? The answer, of course, depends on the child. Some are conscientious when they are very young—they have a list of the assignments and get it done early and study nightly. Sound familiar? I didn't think so. Few parents have children like that.

Instead, we have children who are a lot like us—they need to be encouraged, motivated, monitored, and made accountable. But, this takes time and energy and effort! Yes! Now you know the real secret of parenting.

So, what do we do to help our smaller children and teens during this crucial stage of life—the educational years? I used to make several suggestions in my office—let me share them with you:

1. Buy your child a planner. A planner will help the student keep up with the assignments, dates of projects, extra credit, research paper deadlines, and so on.

2. Check the planner to be sure the daily work is done. If the student says he completed all the work at school, accept the fact that even a genius needs more time to properly prepare for math than ten minutes. Tell your student you want to see the work no matter where it was completed.

3. Set aside a place for homework and study. I always suggest that this place be the kitchen table—not in the kid's room where there are too many distractions and he is on his own to keep on task. "But, Mrs. Knight, we would have to miss T.V. if he studies in the kitchen!" So? Which is more important, your time watching something written on a third-grade level or that your child understands science and algebra?

4. Have a set time *each* night for schoolwork. How long? For grades 1-3 approximately 30-40 minutes. For grades 4-6 no less than 45 minutes. For grades 4-7 approximately one hour—more to study for tests, and for grades 9-12 no less than an hour to one and a half hour per class not including study time for tests. Does this sound like a lot of time? It still leaves four and a half to six hours per night to spend with the family. Did I mention watching T.V. time? No, I didn't. We who have been in education are finding that children are less motivated today because they have spent so many hours in front of a screen that has little or no educational value.

5. Wait for the report card. Tell your child you are looking forward to seeing it. If it doesn't come home on the assigned day, find out why. Call the school if the *excuse* doesn't sound valid (don't believe everything your child says about this important piece of paper). Go to the school and pick it up or secure a copy if the original was *accidentally* lost.

6. Call for a Parent Conference if you are disappointed with the grades. The counselors will set up a meeting with the teachers so you can know first hand what your student is doing in the classroom.

7. Keep it up. For many students, as soon as you back off, they slack off. Your responsibility as a parent continues throughout the educational years—even to college if you are paying.

THE MOST IMPORTANT PART OF
STUDENT SUCCESS: INVOLVED PARENTS

A RE YOU AWARE of the volumes of research being done on student success? The consensus is that it doesn't <u>matter</u> where your child goes to school—in what town, in what area of town, whether private or public. What does matter, as shown in every research finding I have read, is PARENT INVOLVEMENT. You are the most important element in your child's educational success.

A mother once asked me to speak to my husband who taught fifth grade in an elementary school about her son's progress because she was worried that he was not doing well academically or socially. He was perplexed and told the mother that her son was an excellent student, was well behaved, did his homework, and was having little trouble with the new concepts being taught. He also told her that he had met her older son at a restaurant lately. He too, she was told, was polite, mature, and self-assured. Obviously, he told her, both young men were the result of parenting that was disciplined, loving, and expectant.

On the other hand, I know of a student who feels *entitled* because his mother comes to the school demanding to know what the teachers and other staff are "going to do for him" since he is failing. He is a behavior problem, a community problem, even a problem to himself because he has not been disciplined; there are no expectations put on him as far as conduct and grades; and he has no respect for adults.

Another form of *failed* parenting involves waiting until the child fails or does something to get himself in trouble and then whining that he has hurt your feelings or been a disappointment or doesn't love you. That does very little to create a lasting desire in a child to do what is best for him (rather than for the parent). He needs motivation to be the best student/ person he can be for his own good, not to please you or keep you from feeling sorry for yourself.

Still another parenting example is one in which you are too busy or too angry at your spouse (or ex-spouse) to help your child. A student once came to me who was upset over trying to get her mother to help pay for her graduation invitations. The mother got a sizeable child-support check, so the student didn't understand why she couldn't contribute to this important part of her being a senior. The dad's excuse for not helping was that he sends the check which is supposed to be used for the child. Guess who was in the middle and never got the money for her invitations!!

One of our teachers had a student who had not paid for a workbook that had always been used in that classroom. The mother's response, when she was called about this situation, was "This is supposed to be free education, so why do I have to pay for a workbook?" While this might be a good question, guess who had to be taken out of that non-required class because she couldn't keep up with the work without the workbook?

Involved parenting means that your child is the top priority in your everyday life. He is the reason you work, the reason you know what his grades are before the report card comes out, the reason you plan for each year and the supplies he will need to be a good student, the reason you save for his senior year so you can pay for his invitations, his senior T-shirt, and all of those *incidentals* that come that year.

Involved parenting means that you spend quality time teaching your child how to shake hands or meet people, how to talk to adults respectfully (so he can get a job and keep one someday), how to self-motivate (so he can be successful in this level as well as the next level of education and in the work world), how to like himself (so he won't be influenced by his peers to do something he will regret), how to respect you (so he will respect other people in authority), how to set goals and then aspire to reach them.

Parenting takes a lot of physical, emotional, and psychological effort. It is not for the faint-of-heart, but you have learned that as he has grown, right? (And it doesn't get easier.) His present and future success depend on it.

CHAPTER SIX

HELP! I HAVE TEENAGERS IN MY HOUSE!

THOUGHTS ON THE FIRST DAY OF SCHOOL

WHEN YOU ARE just days away from the first day of school, what are some things that you, as the parent, need to do to assure that your child will be successful during the coming year as he gets that all-important education?

First, be SURE that he goes to school. Even politicians are aware that often it is the fault of the parent that kids do not attend on a regular basis. Parents sleep late and take the kids in when they get up—sometimes after the math or science class and then are astounded when the child makes a low grade in that class. They also will require the older child to stay home with a younger child rather than miss work. Then they are shocked when the school and teachers become alarmed over days missed in the subjects that need to be learned. There are parents who are so *sick* (co-dependent) that they have to have the child home to keep them company (this happens more than you want to know). In addition, many parents refuse to be assertive enough with a rebellious child and allow him to use any excuse to stay home. Then when they have missed so many days that they have become impossibly behind in their classes and can't catch up, the parents want to blame the school or the teacher rather than accept the blame themselves.

Let's face it—your child cannot successfully teach himself at home. He needs to be with a qualified educator who has been trained to teach unless you are home every day and are working really hard to be a successful home-school parent and know the avenues the child will need to take to enter public school or college. The students who withdraw from school with the idea of home schooling without the direct aid and supervision of a parent usually come back within a year and want to re-enter school. Why not leave them there rather than let them make the decision to leave and *teach* themselves? You are the parent—you make the decision.

Next, encourage your child and set aside a special time and place to do homework. Most school districts give work to be done at home so the child can learn to work independently and can internalize what the teacher has taught. Don't just naively believe your child when he says he has no homework night after night. Instead, call the teacher at school or set up a parent conference to be sure your child is not working harder at convincing you that he has no academic work than he is at accomplishing it. Most teachers teach "from bell to bell" and give little time to do work at school. Homework is a major element in a real education. Make sure your child does not miss out on it.

Thirdly, ask your child—even your teens—what they are learning in certain subjects. Then don't quit because you are intimidated by his knowledge or if he gives you a typical non-committal answer: "Nothing" (usually said with emphasis on the first syllable). If you have to, look through his books at night so you can be aware and curious and can help your child to be curious too. As we have discussed in this book previously, your enthusiasm for learning will carry over to your children. Your boredom with it will do the same thing—create a negative response.

Finally, support the educators. We didn't become teachers in order to pick on kids or because we couldn't do anything else. We went into it because we actually LIKE kids, because we found that we had a *knack* for teaching them, and because we went to college to prepare to teach your children. We don't, despite what your kids say, pick on a particular kid, call them names, or keep them from being kids. We do insist that children mind and behave so that everyone in the classroom can receive instruction. So, rather than believing everything your kid says about the teacher, get in touch with the school to hear what the adult has to say in a given situation. In return, we promise not to believe everything your child says about you and your home life.

The successful education of a student has a great deal to do with the support the child is getting at home. Work with the school to make your children the best educated people they can be—in that way we elevate our children, our communities, our states, and our nation. EDUCATION IS THE KEY.

A GREAT WAY TO BUILD SELF-ESTEEM
IN TEENAGERS

OES YOUR TEENAGER need an ego boost? Does his self-esteem need a
shot in the arm? Is his self-confidence sagging? I have the solution:
Vacation Bible School! No, I don't mean that he should go and make
popsicle-stick frames and eat cookies and drink Kool-aid. What I do mean
is that he should be a helper with the smaller kids.

I was able to see several incidents in two Vacation Bible Schools one
summer, and I realized that the teens working with the children were
getting as much or more out of the experience as the little ones.

In one situation, a teen came into a room full of small boys and girls
with a silly headband and a mop of dark hair that wasn't his. As he walked
through, his name was yelled by little adoring kids, small hands wanted
to touch him, and all eyes were on him. What a great way to feel good
about oneself! He stopped at each table and spoke to his adoring audience;
he took the cap off one little boy and reminded him not to wear a hat in
a public building; he muscled a bottle top off a drink for a little girl. He
was the center of attention in an adoring crowd, and as he left the room,
his shoulders were a little straighter, his head a little higher, and a broad
smile was on his face. All of this, and a parent didn't have to pay for hours
of therapy!

In another situation, three teenage girls were leading a group of
children from one building to another. They were making a game of
follow-the-leader, and there were giggles and smiles on every little face in
the line as well as on the faces of the girls who were being followed. What
teen doesn't want to experience the success of leading, even if it is kids half
their age?

As I stood in this same big room in a church building, a teenage boy
came into the room carrying a child of about three who had been crying.
The little boy was clinging to the teen and the teen was being very gentle
with him. By the time the teen found the parent, the child had changed
his mind—he wanted to go back with the teen to his group. The thing
that caused him to cry was forgotten—he wanted to be with the teen more
than he wanted to be with his mother at that time. The teen took him
by the hand and led him away with the little boy looking up at him with
admiration. So the teen is learning responsibility and care-taking—not

bad when the parent has probably been trying to get him to be responsible at home for the past several months.

In one Vacation Bible School, at least a third of the leaders were teenagers—both boys and girls. They taught and led music with smart-looking choreography; they taught Bible lessons; they took the children out to play; they gave out craft materials and praised the kids who completed their work. So, not only do these teens have their egos stroked by little people, but they also learn skills in teaching and leading children—something we all could use at one time or another.

Teenagers also helped in the serving lines when the children got their snacks and spoke to each child as he passed. For some small kids, that may be the most they are noticed all day. So these teens learned to pay attention to the needs of the children who were there with them.

Now, you may be thinking, "I can't get my teenager up earlier than 10:00 or 11:00, so Bible School is not an option for me. One of the programs I saw went on from 6:00 to 8:00 at night. So, not only should you be ashamed for letting your kids sleep that long during the day (in case he ever gets a job or goes back to school), but you have no excuse for not telling him that he is going to help in Bible School in your neighborhood since he doesn't have a job anyway.

Your other excuse may be that you don't belong to a church anywhere. Well, shame on you, but some of the teens who were helping have no parent who attends church; however, *they* are faithful to go, and their help was invaluable with the children.

We can all find excuses even though we know that this type of experience can be wonderful for teens who need to learn how to handle responsibility, how to handle little children, and how to deal with different situations daily. It is also a terrific (and free) way to boost the ego of any teen that needs it. I recommend it for them. Find a Vacation Bible School they can become involved in for the next summer—it will change their lives for the better.

A LOOK AT TWO TYPES OF TEENS/YOUNG ADULTS

THE ADULT MAIN character of a novel I was reading was being threatened by three older teenagers. All three were covered with tattoos—both the boys and girl with them. They slouched when they walked and when they stood. All three used foul (filthy) language without regard to the persons who might be listening. The leader of the three made a clicking noise when he spoke, and the observer finally saw the silver bead *skewered* through his tongue which was in addition to the horseshoe in his lip, the ring in his nose, and the stud in his eyebrow. One of the boys had spiked purple hair; the other had long iridescent maroon locks. They all used atrocious English as if they had dropped out of school in the third grade. However, it was a comment that the author made about another aspect of their language that I also found interesting: "I'm like, they're like"—the uneducated must now speak with the word "like", as if they can't formulate a sentence without using this word to stop them so they can think of something else to say.

A generation that cannot think creatively? Cannot formulate intelligent thought and speak well enough that others can learn from them? Cannot express themselves without vulgarities they have picked up from movies or music or TV or (Heaven forbid) at home? If this is true, then our nation is in serious trouble in the future.

And what of those I heard about who disturbed my friend's vacation by being so drunk on the beach that when one of the boys got mad at his girlfriend, he threw her to the sand and proceeded to beat her in the face until the police hauled him away? Or the one who was taken to the hospital with alcohol poisoning? Or the ones who partied so loud and so long that the condo manager kicked them and their chaperones out at 1:00 in the morning? All of this witnessed by two little girls who were just there to be on vacation and have fun with their mom and dad.

I, for one, am concerned about many of the teens and young adults today. Too many are throwing away their lives, their futures, their relationships; thinking, "I just want to be happy, and if I party enough or if I change my life enough—no matter whom it hurts—then everything will all be better". Not gonna happen. Reality has nothing to do with shows on television; it has everything to do with pain, joy, hurt, forgiveness, compromise, hard work, learning, and so much more. Life is to be lived, not avoided by looking for that illusive *happiness.*

On the other hand, there are the young people I see checking groceries, and waiting tables, and selling retail to pay for college, and those who are spending only what they have and are not touching their savings. There are those who are respectful of their parents, who dress nicely, who wouldn't dream of cursing, and who read more than they watch TV or play video games.

What is the difference between the two groups of these teens and young people? Most of the time it is in the type of parents they have—from those who see nothing wrong with the "kids having a little fun" even if it involves drinking or drugging, and who don't require good manners, decent language, or respect for themselves and others—to the ones who are trying to raise well-behaved, respectful, delightful young adults.

It is true, of course, that some teens raised by lousy parents turn out to be wonderful adults. It is also true that some teens raised by terrific parents can make really lousy decisions and ruin their chances of being contributing adults unless something or someone finally gets their attention and they can turn around from the destructive lives they seem to have chosen for themselves.

Your responsibility as parents is to work really hard to be the kind of parents whose kids will make us all proud because of the way they look, act, speak, and how they treat others. It is not an easy task; it never has been, but so many parents have succeeded, we know it can happen. Do your part to make it happen for your kids.

ADOLESCENT GIRLS AND SEX

I AM INCREASINGLY ALARMED over the number of adolescent girls I see and read about and hear about who are having sex. One girl I spoke to had gone with the boy three months, and after the breakup, she told him she thought she was pregnant with his baby (she is fourteen years old; the ex-boyfriend is sixteen). He, of course, told all of his friends, her friends, her enemies, and his present girl friend. The first girlfriend was devastated.

Why are pre-teen and teen girls, and even college-age girls so willing to give themselves so freely? And what can we as parents do to channel our daughters' social energies in a more positive way?

First, a parent's moral values should be apparent to your children from the time they are young. Are you living your life the way you want them to live? Is there a girlfriend or boyfriend in your home without the benefit of marriage? Is there alcohol in your home? Many girls are not even aware they have had sex because they were encouraged to drink until they passed out. Do they see anything wrong with drinking because of your influence?

Second, morality needs to be preached from America's pulpits again. The children sitting in a church building should hear what moral purity is and how important it is for being able to go into adulthood without the burden of guilt, a baby too soon, or a contracted illness that won't go away. Oh sure, some girls who attend church do have sex before they are married, but the majority of them have learned the value of staying pure and waiting for commitment and marriage. I have learned that the reason many girls never hear sermons like this one is that they don't attend church. Is there a lesson here for both parents and preachers?

Third, it is the responsibility of parents to let their daughters know how special and precious they are to you. So many girls think their only value lies in what they can do to please others, including boys and men who will take advantage of their desire to please. A book I read, *REVIVING OPHELIA: Saving the Selves of Adolescent Girls*, by Mary Pipher, Ph.D., (Ballentine Books, New York, 1994) addressed this situation well. The author said that fathers are important in the raising of daughters because they can, even more than mothers, make the daughter feel special and pretty and smart. If a daughter has a comfortable, accepting relationship with her father, she is not so eager to be accepted by boys or men and can take care of herself in most situations.

I was surprised to learn from the author of this book that she had found in her practice and her research that strong girls were usually raised by strong mothers. If the mother is not pushed around by the father, if she conducts herself with confidence, if she is capable of making decisions for herself and the children and the household, then the daughters in her home grow up with a confidence not found in homes of weak mothers.

Fourth, your daughters are growing up in a culture that is different from even the one very young parents in their twenties experienced. The accepted sex and jokes about sex on TV and in movies and in rock music and rap is usually degrading to the female gender. It is up to you as parents to try to overcome this cultural saturation and make sure your daughter sees herself, not as just any girl, but as a special young lady who is loved and accepted by caring parents. Granted she may pull away from you during crucial times in her teen years. But if you have tried to help her see who she is and where she is going, she will be less likely to try too hard to impress her peers with how often she goes to bed with boys and then brag about it at school the next day.

If you are aware of a pre-teen/teen who is engaging in sexual activity and are worried about her, share this information with her. She may not respond openly but you have let her know you are concerned without accusing.

Parenting is not easy, and the pre-teen/teen years are especially challenging. Read books, read articles, ask advice, do anything to feel like you are parenting with all of your effort. The reward <u>will</u> come.

ALL OF US AGAINST DRUNK DRIVING

PARENTS, YOU AND your teenagers need to become active advocates against drinking and driving in your area or county or town.

I had the opportunity to attend a workshop at our Board of Education with approximately eighty teens from the high schools in our County sponsored by MADD, Mothers Against Drunk Driving. The experienced workshop leaders were from Texas. One was a former state trooper who had spent many years being the first on the scene of horrific wrecks and who was usually the one who had to knock on the doors of family members to tell them that the victim would not be coming home.

There were two painful testimonies, one from Greg Kuhl (the son-in-law of one of our local meteorologists, Dave Brown) whose wife, baby girl, and unborn son were killed in 1997 by a drunk driver. Greg often had to drink water to regain his composure as he told about the incident and the sense of loss that will never leave him.

The other testimony was from a young man whose two best friends' deaths were related to a drunk driver—one who died a year later from the trauma he received as a result of the wreck, the other to suicide from the survivor guilt she felt because the rider died and she didn't.

The teens who were listening, sat in silence and sympathy as those men suffered in front of them. Each teenager was also given a workbook which included some terribly revealing statistics that would alarm and depress any reader, but, as parents, you need to be aware of them as well. I will list them and use the exact words used in the workbook:

- Every three weeks the equivalent of the entire senior class at a typical high school dies on the nation's streets and highways.
- With each 12-ounce bottle of beer that a teenager drinks, the risk of a fatal crash doubles.
- In the past decade, four times as many Americans died in impaired driving crashes as were killed in the Vietnam War.
- There are 15 young drinking drivers involved in fatal crashes for every 100,000 young licensed drivers—almost twice the rate for drivers 21 or older.
- Sixteen and 17-year-old drivers are involved in more than twice the average number of crashes per mile driven as are experienced

drivers. These crashes occur most frequently between midnight and 5:00 a.m.

- During 1996, a young person died in a traffic crash on average of once an hour during the weekend and once every two hours on weekdays
- The chance of dying doubles every 10 miles per hour over 50 mph.

One terrific quote came from Greg Kuhl, "When I sat in the back and saw the shirts with SADD (Students Against Destructive Decisions) on them, I saw "Hope"—Hope that we can learn that peer pressure can go the other way—to GOOD decisions that teenagers can influence others, that can be changed because these teens have and will stand AGAINST drinking and driving."

The Texas highway patrolman told the audience that we all stand a 40% chance of being killed by someone who is drinking and driving. He said that MADD also needs to stand for "GET MAD!" over the fact that teens and others are dying because of selfish people who drive after they have been drinking. He challenged them to DO SOMETHING! To say to themselves: "I need to help change this for all of us!"

The leaders also reminded the teens that we already have too many people who are influencing people in negative ways: to rebel against parents, to use drugs, to drink at parties or in groups, to have sex. "Who is going to be a leader toward a positive way of life?"

Finally, they gave a plan for the teens of our County to talk to or write their local community leaders, their legislators, and their peers. They especially urged them to ask those who make and enforce laws to strictly enforce the one banning sales of alcohol to minors and that they could help stem the tide of local sales by taking part in "minor stings" with law enforcement.

Parents, you also have a responsibility to your children, young and old. First, be a good example—don't drink. Secondly, get involved with MADD or with being an advocate to strengthen the laws against drunk driving and alcohol sales to minors in our state. We need everyone to help—our lives and the lives of our families depend on it.

AMERICAN TRAGEDY: TEENAGE PREGNANCY

O NE OF THE most disheartening aspects of my work as a counselor was the continued prevalence of teenage pregnancy despite talks I gave to girls, despite the efforts of the health profession in warning about Aids and other sexually transmitted diseases, and despite the fact that teenagers are actually aware of all of the risks and yet engage in premarital sex anyway.

Within a two-week period I became aware of six teenage girls in the ninth and tenth grades who were pregnant and who had not even told their parents yet. Many of these girls were intelligent and independent, yet their desire to please the boys they were dating left them seemingly little choice when it came to being used as a sex object.

I read an article in the March 1998 magazine Young Maturity and found the following statistics (they are higher now): Each year more than a million teenage girls become pregnant; twenty-four percent of all teenage girls will get pregnant at least once by age 18, and more than 44 percent will get pregnant by age 20; about one half of all teenage pregnancies end in births; four in ten, not including miscarriages, end in abortion; less than 10 percent of teens put their babies up for adoption; U.S. teenagers have one of the highest pregnancy rates in the Western world—twice as high as England's and seven times higher then the Netherlands'; teenage girls who keep their babies are disproportionately poor and dependent on public assistance; pregnant teenagers marry the father of their baby only about 10 percent of the time, and the marriages usually don't last.(page 59, Elizabeth Lange).

Most of the girls I counseled got pregnant in their own homes while their parents were away; many had sex in the home of the boy while his parents were away or even while they were present; and many were sneaking out of the house at night or away from school in the day to be with boyfriends who demanded too much of them.

In addition to the many who were expecting at that time, there were hundreds more who lived in fear each month that they were pregnant. I once intercepted a note from one girl to another telling of her monthly terror that she would be pregnant and of her eagerness to share that fear with her best friend who also lived in fear. I wondered what that constant adrenalin poison was doing to their bodies that will show up as they age.

And this is not just happening to girls of parents who never darken the door of a church. I know of a family who is constantly in church and are active Christians whose son is sexually active. I once talked to the mother of a senior girl who was seriously dating a boy who was different from anything the parents had hoped she would marry—he never went to church; he drank; he dipped; and the mother was so heartbroken that she couldn't talk about it or even think about it. She told me it was like a death in the family to think that her daughter would consider connecting her life to a person so different from them.

Parents, what can you do to try to stem the tide of this progressive problem and to protect your precious teenagers from a decision that may hurt their futures and the futures of your future grandchildren?

First, be sure you have talked to your teen and let him and her know what you expect in a son or daughter-in-law. I truly think you have a right, after all the time and love you have invested in this child, to at least expect them to choose a marriage partner that will fit into your family structure. If your teen has already stopped listening to you, then collect magazine and newspaper articles and leave them on the bed every night that she or he is away on a date. They will not have to feel that they must defend the person they are dating, but they will have the opportunity to think about the information in the article every time they come home. This is was my mother's strategy, and it worked.

Let them know that a decision to have sex before marriage is a choice that has far-reaching consequences, including guilt, emotional stress, possible physical problems, pregnancy, and possible disease, one of which can lead to death. Then you, as the parent, must not be part of the problem. I can't tell you how many girls have gotten pregnant by the boy who is living in the girl's home because, among other reasons, he has been kicked out of his house, he has no other place to live, he is "like part of the family". Young men can find a place to live—you don't have to sacrifice your own daughter to provide it for him.

Above all, be a loving, concerned parent whose principal purpose in life at this point is to be the very best parent you can be while you still have your child at home and can be an influence on him or her.

ARE YOUR KIDS RUINING THEIR LIVES
WITH DRUGS?

Do you know for sure that your child is not doing drugs? Do you have even the slightest suspicion that he or she may be? What are you going to do if you DO suspect that he is taking part in parties or in groups that are smoking it, taking it, ingesting it, mainlining it, or making it?

Do you know that the police are looking for specific cars in neighborhoods, watching certain houses and businesses, learning the names of particular people in your area? If you do suspect that your child is with someone who is selling or using, do you want him picked up with the user or pusher? Do you have any idea what that could do to his future if he is caught with the stuff or with the pusher if <u>he</u> is convicted? Are you afraid for your child? Then let's look at some things you need to be noticing for the sake of your youngster.

Have his grades fallen within the past year or so? Pot (marijuana), alcohol, and most other drugs lead to a mental apathy that prevents him from caring what his grades are like or from being able to remember what he studied the night before if he attempts to study. Even a small amount of most drugs can change a good student into a failing one.

Has he developed a new or different set of friends? Do those friends dress differently—grungier, blacker, sloppier, even more expensively? In fact from the experience of an acquaintance of mine, your child may have a second set of friends—his user friends, that you may not even know.

Is he coming in later and you are not aware of where he has been most of the time? Is he one of the kids who is going to parties where they are either drinking or smoking or doing meth or crack or speed? Are you aware of what all that is doing to his body and mind as well as to his future? Is he almost impossible to get up in the mornings after being out late?

Has he pulled away from you and the rest of the family? A very good adolescent psychologist says that when your child is doing something that he knows you would disapprove of if you knew, he will avoid you for two reasons: he doesn't want you to find out, and he feels guilty over what he is doing because he knows how disappointed you will be when you do inevitably find out.

Does he ever defend drug or alcohol use? Has he ever stolen from you or from a store? Is he sometimes afraid? (Drug pushers can be ruthless if they are owed money and your child can't get it for him.)

If you have even a suspicion because of any of these indications, there are several things you must do. First, you have permission, even the responsibility, to poke around in his room or his car to see if there is anything to substantiate your fears. Is this an invasion of privacy? Yes and no. Yes, a teenager will consider this an invasion of his territory and may even be mad. So? It is your home, his room in the house is one for which you are paying, and the health and welfare of your child is at stake; therefore, you have the right and parental privilege and responsibility to find out what you can do in order to help him.

Second, be sure you know the first AND last names of the friends he is with when he is away from you. We have had teenagers who have run away or have disappeared, and the parents didn't know where to begin to look because they had no idea whom he was with or where he usually hung out. They could not tell the police anything because they were clueless about their child and his habits.

Thirdly, don't be afraid to let your child know where you stand and what you will do if you find that he is doing drugs of any kind or is drinking. I have met several parents who, because they smoked pot or drank in their youth, think they have no right to tell their teens that they cannot do it. So, if you took some stupid, life-threatening chances in your past, do you think your teen should be able to do it too? I doubt it, because you know that losing that child would hurt you so much. So you should be able to tell him that you will not tolerate his using any substance as long as he lives in your house.

Fourth, don't trust even the parents of some of your child's friends. There are many kids who are buying from their friend's siblings, parents, uncles, and others. In fact, there are some sorry adults out there who will do drugs WITH your child. In today's world you must take care of your own, and realize that not everyone is going to do what's best for your children. What if you find out an adult IS selling or providing drugs or alcohol to your child? There is one word for your response—PROSECUTE! It has been done successfully already. Don't hesitate to do the same.

Fifth, if your child has a job or if you give him money, know where that money is being spent. Make him accountable; make him save some of it; don't let him spend it on drugs or the alcohol to take to a party or while driving around in car.

Finally, remember that the most important job your child has at this time of his life is that of being a good student. If his grades are suffering, find out why. If he is missing school, find out why. If he is consistently late for classes, be curious and concerned enough to find out why.

So many kids really want you to make them quit—they want to be normal kids who graduate from high school and go on to live a happy life, and often they will give signals so you will suspect something and get help for them. Take the hint—you owe it to them and you owe it to yourself as a parent.

"BEAUTY FADES; DUMB IS FOREVER"

"**B**EAUTY FADES, DUMB is forever" is a now-famous quote by Judge Judy, the TV judge who has been a Family Court Judge in Manhattan for 25 years. When I think about the YM (Young and Modern) and the Seventeen magazines I see on campuses, I agree with her that our culture over-emphasizes appearance and "catching "a "sweetie" (boyfriend). Judge Judy emphasizes what really should be important in our children's lives: "(My dad) impressed upon me that a bright intellect and a passion for learning are priceless commodities. We have to get this message to girls."

However, in most magazines for teenage girls and young women, there are countless models with skeleton shapes—no hips, no bust; their hair is lustrous and shiny and, according to the ads, smell of strawberry or some other edible fruit; the rest of them have their hair cut as short or shorter than a boys'; their complexion is flawless (teenage models have no pimples?); their mouths are pouty, full and covered with expensive "lip color"; you get the picture! What pre-adolescent/adolescent girl or even young adult woman can measure up? And yet they try.

The emphasis in these magazines is on being attractive to men, usually in a sexy way. Seldom is there an article on self-fulfillment, self-esteem, self motivation, spiritual growth, or intellectual curiosity.

When females see themselves only as sexual beings, they miss one of the most exciting areas of their anatomy—their brains. It's what gives us our uniqueness, our individual personality, our ability to learn, to communicate, our ability to grow as a person. As Judge Judy would put it, they think they have to look great to get a man. So they become obsessed with their body shape, their hair, flawless make-up, the latest clothes—everything but their brain and whether they can think past tonight.

Another Judge Judy quote that got my attention was "For a teenage girl, sex is stupid". Then she went on to elaborate what I have found in counseling—to be part of a couple or because "everybody else is doing it", too many girls think they must "do it" too. A girl who values her worth, who values her unique self, who has plans and goals does not have to find her value in pleasing boys or her friends. We must teach that to our female children.

Judge Judy also said so well what I have implied in counseling sessions before, "Having a baby should be a thought process, not an accident". A baby should be planned, saved for, prayed for, hoped for and finally conceived in love by two married people who really want a child as part of their family. Teenage girls (and boys) so often get the whole cycle reversed—they conceive, then they spend years trying to pay for and raise a child they hadn't planned for. Girls (and boys) should give themselves credit for having more sense and more control than that.

So what solutions can we deduce?

First, accept as normal some of your female child's indulgences:

1. the phone—this attached-to-the-ear phenomenon or texting that happens around age thirteen (just remember that some schools have phone-master systems that report absences between 6 and 8 in the evening, and your "tech-savvy" child may preclude you from receiving those calls, or your child may give his own number to the system).
2. the unusual shoes and strange clothes (our parents were aghast at what we wore too)
3. the "glam" attempts (trying new and different make-up and clothes for the "new look" can be really expensive; you may need a second job).
4. the body reshaping attempts (watch for bulimia and/or anorexia which can become a true and dangerous obsession with weight and, if not caught, can become a mental illness)
5. the giggling, silly, serious, excited, nervous obsession with the other sex.

Second, stress to your female child her value as a unique person who can contribute to the welfare of others through her God-given talents. Allow her to be an individual, to make plans for her future, to grow spiritually and gracefully as a young woman with a mind and a heart of her own. Remind her that she does not have to lose her *self* in order to make other people like her. If she likes herself and is comfortable with who she is, she will be a contented person throughout her life.

God blessed you with this lovely daughter. Give her guidance, give her love, give her protection, give her direction (without nagging), give her room.

DETECTING DEPRESSION IN YOUR TEEN

O N A FRIDAY just after the bell had rung for the students to go home, a girl walked into my office and announced that a boy had told her that he was tired of being treated so "bad" by other students and he was considering committing suicide. My first question was why she had waited until I could not find him to come and tell me; my second question was whether she knew how to get in touch with his parents. For the next thirty minutes I worked frantically to find his mother's work number while continuing to call his home phone number to try and talk to him. Finally, I reached his mother at work and told her about the threat. She seemed very calm and unconcerned. Her first question was for me to name the girl who had come to me (which was confidential); her second question was who I was exactly. I suggested that she leave immediately to see about him or send the police to see if he was all right. She said that she would take care of it and hung up.

Now why was I so concerned about him and why did I take the threat seriously when I just had the word of another student? First, during the previous month two young people from our area had committed suicide, so there is always the possibility of a copy-cat suicide any time one occurs. Secondly, any threat of suicide needs to be taken seriously no matter how many times you have heard it from the same person.

Let's consider teenage depression and how it can get to the point of self-destruction. First, we as parents need to recognize that the mere transition from childhood to adolescence is, in itself, depressing. Not only are these kids dealing with racing, out-of-control hormones, but they are having to deal with acceptance at school, with peer pressure, with wanting to be accepted by the opposite sex, and with feelings of inadequacy and self-consciousness. They have mood swings; they move from complete dependence and childlikeness to wanting to be treated as a grown adult with all of its privileges and freedoms.

The normal depression that most teens feel has to do with external happenings, particularly with being disappointed by friends, a girlfriend or boyfriend, grades, losing an election or honor, or events at home that cannot be handled. This depression is usually marked by apathy, sometimes irritability, difficulty in concentrating, and a desire to be alone. If the teen is healthy emotionally, he can begin to regroup and handle the hurt and go on in time. What you can do as a parent when your teen is mildly depressed is to reassure him that he has enough strength to endure this trial in his life. Never minimize his feelings—they are as serious to him as ours are to us, and we must try to communicate with him and let him know that he has our support and love through his ups and downs.

Severe depression, on the other hand, lasts longer, is more intense, and is disruptive to the normal life of a teen. Clinical depression can be caused by a chemical imbalance in the brain that is triggered by an event that another teen may be able to overcome easily. Let's look at some evidences of clinical, or severe, depression.

1. Feelings of sadness or hopelessness
2. A disinterest in activities which used to be fun to him
3. Isolation and withdrawal from friends and family
4. Crying spells for girls/angry outbursts for boys

Sometimes a teen will cover the evidence of depression by other symptoms:

1. Physical ailments like headaches, stomachaches, dizziness
2. Dropping grades, skipping, and total apathy about school work
3. Inability to concentrate
4. Inappropriate irritability and anger
5. A negative attitude toward anyone who tries to help
6. A desire to sleep too much or too little
7. A display of boredom about things that used to be interesting

Some symptoms may indicate a need to seek immediate professional help

1. Chronic insomnia or too much sleep
2. Losing weight or gaining it too quickly
3. A loss of desire to look nice or to bathe
4. Taking chances, especially indigenous games like recklessness in a car, heavy drinking, drugging, dangerous dares
5. Violent behavior toward family members or girl friend
6. Threats of suicide

Sometimes a teen will never mention suicide but will show evidences that it is on his mind:

1. Giving things away to siblings or friends
2. Staying away from family
3. Getting in trouble at school or with the law
4. Deliberately causing a parent to become angry

What can we as parents do?

1. Know the indications like what you have read here
2. Never ignore a threat of suicide
3. Never have too much pride or too little money to get help from an outside source
4. Never waste your time trying to figure out what you have done wrong
5. Be sensitive to the silent cries for help
6. Pray a lot.

FEMALE BASHING IS MORE COMMON
THAN MOST WILL ADMIT

PARENTS, IS YOUR daughter a victim of female bashing? Is your son guilty of female bashing? Do you know what the term means? Female bashing is mistreating girls/women either physically, emotionally or verbally.

I often had girls come into my office and say that their boyfriends are fine toward them when it is just the two of them. However, when they are around his friends, he cuts her down, makes fun of her and even goes off and leaves her. This is emotional abuse and your daughter may be a victim without your knowledge.

Girls often are so emotionally involved with their boyfriends that they are easily convinced to sneak out of their homes, to skip school, to take a drink, to smoke a joint, to take a dangerous drug, to do many things you as a parent would be shocked to know.

In fact, these girls end up losing their personalities and their right to make personal decisions because everything they do has to be approved by the boy they are dating. Let me give you some examples:

One beautiful girl I counseled was forbidden to wear make-up or to dress in anything cute or colorful because the boyfriend did not want other boys to notice her. This girl lost her beauty, her vivaciousness, her bounce, and actually became a drudge just to please this selfish boy.

Another girl had never skipped a day of school and had very nice grades until she began to go with a skinny kid who totally controlled her life. In fact, she would not listen to anyone but him, including her counselor at the treatment center, her parents, and even the people who cared about her at church. She was totally out of the authority of her parents and was under the control of the boy.

There are two success stories I can relate. Several years ago a very pretty 14 year-old was going with a boy who was considerably older than she. Several times she came to school with black eyes, bruises, and other signs of physical abuse. I found out that it was the boyfriend who was hitting her.

Later, the authorities found out that this boy was actually living in her home with the parents' permission. After several sessions with her in my office, she was able to break the tie that bound her to him and to demand that her mother make him move out. She went on to graduate from school and became a confident, pretty young lady again.

One day I saw one of our graduates at her work and asked how she was doing. Her reply was to cry and say that she was much better—that she had recently recognized that she was in an abusive relationship that had caused her to drop out of college, to suffer physical beatings and injury, and to lose all of her self-esteem and courage. She had become estranged from her family and all of her friends which he had required if she was going to stay with him. As she completed her account, her face began to shine and she smiled at me. She had broken off the relationship two nights before and had moved back home with her family. She is fine now.

Do girls really want to go with boys who hurt them or control them? Remember that girls are different from boys in that they are led by their emotions rather than by their logic.

Every time they are hurt by the boy and become angry, the boy will cry, beg, bring gifts, and plead their case with such emotion, the girl will feel guilty for being so cruel and will inevitably go back with him—very much like a woman who is battered by a husband.

What can a parent do?

1. Fathers, love your daughters. They will not allow a boy to control them if they have received affection at home and been taught they are important and special.
2. Be sure you know how they are being treated by the boys they are dating.
3. Take them to church. God loves that precious girl and does not want her to be mistreated and handled in any way but lovingly.

If your daughter can know how precious she is to the God who created her, maybe she will demand that the boys she dates treat her royally as well.

GETTING READY FOR SCHOOL—THE OTHER WAY

U SUALLY, WHEN I write about getting ready for school, it is about getting them ready academically and preparing them to do the best work they can do. This time, let's look at the social aspect of getting ready for school:

1. Reshuffling of friendships—When I was a counselor for the ninth grade, I spent half of my time with crying girls whose best friend no longer was speaking to her and who had found a new best friend. As a rule, the friendship had been one forged in the elementary or the middle school and the rejected friend thought they were *friends forever*. The present situation was very traumatic for the rejected friend, and her feelings and her self-esteem were taking a dive toward disaster. Sometimes the rejected girl would request a meeting with the other girl in my office with me present, but I knew from experience that event could easily end in more rejection and anger on everyone's part. So what I did was to listen to the hurt and pain and let the girl express her grief. We talked about how hurtful betrayal could be and how long it took to at least face the person again. We even went thorough the stages of grief since the loss and betrayal of a friend is similar to a loss in death. I would assure her that she was a pretty girl who could make friends easily, and that she would be able to soon. Then I would send her to class with the request that she see me again in a week or shorter if she needed to talk again.

In a situation like this, *home* should be the refuge where a wounded teen can run. Rather than get mad at the other girl and over the situation, which will vindicate your child but will not solve the problem, say something like this, "This is typical of adolescent relationships and it usually doesn't matter what kind of friend you are or have been. Tomorrow, and each day after, speak to one girl or boy whom you haven't met before. Say something nice and then go on to class. Don't say anything unkind about your old friend or the new best friend. Just move on and away and enjoy this school year." Parents, for goodness sake, don't get involved—don't call the school, the other child's mother, or anyone else. You will only aggravate the problem and embarrass your child.

2. Having the right clothes—Fashions are so volatile that the new look may be old before you can pay for the new clothes you bought. Having said that, kids and teens think they are being evaluated for their clothes even if they're not, so don't totally dismiss their feelings regarding this. Before you go shopping with the "fashionista", set some hard and fast rules: You have only a certain amount to spend so don't let her/him buy one pair of jeans and that's all; both of you will follow the school dress code and the family values; as the parent, you have veto power on all choices. Help your child find colors that become her; help her choose a style that can be worn more than one time (for school and for church); remind them that wearability is a must; make sure that a blouse can be matched with more than one pant or skirt and vice versa. Finally, compromising on clothes is an acquired parenting art—practice it.

3. Having the strength of character to face social challenges—Your child will face value issues and moral issues that he has not faced before. If you have raised him to know what your family believes and what you consider to be appropriate behavior and that he has you to support him, hopefully he can withstand the pressures he will have from his peers. Encourage him to talk to you or to your spouse and let him ask you questions about certain situations. Don't lecture or act alarmed. When he does handle something well, be sure to praise his judgment and his convictions. He may have to make a few mistakes, but his knowing that you are on his side will give him the fortitude to stand alone.

4. Having the right teachers and classes. She cannot have all of the classes that her best friend has (see #1—they may not be friends after the second week anyway). Most large schools set the schedule and the classes before the first day of school without looking at the names of the students. After the first day, the only way the schedule can be changed is if your child qualified for Geometry and finds himself back in Algebra I. A teacher change is seldom done because the class size has been balanced and changing one student could put a class over the maximum load. However, if your child does not have the classes that will be needed to graduate or to graduate at the top of his class or didn't get a vocational class he requested, then you need to step in and meet with a counselor to see if something can be done. Being in classes away from old friends allows your child to meet new friends and new challenges. That's what life is all about, right?

5. School is a micro-world in which your child learns to handle situations. Give him room to learn but give him the tools to come out of it successfully. It comes from you—don't let him down.

GETTING READY FOR SCHOOL THE OTHER WAY, PART II

P REVIOUSLY I DISCUSSED some ways we need to prepare our kids for school other than academically. Now, I want to cover a few different situations that may occur and for which we should help our students get ready for the new school year:

6. Getting along with teachers—Your child is not going to like all of his teachers; however, this is an opportunity to learn how to handle personal situations with grace and with success. Dreading each day because of one teacher can make a school year miserable, so your child must be taught by you to go into the classroom and to be able to work with that teacher anyway. As a counselor, I used to tell students who were having personality conflicts with a teacher that he was not in there to be friends with the teacher—he was there to get a credit and to learn material that would prepare him for the next level. One ninth grader was so disgruntled that he stayed in trouble with the teacher almost daily and was sent out of the classroom almost immediately after the bell rang for some infraction. Finally, I asked him to "be a desk" in her room. Desks don't talk back; they don't drop pencils; they don't talk to their classmates; they just sit quietly in that room. Each day he came back to my office after the class and I would ask him how him he had done in his imitation of a desk and he would grin and say that he did fine and that he stayed in the classroom the whole hour. Even if all he did was absorb the material she was giving, he gained something, and he learned how to control his emotions and actions—a lesson we all need. Each teacher is also an opportunity to teach respect, not just for the person, but also for the position. There is only one teacher in the classroom and that person should be the one in charge. It doesn't matter how brilliant your child is—he doesn't have the education or the training to take over. Tell him to respect each teacher and her/his position as the leader. Tell him that no matter whether he is a genius or not, he can still learn from other people and that is why he is in school—to absorb

knowledge and go on to the next grade or the next level in math or English.

7. Taking part—Your child cannot feel a part of his school if all he does is go to classes, but he doesn't play a sport or take part in the drama or sing in a choir or any other activity on the campus. The high school kids who were the most unhappy were those who never were on the campus except during the day and who left when the bell rang. They didn't help with Homecoming preparations or attend the games or stay for a club meeting. They were the ones who complained that school was boring. Well, of course it was—they never "bought in" to the rest of what school is all about.

8. Having a boy/girl friend—There should have already been a long discussion before your child wants to have one of these—like how to judge the intentions of others, how not to base popularity on whether he has one of these or not, how to treat a person of the opposite sex with dignity and respect, how not to fall too hard so that the world doesn't come to an end if the relationship ends, how to live up to your family's values while on a date. There should have been an understanding of what will happen if those values are compromised. You've been there—use your experience to help guide your child in this important aspect of growing up. You already know that it would be a mistake to make fun of your child's efforts at being romantic or to downplay his feelings. Never talk about him or her in a critical way where you can be heard and never tell their secrets. Never forget that they need your support in this vital part of becoming an adult.

I used to try and speak to some students of all ages the week prior to school starting asking the usual question: "Are you excited about school starting?" Younger kids are usually ready and waiting to go. Teenagers say something like, "I can't wait to see my friends and to do something different". Whatever the response may be, kids, as a rule, look forward to going to school and being social. The academic part is supplemental.

However, as the parent, you have to be sure it is not so supplemental that it is not important enough to your child.

Don't be negative, don't be pushy, and don't be critical of the school or the teacher. Do be your child's encourager, his support, his refuge, his loving parent. He needs one of those more than anything else.

HANDLING REQUESTS FROM TWEENS
AND TEENS WITH SUCCESS

I FOUND AN ARTICLE in the Feb. 2008 FAMILY CIRCLE's "Ask Dr. Ron", and I felt that it would be helpful to share some of its insights with those who are raising teens and tweens. The problem was presented as this: "All Seth and I do is argue." the writer said of her 13-year-old son. "He refuses to take 'No' for an answer and whines, begs and even throws tantrums until I let him do what he wants. Sometimes he forces me to make spontaneous decisions, like allowing him to spend the night at a friend's house, before I even have the chance to discuss it with his dad. I'm tired of being the policewoman all the time at home."

Dr. Ron's answer was good in many respects, like when he wrote "It's inevitable for tweens and teens to test boundaries—that's how they gain their independence. The way parents respond determines whether kids learn to be manipulative or to communicate their needs appropriately while accepting limitations."

The very first thing the parent must get under control is the whining and the tantrums (a 13-year-old? Sounds more like a 5-year-old!). Tantrums are totally unacceptable behavior. A child (he still is one) should be sent to his room until he can act his age and can be more respectful. A workable tactic with kids this age is to remind him that he is growing up to be an adult but that his actions are those of an immature child. (You can even use the age: a 5-year old). Tweens and teens want to act mature, and a reminder that some of his responses show that he has not quite gotten there often works.

Whining is also unacceptable behavior for kids of any age. If whining has worked on the parent in the past, you can be sure it will be tried again and again. One parent I know simply says, "Do not whine" very emphatically. If another sound erupts that even sounds like it may be the beginning of a whine, she sends him to his room, to the backyard—somewhere away from her. The next time whining occurs, she immediately says "No" to whatever the request is and reminds him that because he whined, he can't do whatever. He has learned that whining will not work and has refrained from that practice since.

Arguing is unacceptable. Why would a mature adult allow herself to be pulled into an argument with an immature child—no matter what the age? As Scripture says, "Let your No be No and your Yes be Yes". If you have taught your child well, there should be a way to say "NO" that lets him know that it is the final word. Many dads drop their voices to a lower pitch to say "NO", and the request is usually not repeated. However, Dr. Ron had some valid points about refusing a request from a child in order not to be consistently negative:

"By using 'yes' much more often, incorporating it into positive-sounding script" a parent can feel better about her answer and can cause each request to be a teachable moment. The crux of this, in order for it to work, is that the child must have chores or responsibilities that can be used. "Instead of, 'No, you can't play on the computer until your homework is done," say, "Yes, you can play on the computer as soon as you have finished your homework". Rather than, "No, you can't go to Devin's house." say," Yes, you can go over to Devin's after you've fed the dog and taken out the trash." Now, this takes practice, but it is a way to communicate more positively to your child and cause him to take charge of his responsibilities in order to *negotiate* his request.

Dr. Ron also suggests that, rather than make a hasty reply that could be negotiated by your child, you should *buy some time* to think about the request. You could give a noncommittal response like "That's a plausible request, but I want to think about it before I answer." or "That is a request that needs an answer from both parents, so we can discuss it with your dad after dinner". Noncommittal answers give you a chance to assess the situation and to make a calmer decision. However, do not allow the child to use the whine or the tantrum or the disrespect to force you to commit quickly.

Raising a tween or teen is a challenge, and the more prepared you are to be a good parent with the correct amount of authority and desire to communicate in order to keep your child safe, the better you will get through these years with fewer scars and regrets.

HELPING ADOLESCENTS ESTABLISH GOALS

RESEARCH SHOWS THAT adolescents and teens who have set goals for themselves, especially long-range, but including short-range goals, stay in high school, make better grades, and have more self-discipline in their lives. Some of the material I will quote was taken from the book WHERE THERE'S A WILL, THERE'S AN 'A'.

First, let me remind both children and parents what goal setting is not: It is not wishing your life away. So many people have spent their lives saying: "When I am 16, I will . . ." or "When I get my driver's license . . ." or "When I am 18 . . ." or "When I graduate . . ." or "When I get that new job . . ." Rather than wishing, encourage your child to enjoy the age he is now. He needs to enjoy high school; enjoy college or a job; enjoy being a child for as long as he can.

Secondly, Parents, help your child to realize that success in school has less to do with brainpower than it does with attitude and determination; that's why they need goals. Approximately 20% of high school dropouts are gifted students, but they had no plans, no direction to keep them motivated. I tell the students to whom I speak that good grades and college success are not dependent on ability, or I may not have finished. But I had a lot of determination; I had a goal—to help and teach kids; and I also had encouragement from home.

Parents, we cannot give our children a goal, and we cannot give them determination and self-motivation; all we can do is encourage and praise and help when they need it.

One goal I have talked about to students is not to be in school just to make good grades and to get a scholarship some day, but in order to *know* something. Be intellectually curious about history (it does repeat itself); be curious about science and know how the trees obey the laws of God through photosynthesis; know where to put commas rather than guess as you write. As the author of WHERE THERE'S A WILL THERE'S AN 'A' says, "Learning can be fun, and it is what you do best. From the time you were born until now, you've done nothing but learn and grow at an astronomical pace—gaining more knowledge perhaps than you will for the rest of your life combined." And, I would add that you are your own best teacher. Use different methods to learn, be creative, and be confident in yourself as a student and a scholar.

When your child is setting goals, another important point to remember is that the goals must never be general—they must be specific. So they should not write (yes, written goals are more effective), "I will make better grades"; rather they should put "I will make a high 'B' in English and will know how to locate adverb clauses so I can punctuate them in an essay."

Another element of successful goal setting is to state the goal positively. You would not say, "I won't eat too much so I won't be fat". You say "I will eat small portions of good food to become trim and fit." or "I will pay close attention to everything Mrs. Teacher says so I can review better for a test and improve my understanding of polynomials."

Another successful part of goal setting is to set goals in more than one area of life. For instance, in addition to a learning goal, our children need a social goal to help them make positive friends who will inspire the quality of their lives; they need a long-range goal which will give direction and purpose in school and in life as well; and the whole family needs a goal to be supportive and loving since the relationships created there are so important.

Yes, your child's goals may change as he gets older, but many of the goals he sets in his early years will actually be aimed in the right direction. If science is his easiest and favorite subject, he may set his goal toward being a veterinarian; if math is his favorite, engineering could be his ambition.

Finally, be sure that your child sets his goals and deadlines *himself*. I know a young man who is twenty years old and is still a freshman in college—he has no goal in life and has no deadline of any kind—he may be a perpetual freshman with a part-time job for the rest of his life. Part of his problem is that his dad set his goals for him. He kept telling him that he could make it in professional baseball—he didn't even make the college team. Parents, let the goal-setting be a personal thing for your child—don't do it for him. If he wants to be a lawyer and his worst subject is English, he will find out for himself that his goal is unrealistic and will change it on his own. If he plans to play pro-football and none of your family weighs over 160 pounds, you might try to steer him toward sports medicine instead so his goal will be more reachable.

Encourage your child to keep a record of the goals he achieves. If he has them written down, he can make a note of the ones he reaches and then set another goal. If there is a goal he doesn't reach, he can assess the reason and decide on its importance and either reset or reject it.

Also realize that your child's maturity comes with time and experience, but it can be accelerated by making good decisions, and that process can be helped by setting high, realistic goals and reaching them.

HOW TO LOVE A TEENAGER

I ONCE ASKED A couple of girls in my office if they ever felt like they never did anything to satisfy their parents. I knew what the answer would be. You have probably heard this cry from your own teenager, "I never do anything right!" and have wondered what caused the remark and what you could do to make your child feel that he does, in fact, please you just because he is your child.

Let's look at some reasons your teen may make this statement, and let's analyze it from a parent's point of view rather than from that of an adolescent.

First, it could very well be that your teen has told you that he never seems to please you in order to put guilt on you. This is commonly called "manipulation" and is a favorite weapon of teenagers everywhere. The purpose of this technique is to convince you that whatever he has asked of you will be granted to make up for the fact that he feels so inadequate as your child. Once you recognize it for what it is, you are no longer vulnerable and can withstand this attempt to outsmart you.

There is, however, the possibility that your teen really does feel that he is not capable of satisfying you with his actions. Teenagers, by nature, already feel like failures because they see themselves as awkward, silly, stupid, and inadequate. They are already battling self-consciousness because of treatment they may be getting at school with their peers; consequently, it really is important that they at least feel accepted at home with you.

How do you, then, make them aware of your love and concern and acceptance? Here are some very practical suggestions:

1. Keep your feelings off your shoulders. In fact, don't have your feelings out in the open and so obvious that they become sport for remarks your teen makes. Often, because he doesn't know what to say, he will appear to be uncaring and hateful when what is happening is that you are too sensitive to his immature words and actions and it causes friction between you.

2. Don't be so tired that parenting is the last thing you want to do when you get home. Teenagers need time, energy, and effort from their parents because they are so complex. If you are constantly in a state of anxiety because of outside work or volunteer efforts or

even taking care of the family, you are cheating yourself and your teen of some valuable years and moments that you can treasure long after he is gone out of your home.

3. Make an effort to find one thing about your teen that you can compliment. You may find his hair absolutely hideous, her clothes outrageous, and their attitudes deplorable, and you may have made many excellent comments about them in the past. However, if you can't find anything to compliment, say something like "You have your father's nicely shaped nose." or "You have a pretty mouth like your mother's." or "Your shoulders are getting broader and your chest is getting deeper every time I look at you." or "That color makes your face glow and makes you look so pretty." If your teenage boy is around while you are preparing dinner, be sure to ask him to open the jar of pickles rather than your husband who is probably tired of opening jars anyway after several years of doing it. Allow your daughter to cook one of the dishes for the evening meal and be sure to say something nice about it.

4. Touch. Yes, the gentle pat of a mother's hand on the cheek of her son as she says something motherly to him; the shoulder squeeze of a daddy as he stands beside his daughter; the hug of a mother when the teen is upset or happy; the back slap of a dad when the son does something well—all are important because a child never gets too old to be touched by a parent.

5. Finally, never forget to say "I love you".

HOW TO RECOGNIZE ANOREXIA AND BULIMIA

WITHIN A TWO-WEEK period, two girls were brought to my attention who were possibly anorexic, bulimic, or both. Both had reached a point where their friends were every concerned about them. One was brought to the office after she had fainted in the classroom.

Parents need to be aware of these conditions, their symptoms, their causes and their cures before it is too late. So when is it too late? The answer to that is, of course, individual, but there are indications that if a girl (90% of the students with one of these conditions is female) is anorexia or bulimic for two or more years, she will become so mentally conditioned to her way of *dieting* that she may never be cured. The result, of course, can be death as it was with singer Karen Carpenter. For the sake of the teenage girls in your home, you need to be educated about both of these conditions.

Anorexia Nervosa is an eating disorder which begins with the desire to lose weight by way of self-starvation. The girl (usually between the ages of 14 and 18) loses weight by simply cutting down on the amount of food she eats, feels happy about her new life, then loses control because the compulsion to continue to lose weight and feel good takes over. She becomes preoccupied with weight loss, and later, she looks in the mirror at an extremely thin body and sees a fat body that must lose more weight in order to be attractive and successful.

She is in turmoil about her weight. If she loses a pound, she is over-joyed, but she must keep that pound from coming back, so, in order to keep from gaining it back, she tries to lose another one. She is by now on a spiral that will be difficult to stop without outside assistance.

The main reason this condition is difficult to treat is because she really does want to look the way she does, which, after this condition has lasted for a while, is *emaciated*. She actually does think that her skeletal appearance is an improvement. She tells her family and friends that she has never felt better. At the same time, she is munching celery, eating tiny bites of the food on her plate then moving it around or disposing of it in the kitchen. She has a horror of feeling full because that will mean that she is gaining the weight she has worked so hard to get off.

The girls who are most vulnerable to this condition are high achievers in school or work, are often perfectionists, and are envious of the apparent control that others have over their lives. One type of family that seems to exacerbate this condition is one in which the parents are often highly demanding and expect their children to be successful. The anorexic feels that she is principally loved for the success she achieves rather than just because she is their daughter. Eventually, she feels that she can never keep up the demands of the parents (especially the father) and she finds another aspect of her life that she can control—her weight. Often too, the parents are highly conscious of their own weight and fitness and may make their children afraid of not looking healthy and trim.

In addition, an aspect of our society that emphasizes being thin—even to the point of emaciation, is the media and celebrities like models, some TV and movie actresses, and musicians. Girls get a negative opinion of their own bodies when they compare themselves to these successful women and wish to emulate them at least by being thin.

Eventually, there are physical indications that the girl has reached a point of danger to her physical health: 1. dry, flaking rough skin and scalp; the hair may begin to fall out; 2. cold extremities due to loss of body fat; 3. fine hair growth on the body; 4. purple nails due to poor circulation; 4. menstruation often stops; 5. finally, and tragically, the cessation of the function of internal organs like the pancreas, the kidneys, and, with the loss of vitamins and minerals, the heart.

A girl (some males engage in this as well) suffering from *Bulimia Nervosa* does the opposite of starvation—she gorges on food, especially on carbohydrates and sweets, then, before it has time to be digested and feed her body, she either gags herself and vomits it up, or she uses laxatives, or, if she can get them, diuretics. Bulimics too are terrified of being fat and of not being in control of their bodies (weight). Another psychological aspect of bulimia is that the purging can give the victim an emotional release and she may become needy of that part of the problem.

Both bulimics and anorexics are not only perfectionists, but they also have low self-esteem and an exaggerated desire to please others. However, even though they have been very social in the past, they become so obsessed with their weight and how to control it, that they begin to be loners—the anorexic so she won't have to answer about how much she eats; the bulimic so she can purge without embarrassment.

Bulimics, unlike anorexics, are aware that what they are doing is abnormal. If caught early enough, they can be treated more successfully.

Physically, Bulimics suffer from malnutrition, as do the anorexics but they can also cause damage to the esophagus from the steady acidic vomiting; tooth enamel and gums are damaged from the acid; digestive problems develop (the stomach wants to vomit even if the girl doesn't); even the onset of diabetes is often predictable.

Parents, there are some very important things to look for if you are afraid your child is developing one of these conditions: if you have a constant battle over the amount of food your daughter is eating (too little, too much); if your child goes to the bathroom soon after a meal; if she is preoccupied with food, even plans and cooks for the rest of the family; if she is showing any of the physical symptoms mentioned above, please take her for a check-up. Let the doctor know your concerns before he does the examination and be sure he is aware of her weight since her last visit.

Remember that the longer either condition goes on, the more difficult it is to reverse. The mental and physical health and life of your child may depend on what you notice in the next few days. Do something now if you are the least bit worried about her.

A LESSON IN IRRESPONSIBLE PARENTING

I WITNESSED A SCENE in a small town on Vancouver Island in Canada that illustrated the fact that teenagers are the same everywhere. I just pray that most parents are not like the one we watched early that morning.

We had stopped our RV in a parking lot beside a community center and ball field to eat breakfast. I was watching a teenage boy with an obvious scowl on his face coming down the sidewalk. He had a backpack strapped to his back and a duffle bag in one hand. He turned into the gravel parking lot and was almost to the fence surrounding the ball field when a family van sped across the gravel toward him. He dropped the duffel and quickly opened a gate in the fence and let himself out before the van slid to a halt in the spot where he had just been.

Out of curiosity (and because I am a student of human drama and psychology), we opened the window to see why this boy was so unhappy and why the adult woman in the van was obviously so angry. However, the mother's language was so filthy, we were obliged to close the window. After she was finished cursing him (he never responded), she retrieved the duffel (was he planning to leave home?) and quickly drove away. The boy strode across the ball field and disappeared down an obvious shortcut to school where his peers would sympathize with him and his teachers will be forced to contend with an angry young man who had left home planning not to return and who had been cursed by a woman in a housecoat who barely missed running over him.

Lesson 1—Teenagers in every country react to stress and to discipline in non-adult ways. Just like the children they still are, they may threaten to run away; they will have a look on their faces that will remind you of the tantrums they used to throw (the look will say volumes—don't believe them); and they will say things long before they consider the consequences. The teenager is ruled by his emotions, his feelings, his desire to please his peers (not his family). These are difficult, trying, painful years—for both of you.

Lesson 2—The last thing a parent needs to do is curse his/her child. Any child any age has the human tendency to remember the negative, harsh words parents say to them. Adults should have control over what reactions they have and what words they use with their children.

I once read an article about getting rid of the "F" word in our society's vocabulary (one of the many obscene words this mother used as she cursed her son). In "One Word We Can Do Without", by Elizabeth Austin (from U.S. NEWS & WORLD REPORT), she says "Public use of the word is a prime example of the 'broken window' theory of social decay. When we put private frustrations and the right to be foulmouthed ahead of public order and civility, we coarsen society and risk an avalanche of rage and violence . . . There is a distinction between necessary frankness and the adolescent desire to shock."

Certainly, this mother has sacrificed her right to correct her almost grown son when he chooses to curse or lose his temper or verbally abuse another person, or later, her. Apparently, this family has no standard of fair play in the child/parent relationship. Obviously, this parent has no feeling for how she has affected a young man who will forever remember how he was confronted in that parking lot that day.

Parents, it is quite possible that during the years you raise your children you will become particularly frustrated, exasperated, and desperate. However, there is a right and a wrong way to handle the discipline of your child and of your own feelings of inadequacy and blame. The very worst thing you can do is to lose your ability to act as a responsible, controlled adult. Your child must see that you can deal with your feelings as well as deal with his lack of responsibility. Don't take away his dignity as you assault him with curse words and loud verbage. Instead, love him enough to be calm, controlled and to be able to discipline in that manner. Both you and your child will be glad you did in the years to come.

MAKING THE TRANSITION FROM HIGH SCHOOL SENIOR TO YOUNG ADULT

H E HAD GRADUATED by the skin of his teeth even though he had a good mind and a delightful personality. He sat down beside me at a local restaurant and I was happy to see him. However, he had sad news: he needed to go back into drug rehab and get his life straight—again. I told him that I had faith in him and would be praying for him as he worked through the problems that had plagued him since his sophomore year in high school. He seemed grateful for the support.

Another young man had not graduated though he had the brain and the family support. He saw me at lunch one day and came over to talk to my husband and me. He had a great job; he was "clean"; he was happy; and he was looking forward to the future. We told him how glad we were for him and how good he looked. He seemed pleased with our praise and with his decisions.

Two young men—one who can't *throw* the habit; one who is making good decisions and is happy with himself.

As I read the newspaper, every year I see the many pictures of seniors who have received scholarships and are making plans for college, or going into the military, or planning to enter a skilled-trade school and I am so pleased with their accomplishments and their plans. I just pray that the ones who have struggled with school, either because of their lack of effort or because they have fought other *demons*, will do as the latter boy has done—grow up into a young person who can look into the future and know that the decisions he makes now will have a lasting effect on the rest of his life.

I will say this about the two boys mentioned: the first one had a parent who was forever taking up for him no matter what situation he got himself into. She was so busy with her career that she may not have even been aware that he was terribly addicted to drugs and to a wild way of partying and had an unstable group of friends. She was concerned that he couldn't seem to keep a job, but that was because he was a drain on her pockets. He looked for approval everywhere else except at home and the addiction may have been his way of making up for the parental concern he didn't have.

The second boy had his parents' continual support, combined with discipline, throughout his high-school years. If he made bad decisions, they did not defend him, but allowed him to suffer the consequences for them. At one time the family went through a difficult emotional time because of a death in the family, and that may have contributed to his growth as a man. I'm not sure, but something happened to help him mature.

In fact, I find that most young adults that I have known as high school seniors make the maturation jump quite successfully. They surprise even themselves if they take the time to look at the difference in the type of person they are now and the one who graduated from school. I think seeing me may even remind them of the change in them, and they are glad to see me so that I too can notice the emotional and psychological growth taking place.

Graduation is an exciting time for seniors and for their parents—the graduation gown and cap have been picked up (and hopefully hung so that the wrinkles will fall out); the family is making plans to attend the ceremony; the party, or dinner, or whatever has been planned; and the family has arranged to be present as the senior receives that diploma. The next step is crucial—the *child* must know that he is expected to do something with his life in the coming year. He should be told that he cannot stay at home unless he is attending a school or has a job to send himself to college or trade school (there should be no option about attending some kind of post-secondary school to prepare him for the future). Unless he is spending his money on classes, he should be expected to pay for some of the household expenses if he is going to stay there. He needs to know that if he does live at home while he is getting an education or getting on his feet, that he still must follow the family rules, like coming in at a reasonable hour, no drinking, no drugging, no friends over until all hours. Unless you make some demands, he has a luxury of never growing up or of taking control of his own life and future.

Yes, graduation is an exciting time, but it is also a time to make some decisions with that senior as he transitions from high school student into young adult.

I wish the best for all high school seniors as well as for their patient, long-suffering parents every May. I hope the future gives you a delightful, mature adult of whom you can very proud.

RECOGNIZING THE FATAL ATTRACTION
SYNDROME

IT IS IMPORTANT for parents of daughters to recognize an obsessive relationship called in some circles the Fatal Attraction Syndrome. There are some indications that allow parents to be aware that your child may be in danger.

A young lady, and sometimes even an adult woman, finds it flattering that the person she is seeing wants to be with her all the time and even acts jealous when she attracts the attention of others. But, beware of this possessiveness. It seldom has your interest at heart, but is the result of his need to control your life and actions. It is born of his selfishness rather than of his *love* for you.

I have seen girls at school begin to wear the worst looking outfits, quit wearing flattering make-up and lose or gain significant amounts of weight. Upon questioning them, I often find that a boyfriend has demanded that she look and dress that way so no other boys will want to look at her or date her. He wants her *just for him*, and she sees nothing wrong with this sweet gesture and is, in fact, flattered by it. She has, by this time, become so dominated by the boyfriend that she is willing to give up her looks to please him.

Another trait that characterizes this relationship is the demand that the girl separate herself from everyone but him. She is required, however subtly, to distance herself from her parents, her friends, her church, and anyone else who may threaten his dominance over her.

By this time, she feels that she must be with him because, by his design, he is all she has left.

Parents, this is not *cute*—it is *sick*. No person should lose his freedom of choice in the name of "love". You need to recognize what is happening to your daughter before it is too late and seek to end the relationship as soon as possible. (More on how to do this later)

Often the girl will go with this boy at first because she feels sorry for him and her maternal instincts kick in. She will nurture him, encourage him, and even give up everything for him as a sacrificial act of saving him. Then, too late, she realizes that everyone else is gone, her personality is gone, her vital relationship with her parents is gone, and all she has left is him.

Because of his extreme need and his total self-seeking nature, he will feel threatened if she even hints that she may want to break up. She may even be terrified to mention it, but would give anything to be free again.

His first reaction to her hint that she may break up is to make her feel sorry for him—the "I can't live without you" plea to which vulnerable young girls are susceptible. He may even threaten suicide and keep her on the phone or in the car for hours trying to talk him out of it; which accomplishes just what he wants—it keeps her on the hook a little longer.

Finally, the unthinkable may be the end result—he really may be sick enough to make her totally unavailable to anyone else. He will feel vindicated in ending her life because she "betrayed" him.

Parents, be sure you can see the person your daughter is dating—for what he is and what he wants out of the relationship. Your child may need your intervention even if she doesn't realize it before you do.

In order to help her to see the need to end the relationship without causing her to become defensive of him, leave materials, like this part of this book, open on her bed for when she comes in from a date with him. If you find another book on abusive relationships in the library, put it on the bed at a specific chapter. In other words, let the breakup be her idea rather than yours. The ending will be much more successful if you handle it carefully.

SUCCESSFUL COMMUNICATION
WITH A TEENAGER

PARENTS, TEACHERS, COUNSELORS, law officers, and church leaders everywhere are watching teenagers make really awful decisions and feel powerless to stop them or even to help them. One of the most difficult aspects of raising teenagers is communicating with them. Some parents who think they have good communication skills find out when it is too late that the conversations were strictly one-sided—the teens were not listening at all.

There are some keys to keeping the lines of communication open with your teen as he struggles through those adolescent years and beyond:

1. Watch your tone of voice. Speak too softly and they will try to manipulate you. Whine and they will tune you out. Adapt an accusatory tone and they will rebel against you. Demand absolute control and they will find a way to take it away from you. Teenagers often say that their parents speak to them only when they want something or to complain about something they have or have not done. Instead, teens want to talk to someone who wants to carry on a real conversation; it makes them feel more like an adult than a little, helpless child, and it gives them some feeling of a developing maturity that needs to happen anyway.

2. Don't be too hasty to give advice. Too many parents want to *jump in* immediately to solve the problem, give the solution, or end the conversation because there is something else that needs our attention. When a teen begins to talk—listen. Actually focus on him and on his feelings rather than trying to think of a solution or to decide again that you don't like the way he wears his hair. He can tell whether he has your full attention or not and it will determine whether he will continue to talk or simply walk away with a "Never mind".

3. When you answer a question that has been asked, don't be *the authority*. This young person needs to learn to make good decisions or he will let other teens make them for him. Play the "What If" game with him. Give him options like, "What if you do go to the party and there are drugs being passed around?" or "What if your friend wants you to say she is spending the night with you even though she is going to her boyfriend's house?" Allow your teen to make judgments for himself. The more he makes decisions while he is talking to you, the stronger his resolve will be to make sound decisions when the time comes to make them—when he is with his friends.

4. Another way to communicate with your teen regarding ways to stay out of trouble is to ask the "Is it worth it?" questions. "Could I be charged as an adult?" "Could I cause serious harm to one of my friends or to me?" "Will I regret this later—maybe for the rest of my life?" Arm your teen with as many scenarios as you can create. If he asks what you think, don't hesitate to tell him, but don't preach, just give him an answer.

5. Listen to your instinct. When she asks if she can go spend the weekend with her new friend and you have an automatic gut feeling that it isn't good to let her, go ahead and say "NO". When she asks you why, you may have to think fast—saying, "I have a gut feeling" isn't going to work with a teen. Instead, have a mental list of things you "were planning to do" that weekend that she will find interesting and pleasant. Believe it or not, often your teen asks you if she can go when she really wants you to say "No" because she already has a bad feeling about it and wants an excuse not to go. You are her best excuse: "My parent says I can't go!" (said with exasperation, but underlying relief).

6. Accept. Accept that your little child is growing up. Accept that he may make a mistake, but unless he is dead, he has a chance to redeem himself. Accept that he doesn't need to have his faults pointed out to him—he is his own worst critic. Accept that he will surprise you and grow into a delightful, responsible adult someday—the journey can be painful, but will come. Accept that you are not the perfect parent—none of us is, but we can read articles and books, talk to friends, pray a lot and do our very best, and the reward will come.

Finally, don't hesitate to ask for help. Parents who have gone through those years and have a responsible adult child, or church leaders, or counselors—there are many who will help you work through this communication gauntlet as you raise a teenager who is growing into an adult, too fast, you think, too slow, you fear, but growing, nevertheless.

SUCCCESSFUL COMMUNICATION
WITH TEENAGERS—PART 2

AFTER THE AGE of ten or eleven, when the hormones begin to kick in, the delightful child who once lived in your home suddenly becomes a surly, non-communicative or monosyllabic, somewhat abrasive person with out-of-proportion arms and legs, and pimples. Teens are aghast that they have to be seen in a restaurant with you, pull away from your embrace, pretend you are not around, and spend inordinate amounts of time in their rooms away from the family (if you let them).

So what are some ways to get this (possibly) human being to want to be a part of your family until he can legally move off to a dorm room or to his own apartment (after he can sign for it and make the payments)?

1. Even if he is involved in after-school sports or has a job, there should still be at least one or two nights when the entire family sits down to dinner together. During that time, the teen should be asked non-prying, non-threatening questions to which he feels safe responding, like "How is your friend (name)?" (or some other person) Allow him to answer; don't give advice; don't judge. Just let him express himself about something without *parenting*.

2. Don't allow him to argue or to be rude to you or to your spouse. Teens that get away with talking back at home are more likely to get into trouble at school because they have no respect for adults. A child (and they still are one of those whether they want to admit it or not) has no right to scream at a parent, to call names, or to storm out of the room or house. Of course, the parent should not "provoke" the child either. So, if a situation cannot be settled in a calm manner, it should wait until both parties can make remarks that are not angry or defensive.

3. Present a *united front*. All children, from toddlers on up, make it a priority to learn how to manipulate their parents. When our son was just walking, he refused to go to bed at night. When he would stand in his bed and cry for long periods of time, I would go and get him until he settled down then I would take him back to his

bed where he would stand and scream and cry again. My husband watched this for several nights then made this assessment: the child was smarter than the mother and was getting his way every night. He suggested that I walk around the block after I put him to bed so I couldn't hear the crying. Sure enough, the toddler was asleep when I got back to the house. Teens too, try to find a *wedge* to divide the parents so they can end up getting their way. Refuse to be manipulated. Stand together so that the child can know that you are going to support each other as well as the decisions each of you make regarding him. This must also be true even if there has been a divorce and the two parents are no longer living together.

4. When your child makes a mistake, and he will, never criticize him—criticize the decision. Never say, "You are so stupid!" Instead say, "That was a very immature, childish decision." In fact, never call him names or derogatory adjectives at all. Whether or not you are saying things in anger and really don't mean them, he will remember what you said and what he was called. Words can cause immeasurable damage, so be careful how you use them with your child.

5. Be a good "teacher". The way your teen thinks about life, his future, and himself will determine most of the choices he will make. Help your teen to set goals for the present (grades, sports, friends, etc.) and for the future (college—or not, career, marriage). The more he sets goals, the better he will do in all areas because he has something to *shoot for*. He can be more focused and less distracted by other things.

6. Help him find friends who will respect his decisions, his plans and goals, his family, and his refusal to do things that will jeopardize what he wants to do in life. If his present friends cannot be those things to him, he needs to find some who can.

7. Teach him to say "NO" when the situation can endanger him and his future plans: when there are drugs or alcohol involved, when there is a plan to break the law, and so many other situations that can cause irreparable harm to him.

8. Always let him know that he is loved and accepted by you. That kind of unconditional love will make him feel secure and will prevent his effort to *please* others in order to feel good about himself.

9. Pray a lot and let him know that you are praying for him. It helps—I know.

TEEN SEX—ARE PARENTS TO BLAME?

FOR A WHILE it looked like the teenage pregnancy rate was going to level off and even decrease. Then I began to see more and more young girls who were obviously expecting a baby during the school year. Most people who create the statistics and those of us in education agree that a good relationship within the home often prevents a child from becoming—a statistic.

Teenagers say that what their parents will think of them and the desire to prevent disappointing them kept them from becoming pregnant or getting a girl pregnant and were even more important than the media or their peers. In fact, if they listen to their friends, they may be tempted to get pregnant in order to *fit in* in some parts of society today. However, if I were to ask the parents if they were an influence on their children in preventing pregnancy, they would probably say something like, "I doubt it".

Too many parents dread *the talk* and wait as long as possible to have it. "They may mentally prepare a quick speech to deliver on the eve of puberty, but the foundation for a child's behavior is laid down in layers, over time, not built in one night at the dinner table." (Let's Talk about Sex", Laura Beil in READER'S DIGEST, March 2008). "Parents need to make themselves "askable" by sharing suitable information as soon as their kids grow curious about love, relationships and their own bodies."

It is, of course, extremely important for your kids to know what you expect of them morally. One boy whom I interviewed for this article said that he knows his parents expect him not to view sex casually or carelessly, and that is what your own kids should know as well.

If you can't think of anything to say to your kids, give them some of this information about casual sex: "A female without a high school diploma almost guarantees that her children will live in poverty—if not permanently, at least temporarily." (Dr. Paul Slocomb, HEAR OUR CRY, 2004). Slocomb also said, "Every child who is left to be raised by a single mother with a limited education is more likely to become a member of a generation caught up in the cycle of poverty, especially if that single mom lacks a high school diploma. The statistics are prophetic".

Teenagers are notoriously short-sighted and unprepared for the demands of parenthood. They cannot see the importance of their influence on the child they bring into the world. It is the responsibility of the parents to let them see the hardship a pregnancy can be on the mother as well as on the child.

And what of the young fathers? Dr. Slocum says it this way, "With a current divorce rate of 50% or greater, boys must be educated about the significance of their role in the lives of the children they will father. Their sexual conquests must be replaced with a sexual conscience and sense of responsibility. Child-support checks from prison will only imprison the children left behind. Dads who stay involved in the lives of their sons produce young men who perform better in school and in personal relationships.

So, Parents, begin from the time your children are little to let them know what is expected of them as they mature. Teach them responsibility to themselves, to your family values, and to others, especially to someone they think they might come to love. Keep the lines of communication open and honest and don't panic when you are asked pointed questions. Don't lecture. Ask questions so that you can determine what they already know and what they need to know. Pay attention to the media they consume. Don't allow them to see sex in movies and on TV or they will have the misconception that no one suffers from AIDS or has a difficult pregnancy or lives in poverty with their children. Remind them of what over two-thirds of the teens I interviewed said about it after they had had sex, "You really can't fully understand it until you make the same mistake." (Notice the use of the word "mistake".)

Remember, "Your influence matters, but know what you are up against". Be educated, be open, be loving to your children. Remember too, that we cannot always be with our teenage children, and often they will make a poor choice that will forever change their lives. Don't accept the full blame. That decision may not have had anything to do with the way your child was raised, but with the influence of another, or of the "moment",

Finally, we must somehow stop this destructive trend for the sake of this generation and the one that is to come.

THE ART OF TALKING TO TEENAGERS

TEENAGERS ARE FASCINATING. They are moody, unpredictable, silly, serious, anxious, self-conscious, and funny. They are pushing away from parents, wanting to be with peers, talking to anyone but their parents, and spending time with the latest *techno* gadget. Yet, everyone agrees with an ad that was once used in a magazine: "Can placemats keep your kids off drugs?" (then in finer print) "Studies show that teens who have family dinner five times a week are 66% less likely to do drugs". (They are also less likely to engage in premarital sex, drink, engage in risky behaviors, and so on and on.) However, it is the *talk* you do with your teens at the dinner table that will help them in their social lives and avoid what could permanently damage their futures.

So how do you communicate with this person who acts like he would rather talk to the wall than to you?

1. Keep it light. If he dreads the conversation because it feels more like an interrogation than a conversation, you have to change the tone and way you converse with him. A good beginning is to ask, not about him or his day, but about his best friend or his girlfriend, or a teacher at school. Once talking has begun, it will be easier to keep it going.

2. If he won't talk, begin with something that happened in your day that could use a solution and ask him what he thinks you should do. Teens love to give their opinions, especially if is an adult situation. Then ask if he has had to use that solution at school or in another incidence, and compliment his insight.

3. Give him time. Most teens, especially boys, talk best when their stomachs are being filled. Keep the atmosphere relaxed and talk of unimportant things until he is ready.

4. If you know of something he did that day in school, like a project or a test, ask how it went or how he did.

5. If he has experienced a difficult time, ask him why he thinks it happened and what he has learned from it.

6. Pay attention to *cues*. Parents have built-in radar that lets them know when something is up with their child. Don't ignore it, but don't try to pry too hard and then lose the opportunity to help him.

7. Don't preach. Even if you find that he has made a bad choice, stay calm and talk through the situation. Let him help decide what he should do to rectify the issue.

8. Be brief. When you do the talking, don't go on until he tunes you out. Say something, and then stop.

9. Watch your tone. Too often, we alienate our teens with an accusatory or a condescending tone of voice that will end the conservation almost before it begins. Even if you are alarmed by an incident that has occurred, don't lose your control.

10. Listen with your complete attention. However, this one has qualifications. Your teen may walk up when your back is turned and he may want it that way. Don't immediately turn toward him, but wait a short time. Listen to his tone, his inflection—whatever—to pick up on his feelings. When you do turn to him, have a kind *parent* face on that will encourage him to continue to talk.

11. Don't get mad or anxious if you discover that he has talked to the school counselor, a teacher, a youth director or other church member or another adult other than you. This is a normal behavior for a teen. They want to feel that they can handle life without your constant input, and they may try a thought or situation on another adult. Don't let your pride interfere with this part of growing up.

12. Be available. When he does want to talk, be there, even if it is over the phone or by text. Your job should not disallow your answering your child's call or text. You are a parent first and an employee second. Make sure this is something that is understood at your place of work. (Of course your child can't call every five minutes!)

Being the parent of a teenager is a challenge but it can also be such fun. Don't be so uptight that you can't enjoy these years and the terrific young person growing up into an adult in your house.

CHAPTER SEVEN

HELP! MY MARRIAGE AND HOME
ARE IN TROUBLE!

Jan Knight

AGGRESSIVE BEHAVIOR AT HOME
LEADS CHILDREN TO ACT AGGRESSIVELY

PARENTS WHO YELL and scream at home lead children to yell and scream as well. We are finding that the school common areas as well as the cafeteria and some of the classrooms have become louder because kids of all ages have the idea that they cannot be heard unless they yell at each other. This is a result of the home and of parents who either yell at their children or who allow their children to scream at home rather than require a *quiet voice* or an *inside voice*. The kids not only scream at each other, but they find it difficult to sit quietly in a library, in a lecture, or in other civilized places. In addition, these same children grow up to be adults who continue to communicate in this way. A friend recently had to move her mother from a nursing home because the aides yelled at each other down the halls and upset her parent and other patients. Adults who have no control over their voice volume are not welcome in quiet places. What parent would want her child fired or put out of a place because she could not teach him to speak in something less than a loud, disruptive voice?

Parents who act aggressively at home show their children that it is OK to act that way toward other people. One night on the news, we watched a video tape of a young woman who was not happy with her burger at McDonald's, so she screamed at the employees behind the counter as she threw large items at them, including three cash registers. What is her home like that would cause her to impulsively destroy over $1500 worth of equipment and to endanger other people? Will her parents pay for the damages and for the court costs and for the fines? And when they do, will they take the opportunity to correct her behavior, and how can they correct it if that is the way they act in front of her? Parents will ultimately pay for the way they act negatively in front of their children whether it is with money or with heartache.

Parents who are verbally abusive at home show children that they don't have to be respectful toward other people. These are the children who get into trouble for calling names, for saying hurtful things to their peers, for picking on younger children, for refusing to be civil to authority. The kids learn fast that they will get into trouble at school because of the very same actions you demonstrate at home, and that they will be increasingly unpopular if they follow your shining example. They will find

224

themselves without friends, unable to maintain a loving relationship and maybe even spending time in jail because they have never learned to be civil and courteous and verbally kind to other people. Eventually, they will either be just like you in an unhappy life or they will resent you for the poor example you set in the home.

Dr. Laura Schlessinger says that people who are rude, selfish, and aggressive should at least be embarrassed about the way they act (particularly in front of their children). She also said, in her book COPE WITH IT! (p. 71, Kensington Books, New York, 1999) that she is worried "that some mutation might have caused too many of us to lose that essential part of our civilized being—a conscience". Too many, she says, "show a hostile disregard for the rights and sensitivities of others". I also agree with her that putting the blame on poverty, discrimination, divorce, and lack of religious influence do not abate one's responsibility for one's own behavior in public or in the home.

In fact, the home is where we learn to be civilized and kind and responsible; however, it is also the place where the adults are failing miserably in helping the younger family members to become a positive part of society. I think that the parents should have to answer for the way their children act in school if it is apparent, from a pattern of behavior, that the actions are the result of influence in the home. I do believe that parents are increasingly going to be held responsible for criminal acts of children under a certain age by judges who get sick and tired of seeing the same ones in front of them for acts of violence and aggression.

If you feel that you are failing your children because of aggressive acts in your home, do something now to correct the situation before you child has to pay for your example.

BEING A REFEREE IN THE HOME

DO YOU SOMETIMES feel more like a referee than a parent? If you are the parent of small children, then refereeing is part of your job description. Somewhere the line has to be drawn between pulling and screaming over the same toy and finding a happy medium.

One family I know has the rule that if one set of hands had it first, then it is his until he puts it down—then it is fair game for the next set of little hands (without argument or tattling). All toys are community property unless it is too old for the younger ones. In that case, the older sibling is required to put the *toy* in a place where the little ones are not to go. (That precedent is already set, and punishment will come if the younger one gets into that space). The mother made rules that are fair and consistent, and the children know where their boundaries are and who gets to play with the toy next. There is also a community property play room where noisy children can be sent while adult conversation takes priority for a change.

Refereeing teenage siblings during disagreements can be trickier than with younger ones. There must be rules that are more important than the end of the argument: First, no name calling. Even though siblings act as though they cannot be in the same room with their sister or brother, they must disagree agreeably. No telling of secrets during a heated argument. If the sibling has confided something, it cannot be used to the *advantage* of the other sibling. No hateful remarks like "I think you were adopted anyway!!" or some such. Hopefully, each sibling has a room and can go there to cool off, and it is your *referee voice* that may have to send him or her there.

Other sibling arguments can cause a good deal of chaos in the home, and no parent wants to spend the day working and then have to come home and referee between half-grown people. So arguing should be limited to something really important. If it is crucial enough, you may volunteer to step in and hear both sides—believe me, they don't want that to happen any more than you want to take part.

One of the most difficult situations in a family is when a child (usually a pre-adolescent or teen) refuses to get along with a step-parent and the arguments are seemingly on-going. The biological parent has the responsibility to referee this issue or it will gain momentum and could cause irreparable damage to the relationship. The parent may be feeling guilty over the divorce and having to move the child or introducing another parent into the equation. However, if you have chosen your new spouse carefully, and he or she is making an effort to get along with the child, then you need to talk to the child about his lack of maturity and respect and refusal to allow the step-parent to move on past being the new parent. If the child knows that the new spouse broke up the marriage between his biological parents, you have a battle that may last for a long time. However, don't allow the child to *bait* you into taking sides or defending him. In this issue you must try to remain as neutral as possible except to correct you child and possibly your spouse if he or she is acting childishly.

Some rules have already been given, but let me share a few more: Listen to the other person respectfully, no slamming doors or throwing things, no leaving the house in anger, no talking back if the other person is an adult, no discussing the issue outside the home except to a counselor.

I have talked to parents who have become afraid of their child's anger. That can happen if you are not a good referee and do not stand your ground and hold the child to the rules you have set. Be a good parent and occasionally a good referee, and your home will be more of a haven than a boxing arena.

"CALL 811-914-DEBT" TO SOLVE
YOUR FINANCIAL WOES?

THE RADIO AD was saying "Are you crushed by debt? Afraid to answer your phone because of bill collectors, don't want to look at your mail, can't sleep because of worry about how much you owe? We can help!" The announcer went on to give an example of a man who was $32,000.00 in debt and this particular company not only helped him *not* pay his bills but also, he bought a house! (I know, too good to be true).

In addition to worrying about our own debt, many are worried that decisions being made in Washington and in the state capitol are getting us further and further in debt and that our taxes are going to drive many more people into debt.

Then I heard that nearly a third of Americans don't know how much they have in their bank accounts and that over a fourth of us don't have a budget or keep track of our money. It would be hypocritical to complain about the national debt if we don't even know what we have (or don't have) in the bank.

I watch so many people use their debit cards in the stores. They are always asked if they want cash as well. Most of them say "NO"; however, there are a lot who say "Yes" and pay for their groceries and take a wad of cash away from the register. Those are some of the Americans who have no idea how much money they have available, but who spend it like it is always going to be there.

Once I was balancing a checkbook and found that two checks had not cleared even though they had been written early enough to have been cancelled. What I discovered was that the bill one of those checks covered had been paid, but the check had not cleared my bank. During my investigation, I found that it was an error on the part of the company's bank, and I am waiting for the problem to be solved by them. What of people who never balance their checkbooks? How will they know that there is not a discrepancy on the part of the bank, or realize that they failed to enter a transaction, or find that there is a lot less in the account than they thought? Will they just pay the exorbitant fee for over-drafts? Will they ever catch up with the fees or continue to lose money because they are too lazy to do the monthly balance? How does one get out of debt when he is continually paying over-draft and other fees because he doesn't know how much is in there?

Parents should be more careful with the money they have in order to care for their children. Every little bit makes a difference in what we can do for them. Are you saving for Christmas presents? Or will you go into debt in December and find out in January that there is not enough to live on while you are paying for gifts that have already been forgotten? Do you need a new roof? Save for it unless the floors are being ruined because of the leaks. There should always be a fund available for unexpected expenses so that you won't have to dig into the only savings you have and then lose it because of one big expense.

So many Americans have not been able to achieve the things they wanted in life because of financial difficulties. However, it is not too late to learn how to manage your money and to set goals that can be reached even if they have to be delayed for a while.

During the economic downturn many adults are learning to scale back travel and other non-essential plans in order to hang onto their money. More people are buying produce in farmer's markets, eating out less, seeing fewer movies, and, thankfully, teaching their children the value of money and the pride of hard work and saving for "rainy days".

The bad news is that some people are using money (or the lack thereof) as an excuse to engage in negative behavior such as drinking and drugging (both of which are expensive), eating poorly (which can also be expensive), spending wildly even though there is no money, skipping work, and causing trouble at work. This type of behavior is self-destructive and cannot help the person or his/her family.

Get serious about keeping your checkbook balanced, about making and keeping a budget, about teaching your children how to handle money successfully. Then, when you have accomplished that, let your state and national politicians know that you expect them to do the same with their budgets and your tax dollars.

CHILDHOOD POST TRAUMATIC STRESS DISORDER

ALL OF US probably recognize the term "Post Traumatic Stress Disorder". We began to hear it more after the Vietnam War when our boys came home and many of them were suffering from the disorder as a result of what they had seen and experienced over there. Research shows that it was also known about after both World Wars, but little was written bout it.

A private practicing psychologist, researcher, and writer I heard says that this same disorder is also showing up in children who are raised in homes that are "war zones". Now, you may say, "Oh, everyone who is married argues and fights every once in a while!" Maybe so, but if your home is a constant battle zone; if the taunts and name-calling are vicious and cruel and damaging; if one of the parents is forever walking out, promising never to return, then the children in that home stay in a constant state of anxiety, apprehension, and fear—very much like soldiers after they have been in battle.

The children who live in this situation even suffer from some of the same symptoms that battlefront soldiers do after their return home: frequent uncontrolled rage, often addictions to substances, arrested development socially, emotionally, and psychologically, altered belief systems. (Many of these children don't believe in God unless He is a God of Wrath—they cannot conceive of a loving God).

In addition, these children and adolescents display intense emotions, whether it is anger, fear, joy, love and/or hate. This may explain some incidences educators see in the classroom.

Finally, many of these children suffering from PTSD lose the ability to learn in the traditional sense. Psychologists say that trauma is stored in the right brain which can affect the learning process.

Now, school teachers are not trained as psychologists and cannot determine whether a child is doing poorly in school or is acting out because of the home environment. However, you as the parents, if you are honest about your situation at home, may recognize some of these symptoms and may realize what you are causing for your children.

Let me tell you the worst part of this disorder. If it persists (both the battling in the house and/or the lack of treatment if symptoms are manifest), the victim (child) can dissociate, which will result in severe psychological problems. The victim can also become so hurt due to the damage caused that s/he cannot *feel* emotionally as others do. They become so unable to sympathize that they become hardened criminals who have no concern for their victims, whether the victim is a neighborhood animal, a small child, or an innocent adult.

It is amazing how much this could be a contributing factor to the violence/crime problems that are being played out in our local areas and in our nation.

Parents, please don't allow your home life to contribute to the problems our society faces today. If you and your spouse need counseling in order to stop the "battling", please go now for the sake of your children and their futures. Things can get better, but you have to want them to improve.

DIVORCE AND REJECTION—TIED TOGETHER
IN THE CHILD

*D*IVORCE SEEMS TO be the American way of life now. It is rare to find a student in school who is still living with both biological parents. Tied to the problem of divorce, *rejection* is a problem that children seem to be unable to handle; instead, they internalize the feeling of being unwanted, and that emotion often causes them serious problems in the future. The problem is that once a divorce is decided upon, one of the parents must move out, and that feeling of rejection occurs in the child even if you have given him the "It's not your fault" talk.

Way too often, one or both parents uses their hurt, anger, frustration, and even *their* feeling of rejection to tear down the other parent before, during, and after the divorce which is a serious mistake for the sake of the children. When I was teaching English, I once had a biography turned in that was entitled "The Divorced Child" in which her feelings of rejection were obvious and painful to read.

I was given an Ann Landers column that gives excellent advice on this subject. The quote is from an official transcript of a divorce proceeding by Judge Michael J. Haas of Cass County, Minnesota:

"Your children have come into this world because of the two of you. Perhaps, you two made lousy choices as to whom you decided should be the other parent. If so, that is your problem and your fault. No matter what you think of the other parent—or what your family thinks—these children are one half of each of you. Remember that; because every time you tell your child what an 'idiot' his father is, or what a 'fool' his mother is, or how 'bad' the absent parent is, or what terrible things that person has done, you are telling the child that part of him is 'bad'.

"That is an unforgivable thing to do to a child. That is not love. That is possession. If you do that to your children, you will destroy them as surely as if you had cut them into pieces, because that is what you are doing to their emotions.

"I sincerely hope that you do not do that to your children. Think more about your children, and less about yourselves. And make your love a selfless kind of love, not one that is foolish or selfish, or causes your children to suffer."

As a counselor, I saw too many students who were allowing their feelings of rejection to damage their lives. Girls usually become too attached to the boys they are dating (or, sometimes whom they have just met), and give them everything—including their virginity. Then, when they have given all that they have, the boy walks away, talks bad about them, and the rejection is amplified, again. The girl's self-worth has been damaged because the father who should be present, loving, and attentive is not there. In addition, the mother too often spends time "putting him down", so the girl keeps looking for love from someone who is not like her father (whatever that is).

Boys, on the other hand, are often just angry. They would never let you know that they feel rejected, but their conduct, their risk-taking, and their rebellion at home are symptomatic of that hidden emotion. If the mother constantly berates the absent father, she will many times find herself alone because the boy will get tired of it and *go see for himself* what the father is really like and what traits he has in common with him. I have known many such situations in which the son never came back home to the mother.

So what is your choice if you are contemplating divorce? First, go for counseling. If the marriage and the feeling and the original commitment can be saved, do it for your sake and especially for the sake of the children.

If it is impossible to save the marriage, have the *talk* with your kids before the other parent leaves and try to have the talk together. Let the children know that this is an *adult* problem and has nothing to do with them. Try to convince them, for each child feels that he is the reason the other parent left, no matter how hard you try to let them know that it wasn't.

Stay involved in your child's life even if you are the one who had to leave. Don't move to Alaska—talking about rejection! Rather, move close enough that you are available for parent conferences, for health reasons, for any need of the child.

Finally, keep reassuring the children that they were not the ones who were divorced. That you still love them and want them in your life. Then show them that is true by just *BEING THERE.*

DO YOU NEED TO HEAR, "OH, GROW UP!"?

"**O**H, GROW UP!" Have you said that to one of your kids? To your spouse? To a sibling? Sometimes it is said out of exasperation or out of frustration or out of hopelessness. However, many times there is a bit of truth in our remark even if the person is an adult. Let's look at some ways many of us should *grow up*.

Small children are so busy growing up that we are afraid they will do so before we get to enjoy their childlike days and ways. We would hardly think of asking them to grow up or to act their age because they are already doing it the best they can.

Adolescents and pre-teens are caught between childhood and adulthood in the most awkward of ages. They will act twice their age one day (or minute) and two years less than their real age the next. They are so unsure of themselves that they will revert to being children at the least sign of conflict; then they will perform the most uncharacteristic *adult* action or express a thought far beyond their chronological age that they will surprise you (and themselves). We may be tempted during their *childhood* setbacks to tell them to act their age, but we are never sure what that age is or what affect the request will have.

Allowing them to grow up too soon may result in their losing some of the youth they deserve and may push them too soon into adulthood. This-age child is so impulsive that they are not sure themselves what they will be thinking or doing from one minute to the next. So allowing them to make all of their decisions is hazardous to their futures. They still need an enormous amount of parental input and guidance. The daughters should dress modestly rather than provocatively and should engage in *girlish* rather than female-adult activities. Sons are almost always two years socially and emotionally behind their chronological age. They need praise, encouragement, and outlets to expend their excess energy.

Teenagers are the ones who get the most "*grow up*" comments. However, it is wise not to actually use those words when you are speaking to them. They already want to be on their own, to test your limits, to be in the world alone. So the best words to use on them are "act your age".

Then, because they are still immature kids, you will have to remind them of their real age. Remember again that boys are behind, so if your son is sixteen, he will finally reach his real age about the time he finishes college or trade school, hopefully without a wife and kids hanging on. Because they are immature, young men don't always make good husbands and dads until they have reached maturation.

Then there are us. Have you asked your spouse to "*grow up*"? It isn't a good way to maintain good marital relations; however, there are times when we must be reminded that we are acting more childish than we think we are. I once watched the movie based on the novel FLOWERS IN THE ATTIC by V.C. Andrews. The grandmother who insisted that the children be locked in her attic was cruel and selfish (and crazy). At the beginning, after the children have been relegated to the attic, you have the sense that their mother is an innocent victim of her mother's punishment and regimen. Later, however, it is obvious that their mother is as selfish and self-seeking and, yes, cruel, as her mother.

Mothers who are more concerned about themselves and their happiness over that of their children do, indeed, need to "*grow up*". Having a child is not a burden even if that child was not originally planned; rather, it is a blessing and a responsibility. Our lives are changed when a child comes, and we must, if we are "grown up", put the needs of our child before our own. No mother has the right to neglect her child for another person even if she thinks she is *in love*. Her first love should be for her husband and then for her children unless the man in question is not the father of her children—then her children come first because their needs are different when she brings another man into their lives.

If you are a father and your priority is not the children you have fathered, you have a lot of "*growing up*" to do. A man who does not accept responsibility for his kids is still a child himself and has no hope of reaching true maturity. Rather, he is running from what real men do—take care of their own before taking care of themselves.

Consider whether you are in need of telling yourself to "*grow up*" because of some of your decisions or actions. Then do some soul-searching to determine how you can grow up and be good for all who depend on you.

FROM THE MOUTHS OF BABES

T HE PREACHER ASKED a rhetorical question from the pulpit: "Do you know a wicked person?" An elementary child said loud enough for all around him to hear: "My mother!"

It was such a sad reply—a comment on a parent who left the child's father for another man who later rejected *her*, a parent whose lifestyle is uncharacteristic of a person whose first obligation is the welfare of her children.

Parents like this, whether mother or father, may think that they are fooling the children or that the kids won't judge him/her because of the way they have treated or neglected them, but the truth is that children are very aware, without anyone else saying a word, of what kind of person the parent is because of the way he is acting. Children have a hidden radar that lets them know whether they are the most important person in a parent's life, and, when they are not, they make their own judgments about whether you are worthy of their respect or not.

In this situation, the discipline you try to administer is probably becoming more and more difficult; the attitude you see in your child may be getting surlier; and the obedience you want is not there anymore. However, rather than becoming angry at your child, look first at yourself and how you have treated them, whether by commission or omission. You may even be really proud of yourself that you have begun this new life for yourself and you have taken care of the kids at the same time. Think again. Any time something becomes more important than your children, they know it, and you have failed them.

I once read about a husband and father who, at first, innocently connected with an old girlfriend on Facebook. Then the meetings became an affair and the marriage was in serious trouble. The twin girls in the equation were not mentioned but once, but I wondered how his philandering affected them. Girls, particularly, want to know that they are valuable, and it is the father who can give that sense of worth to an awkward teen. When this man's affair became the most important thing in his thoughts and actions, where was his attention to those girls? When they saw the way he treated their mother, how will they feel about the next male who does show some attention to them? Will they desire that attention so much that they give too much, or will they be afraid to trust a man in their lives? No one knows until they face the situation, but the father is not helping.

Conversely, I found a card my husband and I had given to one of our parents that summarizes how a parent and the family should be viewed by his or her children:

> "A family's a circle of people who care,
> Who listen and encourage and lovingly share—
> Unselfish and ready, extending a hand
> Their love is a gift that all hearts understand
> With ties that are strong and support that's secure,
> A family shares love that will always endure.

When a husband or wife makes the decision to "break the circle", the security mentioned in the poem is gone, and the children are the ones who feel the loss the most. Children should be raised in a family—people who care about each other and who can help them face the tumult of life because they are safe and loved in the home.

Notice too that the poem mentions the word "unselfish". There is nothing unselfish about a parent who makes the decision to leave that circle of family and strike out *to find their youth* or *to find love*. Too many times the love they seek was in the home all along, but they did not want to go to the trouble to restore the affection of the spouse and keep the family intact.

When one spouse *takes off* in another direction, he or she leaves a trail of broken hearts behind—of both the other spouse and the children. There are too many marriage counselors around for a person not to seek help in maintaining the marriage and the family circle in order to take care of the very people for which he or she is responsible. Not to do so is totally irresponsible and uncaring.

Every family should "share love that will always endure".

LOOKING AT DIVORCE THROUGH MORE RESEARCH

*N*EWSWEEK ASKED ONE of their reporters to do some research on the effects divorce has had on his graduating class ('82). The results were what I expected, but there were some other interesting observations he made as he interviewed and wrote.

He (David Jefferson) put his findings under "culture" and entitled it "The Divorce Generation Grows Up" and the subtitle was "the kids of my high school were raised on 'The Brady Bunch'—while their own families were falling apart." One of the most distressing quotes he made, from the viewpoint of a counselor who sees the problems divorce causes in the children was "My 44-year-old classmates and I have watched divorce morph from something shocking, even shameful, into a routine fact of American Life" (our culture). Then he qualifies that statement, "But while it may be a common occurrence, divorce remains a profound experience for those who've lived through it. Researchers have churned out all sorts of depressing statistics about the impact of divorce."

One of the most difficult situations which most children face is "As their parents remarried, my classmates were left to negotiate the thicket of resentments that crop up between spouses and their exes, step-parents" step-siblings, boyfriend/girlfriends, etc. One of the most disheartening scenes that occurs often in school is "Which name will I go by?" In most states, a student goes by the last name on his birth certificate whether he has ever seen that father or not or whether he has gone by his step-father's name for the past several years. The only alternative is to go to court and have the name changed.

One of the worst parts of divorce is that the kids become their parents' crisis counselor: "As they witnessed their parents' pain, (the children) took on emotional burdens well beyond their years." He said this of one of his friends, "He may have been helping his dad, but he was doing damage to himself, encasing his own emotions in a dispassionate shell". In addition, no matter what the age of the children, divorce jerks the rug of security out from under them, leaving them subject to other pain and rejection.

Many of them deal with the instability at home by acting out: smoking, drugging, drinking, having sex, having babies. As one student said to me after high school, "I think I had a problem because I did not have my dad around. So I was looking for love that was not there".

Some divorces cause harm when the parent(s) move from one relationship to another, perhaps moving far away from the children (adding to that feeling of abandonment and rejection), try to *buy* loyalty from their kids, and/or spy on the ex through the child. Or, the harm may be caused in many other damaging ways.

"Another ugly side effect, according to the research (by Jefferson), is that divorce can be passed from generation to generation, like some kind of genetic defect. Too many children today never see their grandparents or know anything about them because they are no longer in touch with the other parent: A significant loss for everyone."

Then there are kids who are determined not to do what their parents did. They wait to marry until they are older and wiser; they make a concerted effort to maintain the relationship in their marriages; they actually look for character in the partner rather than go by looks or *feelings*. One person interviewed put it this way, "It took me until my late 30's to find a healthy relationship that stuck, probably because I never really believed a union could last without turning ugly".

So, what can you do to prevent becoming a divorce statistic and take care of your children in the process? First, unless there is abuse or the spouse refuses to make an effort in the situation, there is always counseling. A major thing to avoid is trying to find consolation in talking to other divorcees who are still dealing with their own pain, or in falling into the arms of someone else who may be carrying even more baggage than you are. Secondly, there is the supreme sacrifice of taking care of the needs of your children before your selfish ones—that is the ultimate test of parenthood—and of character.

MAINTAINING A MARRIAGE
FOR THE SAKE OF THE CHILDREN

A UTHORS, RESEARCHERS, AND psychologists are saying that maintaining a marriage "for the sake of the children" really is better for children unless there is abuse, abandonment, or neglect. Now, many of you don't want to hear this because you have given up on your relationship with your spouse and you are looking for a good reason to end the marriage—maybe even because you have found another person.

Children of any age, even teenagers, need the assurance that their parents want to be together and want to be in the home with the spouse and with the children they have created. So, because that is so important, I took the time the week before Valentine's Day to interview people who have maintained their marriages for twenty-seven to forty years. I asked them what it took to stay married to the same person for those years.

Some of the first answers, of course, were given by men who could not be serious about such a sensitive issue. They gave answers like "Marry after hunting season", "Don't ever live with in-laws", and "Whoever leaves has to take the kids."

Then when they became serious, they and some wives gave really solid advice. Here are the most prevalent answers on maintaining their marriages:

1. Commitment—One of the men said, "It never occurred to me that I would *not* stay married to that person for the rest of my life." Another man said, "I went into the marriage with the mind set that it would last." So many couples today go into their marriages thinking that if it doesn't work, they can *just get a divorce*. Commitment may be old fashioned, but it has been the best deterrent to the breakup of families and the consequent instability of children.

2. Respect—The husband who had been married forty years said that it was important to *respect* the likes, dislikes, wants, needs, personality, and thinking of the person you marry. This word could prevent many an argument, and as another answerer said, "Being considerate of each other is crucial."

3. Sense of Humor—Would it surprise you if this mainly came from the wives? One went on to say, "Don't take yourself too seriously" that way you won't have your feelings hurt so often. Women are usually sensitive, especially when it comes to words and actions from the man she loves. If she can maintain a sense of humor, she can see that many times the man did not mean to be hurtful—he just is not aware of the woman's feelings. A wife can keep her sanity and still love the man if she can look at many of his actions with humor.

4. Strong Faith—It was deliberate, but most of the couples I interviewed had attended church all of their lives and felt that a faith in God allowed them to work harder and longer on their marriages. Research supports this belief that people who attend church stay married better and longer.

5. Freedom—One wife said that it was important that each partner should be able to spend time alone in order to maintain individuality. We are "One Flesh" according to Scripture, but we are still two people with different personalities. If we are totally dependent on the other for identity, then we have not kept our individual *selves*—we have sacrificed that person we were for another. That is not what God intended.

6. Love—This goes without saying. These couples still genuinely care for each other. One husband said it this way, "It is nice to know that the same person is going to be there when I get home and will be glad that I am there."

7. Two Words—There was also a consensus of opinion that all husbands should learn two words from their wives that make a complete sentence and will keep peace in the marriage—"Yes, Dear."

Parents, I can't stress enough how important it is to be a good spouse so that you can also be good parents to your children. It takes work, but it is worth it.

"MAKING ENDS MEET" NOW AND IN THE FUTURE

IN DIFFICULT FINANCIAL times, the old adage "Making Ends Meet" carries a more serious and dramatic message. Now it simply means: "The end of the paycheck meets the needs of the family". Too many parents who have the responsibility of providing for children have lived with the illusion "It couldn't happen to me", yet there are families living in their parents' garages, in motels, in shelters—anywhere to keep from being on the streets.

Bottom line—you must not think you are immune to financial disaster for you or your family; instead, you must plan now in case the job goes away or you get hurt or your company gives you too few hours per week or something else happens. Unlike the family that always went to Disney World to celebrate each child's birthday, and who had a house note above $2,000 per month and who are now living with friends, you must not spend as if tomorrow is financially secure. Instead, save money, bake birthday cakes yourself, buy reasonable gifts, and downsize on the house. Instead of being embarrassed to tell your kids that you must curb some of your spending on their *fun*, begin to teach them history (remember the Depression?), economics (if they don't understand it, they can't live by it), budget making (you may have to learn this yourself before you can teach it), careful spending, and being self-reliant (like growing your first garden).

Let's look at some practical ways to prepare to make ends meet:

1. Pay credit cards off each month to save the enormous interest they are charging. If the balance is too high, pay the amount required plus more so you can pay it off as soon as possible (and then cut all but one up forever, and use it only for emergencies).

2. Pay more than your house note so you will have a place to live if disaster strikes. If your note is too high, try to re-finance when the interest is low if you can find a bank or mortgage company that will lend.

3. For your own information and to keep from spending foolishly, keep a very thorough account of your spending. I have a book from 1938 in which my mother kept a detailed record of their spending as a young married couple, including bus fare and a package of

gum. They always spent wisely and provided for us even during job losses, farming, moving, and other life-changing events.

4. Pay your bills at least ten days before they are due to prevent having to pay a late fee. Watch the due date each month—they can change it.

5. The keeper of the checkbook should be the one who is the most frugal in your house. The *spender* has too little control and will cause more financial problems.

6. Using a debit card often leads to overspending unless you keep a very accurate record and refuse to use it unless it is absolutely necessary. Refuse to take cash back with the purchase when you do use it unless there is no other convenient way to get cash in an emergency. Some fees attached to these cards can make using them more expensive than other ways of paying for essentials.

7. Many families use the "envelope method" of keeping money available but in restricted quantities. (Some of us were using this method way before Dave Ramsey wrote about it.) Using the budget you agree on and making sure your needs are not more than the monthly paycheck, put the needed amount per pay period for food, household expenses, gas, lunches, etc., in separate, labeled envelopes. When the envelope is empty, there is no more money available. This is an excellent way to control spending and to still provide for the needs of each member of the family. (It's also a great way to build self-discipline.)

8. Teach your children the value of a budget, of spending responsibly, of knowing the value of money to meet needs—not necessarily *wants* unless something has been saved for. The best way to teach is by example.

9. Save. I know this sounds impossible during a time when the family has gotten into trouble by spending. However, looking at the future, you have little choice. I once heard of a single woman who had just lost her job because the company where she was employed was closing down. She was able to live and pay the notes on her house for over a year using the money she had saved. If you set aside only $40.00 per paycheck and if you are paid twice a month, by the end of the year, you have accumulated $960.00, which may allow you to feed your children for another few months.

Our generation has not experienced a Great Depression (yet) and, therefore, has not had to learn "the hard way". However, we can learn from history and can prepare for an extended economic downturn. Make it a family project and learn together how to "Make Ends Meet".

NEW STATUS SYMBOL FOR THIS GENERATION?

URING A TRIP to Vancouver Island in Canada, three instances
occurred that emphasized an institution that is important to the
healthy development of children—marriage.

First, while we were on a nature excursion watching bald eagles
soaring over us or sitting in trees on shore, the nature guide remarked,
in near-reverent tones, that eagles mate for life and that they are both in
charge of building and protecting the nest, feeding the chicks, and finally,
teaching the young eagles to fly before they are nudged out of the nest
for good. Large birds of prey which are respected for maintaining loyalty
to one mate and being good parents? Hmmmmm. Then a conversation
came up as we were watching wandering young adults near Tofino, on the
Pacific Rim. The status symbol of Canadian youth is traveling—all over,
anywhere, with various people. We discussed what the status symbol for
American youth was and decided after hearing a fellow traveler say he had
read a survey that found that the number of years one's first marriage lasted
was now the status symbol. The first marriage? What about the only? My
parents celebrated their sixty-sixth anniversary two months before Dad
died. Many of our friends have been married (to the same person) for
twenty to forty years so far. Could it be true that people are appreciating
long marriages again? It does not appear so if the many divorces I am
seeing are a sign.

Now, I realize that a marriage to an abusive and/or alcohol/
drug-addicted spouse could be reason for not having a lasting first
marriage. (Some people have married that kind two or three times—is
there a problem here?) But working hard at a marriage, even it is "for the
sake of the children", has its rewards—the most important being healthy
children who have both parents to raise them, but also having a companion
who knows you well and still wants to stay married to you.

A quote by Robert Browning had a special meaning for my parents as
well as for my husband and me: "Grow old along with me, the best is yet
to be, the last of life for which the first was made." Traveling, talking to
each other, cooking together, and just being with another person you trust
and who wants the best for you is a terrific reward.

An article in THE SEATTLE TIMES while we were on the trip was
about a mom and dad with four children who were unhappy over the lack

of opportunities their kids had to play organized sports with other kids in their area because the local politicians were unconcerned about the youth there. So, they cleared the raspberry bushes and other brush from a section of their land and created a baseball diamond. Sure, enough, "If you build it, they will come." These parents were not only staying together, but they were making things happen for their children. Like the mother said, "If they weren't playing and practicing ball, they would be watching TV and eating fourteen bowls of cereal a day".

Now, vans drive up to deposit kids for practice and return with parents to watch their children play. There are parents coaching, parents cheering (they don't curse the coaches or the umpires), parents who just come to watch kids play ball. These are parents who want their kids to develop and grow and be responsible. They will know they have done their very best at parenting so, eventually; they can gently nudge their children out of the nest with confidence.

Long marriages and good parenting as status symbols? Wouldn't that be a change in society as we know it now! Let's go for it and see what it does for our children today and for all children in the future!

RECOGNIZING A CHEATER

THERE ARE ADULTS, principally women, who seem unable to choose a
good marriage partner. They are either naïve, too needy, or blinded
by the *charm* of the man. The truth is, some people are perpetual cheaters
and liars. They were able to get away with lying to their parents when
they were young; they have cheated on people in their past and have not
suffered the consequences; they appear to have a need to cheat and lie
because of something in their personality that betrays them.

There are other traits that are characteristic of *cheaters*. Let me share
just a few:

Cheaters are notoriously dishonest. They could even be called
"pathological". When the truth or something honest would be best, they
take their chances that they can get away with the lie or the cheat one
more time. The person married to them can never totally trust them and
so the marriage is perpetually in jeopardy.

Cheaters are actually afraid to be alone. They lack the self-confidence
that comes from knowing and liking who they are as individuals.
Consequently, if they cannot be with one person long enough, they will
find someone else to be with. Sadly, cheaters can even be afraid of sharing
a spouse with the children. Many of them betray the marriage vows for
someone who can pay attention to them only.

Cheaters seem to find it impossible to accept responsibility for their
irresponsible behavior. When confronted with the lie or the cheat they
have perpetrated, they will inevitably blame the spouse, the lover, the
children—anyone but themselves. This type of behavior keeps the spouse
in perpetual confusion and self-doubt. When the spouse finally recognizes
that it is the fault of the cheater, then anger sets in and rightfully so.
However, the spouse of a cheater is usually too needy to be angry enough to
actually cast blame on the one who should have it, and therefore lives with
quilt as well as the anger—a sad combination that is self-destructive.

Cheaters have a totally selfish mindset. They don't care what effect
they are having on the spouse or the children or any others who may
be affected by their behavior. In fact, to the consternation of the family,
they appear oblivious to the damage they are doing to others. When
confronted, they refuse to be at fault, so the confrontation is useless and
even frustrating to the one who confronts.

In trying to save a marriage, the two partners must, individually, agree to turn toward each other and work together or separately to make the situation agreeable for the sake of the union. The cheater, by nature, turns away from the marriage and finds a way to justify what he is doing to prevent reconciliation.

Many times the life of a cheater begins when he is a child. As stated earlier he is able to lie to his parents and there is no consequence; in fact, he learns that lying often gets him what he wants. It becomes easier to lie than to tell the truth, and he gets in the habit of fabricating every kind of excuse to fit the situation. If he cheats on a test, he finds that it was easy to get the grade without having to work for it. If he cheats on a girlfriend and loses her, he just finds another one. So his entire life becomes a lie and a cheat. He is incapable of maintaining a healthy relationship because he has become mentally unhealthy.

There are two reasons parents should be aware of this type of person. First, mothers who find themselves in relationships that meet this description should evaluate their own mental health to determine why they are so eager to accept the conduct of a person like this. Many times she is so unsure of herself or so self-destructive because of a trauma in her background that she will take just anyone as long as he shows her some affection. The problem is that he will be affectionate as long as his own needs are met no matter whether she is being taken care of or not. If you find that this is your situation, please, for the sake of your children, go for counseling and learn to like who you are so you will not be so emotionally needy.

Secondly, as mothers and fathers, we must not allow our children to lie and cheat and not have to suffer the consequences. We are causing our children a multitude of problems if we defend their bad behavior or ignore it.

Finally, we must give our daughters knowledge about this type of person and how unsteady a relationship they will experience if they continue to date him. Cheaters are often charmers, and a girl cannot see past their looks or their charm into what kind of person they actually are. Ask your daughter to take a long time to evaluate him before she commits to a relationship with him. Of course this cheating behavior is not just limited to the male gender, it is just more prevalent among men.

Parents are the defense against our children's unhappiness in relationships if we can give our kids some preconception of the people they date. They may not believe us at first, but they will begin to look for the problems we have pointed out and may succeed in seeing them before they are "duped" by a cheater.

SECRETS OF A SUCCESSFUL MARRIAGE

EXPERTS AGREE THAT a crucial element in the lives of children is a stable relationship between the parents.

Several years ago I read two novels suggested to me—THE ACCIDENT by Danielle Steele, and A WOMAN'S PLACE by Barbara Delinsky. Both involved the dissolution of seemingly happy, perfect, two-parent, two-child families. It seems the husbands/fathers in both books became disenchanted with their wives and found a more "independent" woman who made them feel "young" again.

While the reader is observing the hurt and disillusion of the wife, the authors also let us see the pain in the children as the marriage disintegrates and the security the children need falls out from under them.

On the other hand, our family celebrated my parents' sixtieth wedding anniversary that same year and the strength of that marriage and the commitment of these two people is a rock on which their children could always depend.

As a close observer of a relationship that has lasted over half a century, let me share with you what has made it last:

A willingness to give—As their lives changed during those 60 years, each partner was able to adjust, re-adjust, and adjust again. Through children, moves, job changes, war, and death, they have been able to take care of the needs of the other and build a home that stood firm and a marriage that endured.

Patience—a trait many younger married couples lack. So many husbands and wives find fault with each other, belittle the other, pick fights, and just give up. And when they begin to yell things that will damage the trust of the other, they cannot love enough to back off and save the situation and the relationship. Why is it we are less patient with the person we promised to love and cherish to the death?

Commitment—a word we have lost in today's fast-paced "all for me", "it couldn't be my fault" world. When they stood before the preacher and witnesses over sixty years ago and vowed to love each other through sickness and health, poverty and wealth (sick children and college tuition), they committed their lives and futures to each other and kept their word.

Humor—They are both blessed with a sense of joy in life. Their fun has never been at the expense of the other; rather they have sixty years of delightful memories that still make both of them laugh when they begin to recall them

Affection—They still hold hands, kiss, call each other sweet names, and take care of each other. We children grew up seeing our parents show affection. She has always known that his lap was available to her. He knows that she will brush his cheek with her hand as she talks to him. What security that gives to their children!

A strong sense of loyalty to family—to their parents and parents-in-law when they were living, to their children and spouses, grandchildren, and great-grandchildren. There have always been birthday and holiday reasons to get together as a family and remember who we are and how we are connected by blood and by love.

A love of simple pleasures—Since we were young, my brothers and I were taught to find personal pleasure in a sunset, a walk in the woods, a lesson on bird calls and names of trees, or a visit around a campfire. We never had to spend exorbitant amounts of money to have a good time—just the company of each other and nature.

A love of God—Research shows, even today, that couples who attend church and have a personal faith in God live longer and stay married better. Mom and Dad belonged to the same church for over 50 years.

We can learn a lot from the examples of committed couples and parents.

"SLAY SUSPECT HAD VIOLENT PAST"

IN OCTOBER 2010, we drove to Waynesville, North Carolina, to see the fall foliage and to visit a favorite aunt. The day after we arrived, the ASHEVILLE CITIZEN-TIMES (Tuesday, Oct. 19) headlines read "Slay suspect had violent past", and the subtitle read "teacher's husband held on $2 million bond".

This violent man, who still had a restraining order on him by his former wife, had all the signs of being an abusive partner and, because his current wife did not see the signs soon enough, she had been murdered. Among the ones she left behind was her son by another marriage who was the kicker on the local football team. Also, that entire team was affected because she was at every game and helped serve snacks and food. The members of the team called her "Mom". Others who were sadly affected were her seventh-grade math students and the faculty of both schools.

Since that week, I have talked to two other women who are afraid of their husbands but are not sure how to get out of the situation. So let's look at some of the signs of a potentially abusive partner and how to escape them when the abuse becomes intolerable.

1. He separates you from family and friends and is controlling. In this woman's request for a protective order against him she had written this complaint: "(He) controls everything I do. I'm not allowed to go any place with anyone, including my parents, without having to check in every ten minutes".

2. He becomes irritated easily and escalates in abuse. He may begin with verbal abuse, then continues into threatening. He may even say that the wife will never see the kids again or he may hurt or take a pet away. As he becomes more violent, he may do as this man did—choke, hit, pin the victim against a wall and/or threaten with a weapon.

3. He will accuse the partner of having an affair. Abusive men are unusually jealous and, even if he knows it is not true, he will accuse her in order to maintain more control over her or to have an excuse to hit her. It is useless to argue with him because he is using it as a wedge to maintain control, not because he knows it is true.

The abusive man in Waynesville also did what many others do—he threatened to kill himself which caused the wife to drop the charges she had filed previously. The threat, usually, is a manipulative effort to gain the control he sees slipping away. Dropping charges is never a good idea—it gives all control to the abuser; however, most police departments keep the charges on file and they can be used against him if the abused has to go to court to escape him.

As in the tragedy in North Carolina, counselors and law enforcement will tell the victims that the most dangerous time for her is when she leaves, or tries to leave, the abuser. The reason is obvious—his loss of control over her. Consequently, she must leave only if she can find a safe haven (which, by the way should not be to a relative's home if he knows where it is), and she must never return to him—the abuse will only get worse.

Now, how to escape an abusive situation? The ASHEVILLE CITIZEN-TIMES put it this way: Women in this situation "should call their local women's shelter for help in creating a safe plan to get out". Some women's shelters are not close to where you live, but they will come and get you if yours or your children's lives are in danger. Often the police department will take a woman and her children to a shelter and safety.

Most women's shelters also have a counseling service as well as a support group in which the woman can find other women who are in the process of overcoming an abusive situation. If you can get to one, they will help you get to your out-of-town family if you know he will not follow you there; they will provide clothing if you have left with none; they will go to court with you as your advocate, and they will recommend a lawyer who will understand your plight. They can refer you for medical help if you are injured. Later in the process, they can refer you to housing placement, job placement, and other health assistance.

They are your hope in getting out of a seemingly hopeless situation, and you will be safe from the threats of your partner possibly for the first time since you married or moved in with him.

Please seek help today if you have recognized yourself or your situation after reading this. And God bless you.

SOME PREDICTORS OF DIVORCE

D IVORCE IS HARD on children, no matter what age they are, unless there has been so much yelling and cursing and abusing that it was better for everyone to just end the chaos. However, most divorcees say that they never saw it coming even though there was little communication and no overt affection. So let's look at some issues that can undermine a marriage relationship and set it up for failure.

"We were more interested in getting married than in trying to maintain a marriage". The romantic part of getting married often does not allow a couple to look into the future and realize that moving two people into a home and hoping they will forever get along will be next to impossible without a lot of work and emotional effort. They give up too easily rather than invest in the relationship. The words "for better or worse" have been in marriage vows for generations, and they are there for a good reason. Most couples haven't seen the "worse" of the other person until they marry and move in together. However, if they are committed to the marriage vows and to each other, they accept that neither is perfect and they determine to stay true to the relationship and the commitment they made.

"We don't fight fair." Any married couple who says they never have disagreements must never talk to each other. Two people from two different backgrounds, different family structures, even different cultures, and who are visibly different (male, female) are not always going to get along all of the time. There are going to be clashes unless one of the spouses is so dominant that the other has no opinion (which will eventually lead to marriage conflict as well). There are some things you can do in a "fight" that will actually predict divorce: name calling, belittling, attacking the character, sarcasm, mocking, cursing, not allowing the other to retreat with dignity, not staying on the subject (bringing up other conflicts from the past). The goal in taking part in a disagreement must not be to win ("If I win, my spouse loses".) but to protect the marriage and to reach an agreement that is good for each spouse, the marriage, and the children.

"We can't get out of a financial strain." Struggling financially usually leads to blaming: "You spend too much on the kids." "You spend it on golf and your other toys". "Why do you have to have your hair done every week?" "Why do you have to meet your buddies at the bar so often?" Rather than blaming, a married couple must find a way to list the necessities for maintaining a home and a life and budget for those. The rest must be sacrificed if money is tight and is causing marital discord. One family was ordering pizza at least two nights a week but could not figure out where their money was going. Determine to use your income for the health and welfare of your children and each other. Leave your petty, selfish wants outside the budget until you can afford them again.

"We don't think flirting can do any harm." Flirting should stop when a person says, "I do" to another person. The purpose of flirting is to find someone you may want to spend time with. Once you have married, you have made that decision. The only other two reasons to flirt are to stroke an ego or to make a spouse jealous. Both can lead to hurt, anger, and distrust—all can lead to divorce.

"One of us is addicted to _____". Drugs, alcohol, porn, sex, whatever—a person who is addicted puts that desire before the wants and needs of anyone else and that selfishness leaves others out of any kind of acceptance and love.

"We don't take care of each other." Research shows that a man needs praise; a woman needs affection. If a spouse is not meeting those needs, it can cause conflict in a marriage. Taking care of the needs of each other takes an unselfish position—you have to give of yourself to another person. Too many adults are too self-serving to tend to another's needs in order to save a marriage.

One of my favorite sayings is "Marriage is really hard work." However, marriage is worth it. Research shows that long-married people live longer, have more money, are more satisfied with life, and are healthier. It is worth the effort, the compromise, the kind words, the touch, the little surprises, and the attention.

Say to yourself, "My goal is not to take care of myself, but to take care of the person I married and to preserve the marriage". Your children will thank you.

STRAINING AT MARRIAGE *GNATS*

HAVE YOU HEARD the phrase "straining at a gnat"? Too many couples spend too much of their time straining at their marriage. The least little thing sets one of them off which begins one of two cycles: 1. The *set off* spouse yells or screams or both and the other spouse, in defense, yells and screams back, or 2. The screamed-at spouse refuses to respond but leaves the scene angry and hurt and there is no solution to the problem. Both situations create an enormous strain on the marriage and the stress accumulates over time. Let's look at some *gnats* that can strain a marriage and what to do to prevent the stress and the collapse of a union.

1. Finances. Whether you have a lot or a little or just enough, money can cause a strain in even a strong marital relationship. Marriage is a partnership, and both parties should be able to make financial decisions—but always together—never individually. Sure, one partner is usually better at saving and handling money than the other and should be in charge of the distribution of funds, but never without the knowledge of the other spouse. Budgets should be discussed and agreed upon and followed explicitly, especially in times of economic downturns.

2. Children. I read about a child who was never taught to respect his parents, and, as he grew older, he refused to obey and often back talked. Parenting became a screaming match with both the child and the parent acting like two-year-olds. The spouse who was not engaged in the battle of wills felt a strain because there was such chaos in the home and the one he blamed was the spouse—not the child (and rightfully so unless he contributed to the spoiling of the child). In addition, raising pre-teens and teens creates stress unless the parents agree on what will be acceptable behavior in this growing, maturing person living in the home. Disagreements over parenting can be a troublesome, irksome *gnat* unless the two adults can sit down and make some decisions together about the welfare of the child, of the home and, yes, of the marriage.

3. Home Responsibilities. Whether one or both parents work outside the home, there must be a division of responsibilities to maintain the house (and yard) in reasonable order. Granted, if only one does work, the bulk of the household chores would be on the non-working spouse and only what that spouse could not do should be delegated to the other. If both work, the division of responsibilities should be as evenly divided as possible—even the cooking/grilling of the evening meal and the shuttling of the kids from one activity to another. Additionally, of course, children should be required to help with household chores just because they live under the roof and because it is one of the best ways to teach personal and familial responsibility.

4. Leisure Time. If the spouses have no joint interests except the children, they will find themselves drifting farther apart as the years come and go. Too often, we become more selfish as we begin to take the marriage vows for granted and ignore the emotional needs of the other spouse. If you enjoyed going to a movie or going on picnics or walking in the woods, or whatever at one time, that could still be a together time for the two of you or even for the entire family. Wives should take the time to at least try to know the name of the quarterback of his favorite team and whether they have lost all of their games or just one. Husbands should pay attention to her when she tries to show him the new paint swatches for the foyer. The *gnat* you avoid by just taking the time to show interest and by taking part together could be the one that would have destroyed the marriage.

5. Emotional needs. Did you tell him (her) that you loved him (her) while you were dating? Then why isn't that being said regularly now? Did you tell him why you cared about him back then? Are you still doing that? Did you tell her she was pretty? She probably still is but you haven't noticed. We do not stop having emotional needs just because we have taken on the roles of spouse and parent. We still have them and we want them fulfilled by the person whom we loved enough to marry and to whom we committed

our futures and ourselves. The strong marriages of many years are the ones in which the partners still let the other spouse know that they are cared for and that they are truly wanted in that person's life. If this doesn't happen, the *gnat* of dissatisfaction will become bigger and bigger as time goes by.

The saying goes, "Take care of the little things and the big things will take care of themselves". That goes for taking care of your marriage, your spouse, and your future. Keep those pesky *gnats* from working their way into your marriage and your lives!

THE TWO PRINCIPLE REASONS FOR DIVORCE

I LOVE IT WHEN there is research that comes along to support something I have said in my columns, especially when it may help someone who reads it.

In a far-reaching survey by a nationally distributed ladies' magazine, the results revealed that the principle reasons for divorce in today's society are *immaturity* and *selfishness*. In those two words lies all of the so-called *reasons* people say they have for breaking up a family, a relationship, a commitment.

Even spousal abuse is the act of a selfish, self-centered person who ignores the feelings of the spouse and gives the blame for the abuse *to the abused* because he is too immature to accept responsibility for his own actions. The abuser shows his immaturity in his inability to control his anger *or* his angst. Instead, he finds it more convenient to hit another person or to speak to a spouse in a belittling way to try to make up for his childish way of handling life's difficulties.

So many adults leave a marriage commitment because they "just don't seem to love that other person any more"—a very immature way of facing reality. There is no marriage that is perfect or gratifying all of the time. However, the mature adult looks for reasons to stay in the marriage rather than looking for all the spouse's faults and short-comings so they can have an excuse to find someone else who can satisfy the temporary problems in the marriage. Leaving a marriage unless there is abuse or infidelity, especially if there are children involved, is one of the most selfish acts one can commit.

Another selfish act in many marriages is the inordinate amount of time spent on FaceBook and Twitter and the guilty spouse is neglecting the relationships at home. It has become an *escape* from trying to maintain communication with the spouse and allows the user to emotionally separate from the spouse even if they are still in the same house. Not only is this selfish and self-serving, it is also immature. Life hands us difficulties even in our relationships, but we should not try to avoid trying to correct our own actions that are contributing to the problem. Psychologists are suggesting that we spend at least thirty minutes a day communicating with our spouses without kids or technology or any other interferences. Just that one act could save a relationship.

I have written often about the extra burden that addictions add to a marriage. Addicts are, by nature, selfish because they cannot give up something that not only will destroy their bodies and minds but also their relationships. So when a person refuses to get help with his addiction, he is committing a totally selfish act that tells his spouse and everyone else who cares about him that his addiction is more important than they are. So many addicts got into drugs or booze because they thought it made them appear to be more mature. Actually, anything that takes away inhibitions causes the person to act in a very immature way and makes him or her look silly and foolish. What they were trying to do ends up being the very opposite. Then, later, they can't control what they thought would make them look good, and they end up destroying the people and the commitments they wanted in their lives and their own lives as well.

Too many divorces also occur because one spouse refuses to *grow up*. They are committed to their toys, their games, their friends, their jobs. Being so involved with other things allows them to avoid working on the family commitments, on relationships, on the truly important things in their lives. Their immaturity is evident. So is their selfishness. They end up cheating their families but also cheating themselves because they will have nothing left in their lives when they are older and find that their pastimes give them no lasting pleasure.

If you have contemplated divorce lately, examine yourself to determine whether you are acting selfishly or immaturely and whether, with effort, you can find a way to salvage your relationship and your commitment again. I hope for your sake and that of your children, you can.

CHAPTER EIGHT

HELP! I WANT TO BE A GOOD DAD!

COULD VIOLENCE BE CAUSED BY ABSENT FATHERS?

PEOPLE ALL AROUND us are asking it; newscasters and commentators are asking it; writers and researchers are asking it, "Why is there so much violence in our society today?" I have researched a book recently and also was able to watch an Oprah segment both of which sought to answer that important question. Both claim that the vast majority of violent incidents are perpetuated by young men who are victims of what the guest on Oprah called "The Prodigal Father" and what author David Blankenthorn calls "Fatherlessness."

Blankenthorn says in his book *Fatherless America* that the parallel between increased violence and the increase in fatherlessness cannot be ignored. He adds that over 40% of American children are going to sleep in a home where their fathers do not live. Mark Bryan, author of *Prodigal Father*, says 10-12 million men are living away from their children. Before they are 18 years old, more than half of America's children will live part of their childhood away from their dads. Blankenthorn puts it plainly but painfully, "Never before in this country have so many children been voluntarily abandoned by their fathers."

Fatherlessness is now recognized as a cause of crime, teen pregnancy (which just perpetuates the growing problem), child abuse, and domestic violence. Yet this subject is seldom debated on state or national levels, and laws are being passed that make divorcing easier and out-of-wedlock child-bearing less difficult. In fact, we are seeing movie stars who choose to raise children without the benefit of a father. The authors say that there should be more attention on maintaining marriages so children could grow up in two-biological-parent homes.

Many teenage boys seem to think it is the mark of a *real man* to be able to get a girl pregnant. Yet the truth is that a real man does not *father* a child—he willingly acknowledges the child and nurtures him/her into maturity. The opposite of involved paternity is narcissism—a total *me-first* mentality that wishes only for the basic pleasures without commitment.

Another sad commentary on many men today is that, in the past, fatherlessness was caused by death (often war), Today it is by choice. When a father dies, the child grieves ("I have lost someone I love"). When a father leaves, a child feels anxiety and self-blame ("What did I do wrong?" Why doesn't he love me?"). A little boy interviewed on Oprah said, "When I don't hear from him, I think he is lost." A teenager said it this way, "A dad is a dad for life—but not for me." Isn't that sad?

Who is to say that that sad, depressed boy will not someday become angry and turn that anger on family or others in order to vent his frustration? And will he shoot students at a school, or beat his wife, or hurt his children?

If fatherlessness truly is a part of the problem, could fathers everywhere not care more for their own children and for society as a whole and stay home?

I recommend both of the books mentioned above for those of you who wish to learn more about this problem. In fact, *The Prodigal Father* is a handbook for those fathers who have lost contact with their children and wish to be in touch with them again.

If you are a dad who is trying to be back in touch with your child, just be sure that your contact with them will be for their sake, not just for yours. And be sure too, that your influence on them will be a positive one once you have reestablished a relationship.

Jan Knight

FATHERS NEEDED IN THE LIVES
OF THEIR CHILDREN

OUR CHILDREN IN America are at risk today due largely to men who refuse to assume the roll of loving, providing fathers.

One of the most endangered segments of children is our girls. Author David Blankenthorn says in <u>Fatherless America</u>, "When a girl cannot trust and love the first man in her life, her father . . . . she loses. As more and more girls grow up without fathers, society loses." Another comment he makes that we also see in schools is that when a girl is not raised by her father, she grows up anxious about her relationship with men—too eager to have a relationship or too afraid to have one. The author says that these girls speak often of male betrayal and abandonment. It is hard to trust men when your own father has not wanted to be part of your life. Yet these women find themselves needing men to complete their lives due to the earlier emptiness, and they often set themselves up for abuse, battering, even death.

In addition, because there is no protective father in the home, more girls are subjected to sexual abuse by unrelated males who live in or often come to the home. They are also more prone to childhood pregnancy, divorce, and confused sexual identity. Fathers are so very necessary in the lives of their daughters.

Another problem in our prevalent fatherless society is childhood poverty. All educators have experienced the child who cannot take part in the party or go on the field trip because he has no money. According to statistics, single-mother homes account for 66% of children who live in poverty in our country. In fact, fatherlessness is now more of a factor than race, religion, or education. Changing-family structure is the greatest long-term threat to U.S. children and their futures.

There is a growing refusal of fathers to spend their money on their offspring, especially if they are living apart from them, yet a man's children need his financial support no less, and even more, when they are not living with him. Blankenthorn says that the pervading question today is not which men will pay child-support, but which men will be fathers—they are certainly needed more.

Finally, *Fatherless America* also mentions that when crime statistics are being studied, a common denominator is becoming more and more prevalent—fatherlessness among the youth and adults who spend time on probation or in prison. Whether this statistic is caused by the poverty, by the young men trying to prove their manhood, or by the lack of a father's guidance is unclear—maybe it has to do with all of the above, or, perhaps *fatherlessness* is the root cause of the other two.

Now, I know of very successful, very happy people who were raised in fatherless homes. I also know that they have overcome significant odds to become content adults. It is also true, as Hemingway said in *The Sun Also Rises,* "We are stronger in the broken places". But if you are a father who can find a way to maintain your marriage through counseling or sheer effort or remembering why you loved your children's mother in the first place, or if you can just be *man* enough, stay home with your own children. Or if you are a father who is already divorced from the mother of your children, please make a supreme effort to be a good, supportive, loving father. Don't be the handicap in their lives, rather, be one of the advantages they have because of who you are and the good example you are.

For legislators, pastors, marriage counselors, and parents who are reading this, here is a powerful quote on family from *Fatherless America,* "The best anti-poverty program for children is a stable, intact family".

Let all of us make a commitment to our spouse and to our children so we may live in contentment and may enter our older years with a philosophy like the character in "City Slickers" when he saw the faces of his children and wife—he said that being with them was the most important "one thing" in his life.

GOOD FATHERS ". . . EASIER TO BECOME ONE THAN TO BE ONE"

GOOD FATHERS ARE necessary. Oh, I do not mean the men who *father* a child then never see or acknowledge the mother or the child or who leave or divorce the mother, and the child or children too. They are not real fathers—they have instinctively procreated and then, unlike most of the animal world, have abandoned their young. It *is* much easier to become a father then to be one.

Good fathers are the men who are committed to the mother of their children, or, if not to her, at least to the child or children they conceived. They are men who keep their word, who show up when they say they will, who put their family before their play or their work, who never assume that money can take the place of their attention or their effort.

Good fathers are men who are represented by some of the quotes I found several years ago. My comments follow:

"One father is more than a hundred schoolmasters." (English proverb) A good father is the best teacher for his child, not just by what he says (some fathers tend to *preach* rather than teach), but more by their example. Never allow yourself to be guilty of *hoping* your child will go by the old adage, "Do as I say, not as I do." Be an available, encouraging father, not like the father of a girl who said, "My dad always has friends over; he never has time for me." Notice too that I said a "good" father, not like the father of two boys I know who has spent his parenting years as a verbally abusive drunk. They have learned from him, all right. They have dropped out of school early, and one is already a self-destructive drug addict. Never be guilty of hoping someone else will be able to teach your child what a father should teach—that is your responsibility.

Another very poignant quote: "I can not think of any need in childhood as strong as the need for a father's protection." (Freud) That means, as Dr. Laura Schlesinger says, that you should live in the home with your children or at least in the general vicinity, not a state away. Some of the saddest children I counseled were those who said, "I never see or hear from my dad", or "My dad doesn't care anything about me". No matter how old your child is, you are important in his life. For years, I have noticed that boys about the age of thirteen to fifteen want to know about their fathers even if they have never seen them before. They know that, genetically, there is a connection, and they want to know how they compare. I also notice every year that many boys, and girls too, have a tendency to give up on themselves if they don't have the love, support, and protection of their father. What a responsibility—what a privilege!

Is being a father easy? Not according to some of the other quotes I found:

"A father is a banker by nature: (French Proverb)

"When I became a father, I learned that insanity in children, like radio transmission, is liveliest at night." (Bill Cosby)

"Before I got married, I had six theories about bringing up children; now I have six children and no theories." (John Wilmot, Earl of Rochester)

"Raising kids is part joy and part guerilla warfare." (Ed Asner)

Finally, two quotes that fit very well in my life as a daughter:

"The most important thing a father can do for his children is to love their mother." (Theodore M. Hesburgh) and "We never know the love of our parents for us until we become parents." (Henry Ward Beecher)

A SPECIAL CHALLENGE
TO FATHERS AND HUSBANDS

ONCE I HEARD Ted DiBiase, of wrestling fame, talk about the changes in his life. One particular portion of his talk was especially poignant when he admitted cheating on his wife and consequently almost losing her and their marriage. Her words to him when they met with a pastor friend to try to work things out were, "Who are you and where is the man I thought I married? I don't know you!"

Men, you need to realize that two of the most important things a woman must have in her relationship with you are **trust** and **caring** (affection). She must know that you will be faithful, constant, and true to her and to the vows you made with her. She must also know that you care about her and will for the rest of the time you are together on this earth. Even into his nineties, my dad complimented my mother. On the other hand some men foolishly say, "I do things for her around the house, and I bring her my paycheck; what else does she want?" Love her—but don't just tell her—show her! Flowers are nice, but so are tender caresses, notes, and whispers that are meant only to fulfill her need to be cherished—for no other reason.

They used to say that women were fickle because they couldn't be satisfied with one man. I think they had the wrong gender. Men are fickle as husbands because they let other things become more important than the women with whom they share marriage vows. I realize you have to concentrate on your career so you can provide for her and for the children you have brought into this world. However, your job must never be as important as she is. In addition, she must always be first in your life—not hunting, fishing, four wheeling, golfing, or other recreational activities you do. Surely, there are also things you enjoy doing with her. If not, find something so you can enjoy being with each other. I have friends who are no longer together because he let his gambling break them financially and because she could no longer *trust* him—his addiction had become more important than she was.

On the other hand, I see couples out who are eating and having a good time together. Other friends go to the theater—maybe because she likes to, but at least he is there and in good spirits for her sake.

Still more couples and families are involved in their churches and the friends they share there.

Finally, if your wife cannot trust you to be available for her emotionally, your children see you fail in this very important part of their lives as well.

Your daughters grow up thinking that they should not expect the man they love to be loving, supportive, and caring. Your son, if he models your behavior, will never succeed in married life because he too will ignore the special needs of the woman he loves and marries.

Men, you have a significant role to fill in your household, and it is not just as provider. You have people in your home who need your attention, your affection, your care. You also have people who have a need to know that they can trust you to be faithful to all of them for all the years of their lives. Don't disappoint them.

POOR AND GOOD EXAMPLES OF DADS

A Florida beach and the accompanying stores and restaurants were good places to observe Dads and their children. There were the poor examples of what real Dads should not be (thankfully there were only a few of those), and there were examples of attentive, good Dads (saw lots of those). Have are some examples:

POOR:

1. The loud-mouthed, rude, obnoxious specimen who was disturbing the marketing director at the traditional guest breakfast. Several people tried to shush him which he summarily ignored and kept talking too loudly, too stupidly. The saddest thing to me was the adorable twelve-year-old boy who was hanging over his shoulder and on to his every word—an example of how a grown man should not act in the presence of others.

2. The one who sat at the table with his wife and children and never lifted his hand or his voice to help discipline the kids. When the little boy began banging his silverware on the table, the wife corrected him and then had to take the utensils away when he continued to use the table as a drum, disturbing the folks around them. Dad said and did nothing to help. When the little girl began to cry because she couldn't leave her seat, the mother corrected—the dad ignored. Will these children forever be corrected only by the one parent?

3. The one who never left the beach during the day, but sat in a chair in the sun and drank beer. His son and friend were never supervised, never given attention. The last night of their vacation, he was so drunk that he had to be half carried off the beach and helped into bed, couldn't get up the next morning for breakfast and the wife packed the car and planned to drive back to Texas herself with his semi-conscious, drunk self riding in the front seat.

GOOD:

1. The Dad who spent hours hauling umbrellas, a blow-up wading pool and buckets and toys to the beach and back every day and then sacrificed his pasty white skin to the salt water and sun so his kids could be in the water and the Florida sand with him. He told his two little blond-haired children not to do something only once and was obeyed. He played with them, loved them, gave them attention, and then took at least one of them, sound asleep, on his shoulder each evening as they went back to their condo.

2. The Dad who couldn't locate his two pre-teen daughters in the Gulf water or on the beach and stood until he saw them way down the shore. One ear-splitting whistle later and they were standing in front of him. His correction, to be where he could see them, was accepted and obeyed—no whining, no "But, Dad!"—nothing. They acknowledged that their safety was his concern, so they did it.

3. The Dad who brought his daughter to breakfast at the local restaurant. As they sat next to each other waiting for their food, she took his hand and put it against her cheek. I don't know where the mother was—maybe working, maybe divorced, maybe deceased—but here was a Dad who loved his little daughter and was loved in return. When their food arrived, she was the one who asked the blessing as they both bowed their heads.

There were others who threw footballs, who held little hands in their big ones, who drove jet skis with kids behind them to see dolphins up close, who were human diving boards in the pool. It was great to watch the good ones, sad to watch the poor ones.

Thanks to all of you who are good Dads whether your kids live with you or with their Mom if you're divorced. You are a valuable part of your child's life. Please don't think that if you correct your children that they won't love you—they will love you more if you do because it is a way of demonstrating that you truly care about them. Please don't allow your life to be so full of *other* things that you neglect your children—they may never forgive you. Please remember that they are only children (including teenage children) for a brief time and that your importance actually increases rather than diminishes as they reach adulthood and have families of their own if you have been a good example of what a real Dad should be.

THE IMPORTANCE OF A MALE AUTHORITY FIGURE
IN RAISING TEENS

I CAN SPEAK FROM authority because I can look back and see the importance of a male authority figure in my life and development.

I think that the first priority of the father in the home, whether he is a dad or a step-father, is for him to love the mother of the home. If the children see love there, the father automatically gives a sense of security, stability, and peace to the home and to the children.

The role of the father to the daughter is what my father gave to me: a gentle, loving spirit, a hand to walk with, an arm to escort with, and a security to hold on to. If you do these things, Dad, then when your daughter is older, she will look for someone who gives her that sense of peace she found with you. She will bring to her marriage a trust, fidelity, and a loving spirit that she found at home. In addition, she will not accept being treated any way but like a lady if she has been taught by her father that she is valuable and special.

The role of the father to the son is as a role model. If your son is a teenager, he may not seem to be copying you; in fact, he may seem to be doing the very opposite. Just remember, he is probably testing you to see how strong you are, not just physically, but how firmly you can stick to your word and how determined you are to raise him according to your values and principles. As he tests you, he will be going against what you have taught him. Will you pass the test he is giving? Or will you wimp out and let him get away with too much and then both of you will live to regret it? If you tell him not to drink and there is alcohol in the home and he sees you drink socially, how much will he believe you when you try to teach him about other things? If he follows in your footsteps and copies your habits, are you going to regret the fact that you never could put down that cigarette, or turn off the TV, or come home to be a father rather than work all that overtime so you could buy *things*?

What are some of the other roles of the male authority figures in the home? One is a teacher—and I don't mean in books. I learned from my father to love nature, and music, and family, and simple pleasures. Another is as an example—two of my examples, my father and his father, taught me the value of hard work and of keeping my word. Another thing

I learned, especially from my grandfather is to love the Lord, His word, and His work.

Now, for you single mothers, what can you do about a male figure who can help you as you try to raise a teenager, especially a son? I recommend that you solicit help from a gentleman you can trust. Your own father may be the mainstay your teenager needs to fall back on when he needs advice and encouragement; your brother can be a help to you; a coach can be of valuable service if your child is involved in sports. There are male teachers that boys, especially those with dysfunctional families, have learned to trust. A youth director can be a valuable help to you. In our family, my mother-in-law, who was a widow raising a big teenage son, solicited the help of the school principal who forced him to leave the study hall where he was wasting his time and go out on the football field and play. There he learned the value of team play, of cooperation, of working hard. And it was not until later in life that he realized how much that man meant to him.

Too many children are being raised without a male figure at all or they are influenced by men who are into drugs, gangs, foul language, stealing and mistreating women. What kind of adults will their sons and daughters be and what will happen to the next generation of children?

Dads, take your role in the family seriously. Too soon your children will be out on their own and away from you. You will still be able to fish, to hunt, to watch TV, to work, but the time to teach and influence the lives of your children will be gone. Don't let this important time in your life go by without your effort, your time, and your love.

WATCHING FATHERS ON SUMMER VACATION

IN THE MORNINGS we would sit drinking coffee on our balcony and watch the parade of daddies burdened down with umbrellas, coolers, plastic buckets, and beach chairs who would be accompanied by talkative, excited little boys and girls. The children would run ahead of them on the raised walk going to the beach, but they wouldn't go far from the safety of the dad who was coming behind them.

Then in the afternoon, the same burdened dads would be accompanied by crying kids: "Why do we have to go in?" cranky kids: "I don't want to eat supper!" or sleeping kids hanging off of broad shoulders. Dads apparently have lots of responsibility when the family is on the beach, and they handle their chores well.

Dads were also playing in the sand, holding little bodies above the waves while the little ones squealed, throwing balls with older boys, and watching carefully for the return of their young daughters from their strolls down the beach and back. They were enjoying showing their children what they apparently had learned to love when they were younger.

Dads are wonderful people to have around when they are doing what they do best—being dads. Mine loved to be in the water and taught me how to handle the waves, to swim parallel to the shore, and to avoid panic when I realized I had gone out too far. He also loved the mountains and spent time teaching me to look for the things that make them so spectacular.

Dad taught us to appreciate the simple things—the song of a particular bird, the sound of water in a stream, the rays of the sunset, the beauty of a mature tree. He was very comfortable in nature, and it was there that he held his classrooms and became the instructor and we became the students. He believed that a man must be worth his word or he is not fully a man. He taught that men were to take care of women even if the woman could take care of herself. He gave more value to a daughter's character than to her looks. He was tall and fairly quiet, but there was a strength there that not all men have.

Like my dad, my son's dad taught some truths that are now being taught to his children, like the value of hard work. He is not only an example of what hard work can accomplish, but he taught a saying that I hear our son use with his children: "Once a task has first begun never leave

275

it till it's done. Be the labor great or small, do it well or not at all." I expect those kids will quote it to their kids someday—it's worth repeating.

Children expect Moms to appreciate them, but it means something special when their dad approves of what they have accomplished. Just watch their faces when you compliment them—Dads carry a lot of weight when it comes to self-confidence brought on by their approval.

Girls who have made up their minds that they must be the ugliest one in the school will go the next day with a renewed confidence if her dad tells her she is pretty or has a nice smile or has expressive eyes. Boys who are told by their dads that they are growing up fast and adding muscle will have more confidence to face a critical world among their peers. All children should be taught that their worth is not in their looks or in what they possess, but in their value as good, kind, thoughtful people. Dads can teach that lesson.

So Dads are necessary. Men were not made just to be sperm donors—they were made to take on the responsibility of maintaining a family and providing shelter and food and for teaching their progeny. They see the future for those who are coming behind them; they are the safety for those who are venturing away from them; they are the instructors about life and work and handling difficulties.

Hopefully, you who are reading this have or are fulfilling your responsibilities toward those you have brought into the world; you are being a good example that your children can follow with the assurance that if they do as you do, they will not go wrong; you are a good teacher so that your children can take your words to their own children; in other words, you are a good Dad.

WHAT IS A DAD?

WHAT IS A dad? Well, let's look first at what he is not:

1. He is not a *buddy* to his children. Your kids have enough friends with whom they can play. If your only relationship with your children is to have fun, to go places, to spend only *play* times, then you have misunderstood the role of being a father.
2. He is not just a *bankroll*. Too many dads spend too much of their time at work or being involved in their own *games* and then they throw money at their children in order to diminish their guilt over the time and effort they should have spent with them. I had a very angry young man come to me and say that he couldn't believe his dad had bought him another expensive set of golf clubs. "He thinks that I won't miss being with him since he has to spend all of his time at work and with his new wife. I don't want his 'stuff'—I want to be with him!"
3. He should not be just *someone else's husband/father*. I hear it all of the time, "My dad has another life now, so I never hear from him." Your children are your children whether you live with them or not. At least send a card on their birthdays and a small gift on Christmas! They remember, whether you do or not.
4. He is not a permanent part of a recliner. He should not immediately flop down in his chair and stay there until and even after his children's bedtime. You may be tired, but you are neglecting such a vital part of your life—your family.

Truett Cathy, the founder of Chick-fil-A, once said that the role of dad, in his opinion from working with foster children and teaching 13-year-old boys in Sunday School, is this: "Homes were much more stabilized back then (fifty years ago). Nobody thought about divorce. It is particularly important that the father realizes his responsibility. He is the CEO, president, and chairman of the board of the greatest institution in the world, and that is the home".

Parents tell me that they cannot get their teenagers to talk to them, Truett Cathy has a solution—one I used for years with my son: "I advise parents to talk to their children when the children want to talk. A lot of times fathers don't talk to children except to scold them. Time is the greatest gift we can give to our children." I found that our son would talk best over a hamburger and fries whether he was at home or at a restaurant. Want to know what's bothering him/her? Sit at the table and eat with them—you'll know soon enough.

Cathy also had this to say about parents: "I've seen a lot of people be very successful in business, but be a total flop when it comes to responsibility for the family." It may come down to another quote I used recently: "My greatest fear is that I will look back on my life and wonder what I did with it". I think there are going to be a great many parents, especially fathers, who will regret the lack of time they spent with their kids. Those kids will grow up and away from you and possibly treat you the very same way you treated them when they were young—with unconcern and neglect.

Finally, Truett Cathy has some sound advice for dads and all parents: "My dad was the last person I'd go to if I had a problem because he'd end up scolding me rather than showing any interest. I tell fathers not to be so concerned that your teenager does not listen to you, but be very sure he sees everything you do." Setting an example! Your child will do what you do faster than he will do what you tell him to do. Do you drink? Do drugs? Curse? Smoke? Become angry and lose control? Then don't be surprised is your child gets into trouble for doing the same things.

Dads have such an important role in raising the children of this nation. I pray they will take that role seriously and will spend more time considering what they are doing wrong and what they can do that is right. Then I pray they will spend more quality time with their children.

CHAPTER NINE

HELP! THERE IS SO MUCH MORE TO KNOW!

Jan Knight

A GROWING SOCIAL PROBLEM—PARENTS IN PRISON

THERE IS A growing crisis in our society. It has been going on for many years, but it is increasingly affecting the families, the economy, the social-welfare, and the attitude of our nation. It also hits close to home more often than we imagine. The crisis is parents who are spending time in prison.

We have many children in our country who have at least one, and sometimes both, of their parents serving time in prison and who are living with grandparents, parents' friends, anywhere they can until the parent has served time and is released, if ever. There was one student who worked an almost full-time job so that she could pay rent to a friend of her mother's and help pay for the food while her mother was in prison. She also paid for all of hers and her younger brother's school fees, clothes and incidentals. If she hadn't been so responsible, they would have been *housed* by the state and, therefore, would have been separated. She told one of her teachers that she would do anything to keep that from happening.

As of 2010, about 7.7 million adults in the U.S will have served time. That means that a growing number of ex-prisoners will have difficulty finding jobs because they have felony convictions and they are also more likely to have family issues or emotional problems. (numbers from Bureau of Justice statistics). That number also means that children may be homeless, hungry, living in children's homes, and/or continuing the same life style that put their parents in prison in the first place.

In the Book HEAR OUR CRY: BOYS IN CRISIS, the author, Paul D. Slocumb, says that we as a society are making it more difficult for young males to succeed and that "male aggression contributes, at least in part, to female aggression." (A reason many women are incarcerated) He also gives these statistics: "Of the 1.3 million children who have mothers under the supervision of justice system agencies, there is probably a missing father for these children, and, with mothers and fathers absent, the probability of children repeating the cycle of violence increases".

One evident contribution to this problem in society is the fact that too many young men are fathering children and then refusing to parent them. Without a male role model, male children have to depend on their peers to show them how to cope in the world, and too often those peers may be gang members or family members who themselves have served time which may, then, lead to the boy eventually serving time as well. Girl children raised without a father, too often crave male attention and have babies who will not have a father present and who will, again, grow up without that role model. These single mothers also usually find it difficult to parent successfully because they are busy trying to make a living and so will perpetuate the problem. Statistics also show that single mothers make up a significant number of families living in poverty with little hope of getting out of it. Though poverty has not been proven to be a road to incarceration, still, frustrated poor people are too prone to try to get money illegally and end up in prison. In addition, a mother without a high school diploma almost guarantees that her children will live in poverty—sometimes permanently.

So, why are parents going to prison, you ask? I have no statistics to make a definitive statement, but I do know that many of them are there for drug sales, meth manufacture, robbery, driving under the influence (several times, and sometimes with death of another driver as a result), violent, aggressive acts, and so many more. There are also parents in prison for so-called "white collar crimes"—stealing from the workplace, embezzlement, extortion, and more.

Parents, you have an obligation to your children to stay out of trouble with the law. You are obligated to take care of your kids and that does not include leaving them with others while you are serving time for some stupid act. You also owe it to them to be a good role model and that does not include incarceration. You must make good decisions, good choices, and good memories for your kids. They are depending on you—don't let them down.

ADULT SONS DEALING WITH PARENT ABANDONMENT

QUITE A LOT of research has been done on the affect a parent's abandonment has on the lives of their children both at the time of the leaving and on into those children's futures. There are few who enter adulthood unscathed emotionally if one or more of the parents has left the child and gone on with their lives.

At one time, I was faced with the affect that abandonment has on adult men. One man with whom I spoke is still angry that not only did his father leave him and his mom and siblings, but he never calls, never sends cards, never acknowledges a birthday or a graduation. The compounding of the neglect is magnified by the father's consistent refusal to have anything to do with his son. The anger this man feels is often manifest in his relationship with his mother and his siblings and he seems unable to keep from hurting them with his words and his actions. He may even have an alcohol problem—escaping the pain by attempting to drown it. He will regret his decisions, his *ruminating* over past and present hurt, and his inability to face truth.

I have found during my years as a teacher and counselor that the connection between father and son has a dynamic that is totally different from that of a father and daughter. If the son does something that disappoints his father, the guilt and pain are almost palpable in the dad. The father takes on the responsibility that does not belong to him—he blames himself if the son takes the wrong turn when it had very little to do with the father—it was just a bad choice on the part of the son.

Then there is the situation where the son decides to go live with the father with whom he has had little interaction since the divorce—leaving the mother wondering what she did wrong. I have told many a crying mother that it has less to do with her than it has to do with the son's curiosity about the father who has contributed the genes that make him who he is. He wants to know if he is anything like his biological father in personality or character—whether good or bad.

On Dr. Laura Schlesinger's radio show one of the callers was a man who could not get over his father's abandonment. "He told me that there are over a thousand minutes in a day, and that he didn't have even one for me . . . . it really hurt . . . . I am his only biological child. I feel that he must have a lot of anger toward me and I don't understand why." Dr. Laura asked how he thought the father could make a judgment about him when he did not even know him. She reminded him that he was assuming that there was something wrong with him and that is why he felt rejected. "That's a dangerous place to go because you end up undermining your own lifelong happiness because of a false assumption."

Then she made the ultimate comment that few people will face: "There are some men who can't love, who can't face responsibility, who are unbelievably self-centered, who rob, cheat, or murder—there are some bad men out there and one of them is your bio-dad. It's not personal, and when he looked into your face, what he saw was his bad self for abandoning you and he slapped you (with his words and actions). That is how we know that he is still a loser." (The caller seemed relieved to face this truth.)

That is the beginning of healing—when the abandoned child lays the blame on the parent and refuses to take on the guilt and shame for himself. As Dr. Laura said: "Not having your mommy and daddy in your life is a painful loss. However, blaming or punishing yourself for your parent's choices in life is an avoidable hurt (that you can do without)." What the adult child must do is move beyond that hurt and get on with his life—to break the dependency of trying to please a parent who could care less and to spend his energy loving the people who can give affection back.

Staying in the blaming/guilt/anger place prevents a person from being able to make and keep lasting, loving relationships. If you find yourself in that situation now, you must make a supreme effort to let go of your past, live in the present, and give yourself permission to be happy and healthy and productive for your sake, for the sake of the children in your life and for the sake of the loving relationship you can have.

If you are a parent who has left your children, unless you abused them (in which case you *need* to leave them alone), you should make the effort to make amends. They may reject you at first—you deserve it, but you, as the parent, should be the one to make the move that will heal some of the hurt you have caused. Do it soon.

"AT RISK" PARENTS AND KIDS

A S PARENTS, ONE of the labels we never want to have attached to our children is "at risk". Let me share with you the definition of "at risk" from a Master's college course I took (paraphrased): "At risk youth are children who are not likely to finish high school or who are apt to graduate considerably below potential. At-risk factors include chemical dependency, teenage pregnancy, poverty, disaffection with school and society, high-mobility families . . . and learning disabilities that do not qualify students for special education but still impede their progress."

Now, I realize that many of you have parented with all your heart and effort and yet this definition, or parts of it, apply to your child. The parents I wish to address are "at risk" parents. Those who never finished high school, those who can't control their drinking or drugging, those who have unstable marriages, those who are discontent with their lives and/or jobs, those who are so busy trying to succeed that they neglect the important people in their lives. All of these parents are labeled, whether they want to be or not—they are called "dysfunctional" because they are not successfully functioning as parents.

Well, you say, it is too late for me to finish high school, so what do you suggest? First, you will have more difficulty convincing your teen to stay in school even with the argument, "Look at what kind of job I have because I don't have an education!" Your child can only see that you are at least making a living—they only look at the present, not the future, so they really don't believe you. What you can do is, beginning early in your child's life (or now), emphasize that the importance is not education but the knowledge—of *knowing stuff.* My grandfather, who completed the eighth grade, loved learning, knowing, seeking for more. His grandchildren all have college degrees in education, engineering, finance, and medicine and two have Master's degrees. Why? We love to learn.

Don't interrogate your children about school. Instead, make them excited about what they are learning. Don't let them dwell on the few negatives; rather let them see the positive things that are happening to them as they learn every day. Encourage them during the summer to be curious. Get them from in front of the TV and take them to the library to find a book they will enjoy. Don't just answer their questions; let them search for the answers.

Also, why can't you go back to school? There are as many adults as there are young adults in GED courses everywhere. Take advantage of the one nearest you. Then, if you want, you can take the ACT and go to the nearest college for classes or to pursue a degree.

The second group of dysfunctional parents who drink and drug have little argument when your kids are doing the same. They are already "at risk" in two ways—genetically (your addictive genes) and because they see that you are able to carry on with life and still use. In fact, some of you even use these dangerous elements with your kids—talk about risky activity! Do you really want your precious child to have as much trouble ending the habit as you have? If not, STOP! For the sake of your child, love him more than the booze or the pot or the other drug, even prescription drugs.

The third group of parents are actually creating a dysfunctional situation because you spend your time arguing and fighting with the other adult in your home, or you are living with a person who is not married to you. No wonder your child is "at risk"! In fact, as soon as they can, in whatever way they can, they will get out of your house—even if it is by having a baby of their own. Spend the next few weeks finding a counselor who can listen to you and help you see your relationship with less emotion and with a more positive attitude. You must for the sake of your children.

The fourth group, who are miserable in their jobs and lives, are usually miserable to live with as well. They either come home angry and blaming, silent and sullen, or drunk/drugged. How could you be so selfish that you end up damaging the atmosphere in your home for everyone else? I realize that some of you, because of your lack of education or lack of skills, or because of the need for insurance or a future retirement fund are staying in a job that you don't like. So, what's the answer? As I've said earlier, "Why not go to school?" I know that takes you away from home, but you are causing frustration there anyway. So why not hone your skills, learn more, become a better worker so you can come home happy for a change.

However, don't be like the last group of parents who are so busy being successful that the very people they are working to provide for are being neglected. Your family doesn't need just food and shelter—they also need your attention, your concern, and your time. Come home earlier, eat with the family, and listen to your children. Be more of a parent than you are an employee.

Don't be an "at risk", dysfunctional parent. Be a giving, caring, involved parent. You don't have much time with your children during their formative years. While you have them at home, concentrate on your parenting skills so you will not have to live with a negative label attached to you or your children.

BEING COMMITTED, RESPONSIBLE ADULTS

D O YOU REMEMBER some of the positive ways one of your grandparents impacted you or your thinking? Did one of your parents teach you some values you have brought into your adulthood that have been invaluable? Now, the hard question: What and how are you teaching your own children or grandchildren, not necessarily by what you are saying, but more by how you are living?

One year in our Sunday School class, we looked at the word "Commitment", and we discovered that it has been through the commitment of those generations before us that we have become the adults we are today. So, let's look at several areas of our lives that may need a new level of commitment so we can positively affect the generations behind us.

First, our initial commitment should be to our marriage. Whether it is the first marriage or the second, we literally have to work hard to maintain one that is actually successful. A parent in my office one day was angry at her husband for the failure he has been as a loving husband and father. She wanted to blame him for the problems they were having with their teenager and with the home as a whole. During our meeting, she decided that the husband had many good qualities and that she should seek his help in the raising of their child.

Research shows that a divorce is a traumatic experience for the children no matter how much you prepare them or try to make the new home compatible and comfortable. Their grades will fall; they may experience depression; they will be angry; they will probably blame themselves for the divorce without saying anything to you; they may become self-destructive with drugs or alcohol or other alienated friends. So, what should you do? Try to really **work** on keeping the marriage together and going forward. But, you say, what if I am the only one working to make it successful? Answer: One of you is better that none of you. And for Heaven's sake, don't spend your time with your child belittling and fault-finding the other parent! Your child does not need to have to take sides against one of his parents—it may feel good to you to be that vindictive, but it does irreparable damage to your child.

Secondly, but not less important, we must be committed to our children who are still living at home and are going to school. I qualify this because there is a time when we must let go—when we become enablers if our child is grown but cannot keep a job or stay in school or maintain a successful adult life. There is a time in their lives when we must send them out on their own whether they want to go or not. It is the only way to "grow them up".

The (non-adult) children who are still in need of your home are in need of your unconditional commitment to their well being—physically, emotionally, socially, and spiritually. They should be the reason you put off being selfish and self-centered. They should be the reason you and your spouse spend time with each other deciding the best ways to discipline, to teach, to nurture. Children of all ages can tell if you as parents have not committed to support each other, especially regarding discipline. They sense a division and can manipulate both of you to the point where you are fussing at each other rather than taking action to assure the child that any misbehavior on his part will be dealt with swiftly. So spend some time working to be committed to each other and then to be committed to your children.

Thirdly, you need to be committed to a life of values and morals. As I said before, your life will be remembered by future generations—whether you are the alcoholic uncle everyone talked about while they felt sorry for your family, or the grandmother who told her grandchildren that you prayed for them every day no matter where they were or what they were doing. But you can't just SAY things that will be remembered. You must live a life that can be remembered with affection.

So many people I meet today are living their lives so selfishly that they are hurting the chances of their progeny being people of morality. There are the grandmothers who are living with a man because it is *convenient*, grandfathers who have left their spouses of many years to begin a family with someone younger and sillier, mothers who spend more time in bars than they do with their children, fathers who would rather be at the race track or casino or with their friends or at work than with the children they have fathered. What is WRONG with these people? Don't they see that they are being watched by the very people who were born with their genes? Why do they act surprised and disappointed when their son or daughter does exactly what they have done? Why is it impossible for them to see several years down the road and change their lives so that they CAN be a positive influence on their own flesh and blood?

The answer to all of the above questions is a lack of commitment to a marriage, to children, to moral living, and to yourself as a decent person. Could be we ALL need a lesson in being committed to that which is of value in the lives of those we love.

CYBER WARNINGS FOR THE WHOLE FAMILY

S HE DIDN'T KNOW that he was seeing someone else until she saw it posted on his Facebook. When she confronted him, he lied. When she said she had seen his picture with her on the internet and the words he had said about her and their relationship, he finally told her the truth. She is devastated. Not only has she been betrayed by someone she thought she could trust, but also the rest of the world is aware of their breakup and the reason.

She was a depressed widow; he knew she was vulnerable. They began a cyber-chat relationship that went on for many months and became more and more personal. He sent her some pictures of him (not really him) and asked for her pictures. Then he asked her for more intimate pictures and made suggestive remarks. She sent the pictures; he blackmailed her. She was *hooked* because she didn't want her innocent daughter to ever see the pictures. She lost a lot of money and is still afraid he will send the pictures to *everyone*.

He is a sophomore in college. Actually, he should be a junior, but he spent so much time in cyberspace that he didn't study, prepare papers, do research, or other required activities that guarantee some credit hours at the end of a class. He is worried that he will fall into the same pattern this year and will flunk out of college. What will he tell his parents? What will he tell his friends (the ones who are not having daily chats with him)? Actually, he may have more company than he realizes—there are many college-age students who are so hung up on the internet on various sites that they are ignoring their academic work.

She thought she was chatting with a new friend; however, she found later that she was actually writing the new *love interest* of her husband and this *friend* was milking her for information that would allow her to have an advantage in the relationship. It happened; the marriage is over; he is gone; and she feels partly to blame.

So what does this have to do with parents? Several things:

First, if you or your spouse is spending time on the internet and it has nothing to do with work, it could lead to problems in your marriage whether it is because he/she is *chatting* with someone of the opposite (or same) sex and could lead to unfaithfulness, or because he has become addicted to pornography, or because the person is neglecting the relationships in the home.

Second, if you are the parent of a college-age student, warn him about the fact that on-line social media of any kind (including texting) can become addictive and time consuming. College students don't have the time to be on the computer all of the time and still do the academic work that it takes to be a fairly good student. You don't have control over this situation, especially if he is away from home, but you can be concerned and at least give him the warning.

Third, if this can be a problem for adults, how much more serious can it be for a child or an adolescent? No one in your home should have absolute access to the computer if he is still in high school or lower. Too many kids have had great difficulty because of something they have *posted*: from innocently *talking* to a pedophile, to making "slam" remarks about another student, to becoming involved in an abusive relationship in which they must account for every minute spent away from that person, to attaining access to pornographic sites and becoming addicted to that filth. There are just too many *red flags* in relation to internet use for you to be negligent in monitoring what is being seen or read or written on it at all times.

Parenting takes your time and your effort and you too don't have the privilege of spending inordinate amounts of time on the computer whether the kids are asleep or not. Too many of you have complained to me about the time you spend on it, but you seem unable to stay away from it. Like all addictions, it takes a lot of willpower, a lot of self-control, and a willingness to admit that you have other responsibilities that you are neglecting because of it. Take control of your life and of the time you and/ or your child spends on it. You will be glad you did.

DEALING WITH THE PAST TO HEAL THE PRESENT

EACH OF US is impacted by our childhood—whether it was pleasant, secure, and full of warm memories or was one of unhappy events, poor relationships, even trauma. However, too many people spend their adult lives blaming their dissatisfaction with who they are, with their failures, and with their addictions on their parents.

As Dr. Laura Schlessinger said on one of her radio shows, (paraphrased) "Your life may be compounded with the pain of 'yesterday' mixed with the disappointments and frustrations of 'today'". Many people try to survive each day using alcohol, work, promiscuity, drugs, and other compulsive behaviors to drown out the inner noise of hurt, anger, and despair. At some point, though, it has to become clear that these attempts to avoid pain paradoxically bring even more pain and problems.

"Those who have successfully overcome victimhood force themselves in directions that they know are healthy, in spite of tremendous doubts and fears that pull them back.

I don't believe anyone does life well alone; I believe you lose your humanity by isolating yourself. It is up to you to reach out . . . . You should neither be satisfied with being a victim, nor with being a survivor. You should aim to be a conqueror." (Dr. Laura)

As one of her listeners said, "Too many people blame their disappointments with their lives on their parents and the childhood they had. Please, that was ages ago. Let it go and move on."

One of my friend's sons was being treated for drug addiction and during treatment was told to tell his parents how he felt about his childhood. He proceeded to unload every real and imagined pain he felt that they had inflicted on him. He even blamed his brother because, during a time of convalescence after a skiing accident in which the brother was almost paralyzed, the parents spent "too much time" at a hospital and neglected him.

The hurt the *therapeutic confession* caused his parents was almost too painful to bear, and there was no actual basis for it! He had been given many opportunities to pursue his interests in sports, music, academics, in everything—and his parents were always there to support him. He was loved, cared for, driven to all events, and cheered on by both of them. Yet his response was to give them all the blame for his own foolish choices.

There <u>are</u> those, however, who have been injured by words, by neglect, by physical abuse, by sexual abuse, or by abandonment, and, as Dr. Laura says, "I believe that many people don't even realize that their childhood history has impacted their adult thought and behavioral patterns in unproductive ways. They don't realize that some of their less pleasant or destructive adult reactions are reflexive responses forged by their unfortunate youth. They don't know that much of their adult life has been dedicated to repeating ugly childhood dynamics in an attempt to repair deep childhood hurts and longings."

What an adult in this category must do is find help in evaluating his or her adult responses that are reflex reactions to a traumatic childhood. It may take professional help; it may take group therapy; it may take a close self-examination of the poor choices you are making that may be a result of your years as a child.

The principle reason you must do something about it is that you may be doing the very same things to your own children and not even know why. You may find it difficult to love them, to care for them properly, to make them a priority rather than someone or something else in your life. You may have wondered why you become so angry and out of control and have forgotten that you were treated the same way as a child. You may have a residual reason for your drinking/drugging/or other addiction problem. However, unless you ask for help with these issues, it may never come and the people you will be cheating will be your children and yourself.

Don't wait too long to get help. You may think that you have a long time to change, but time may be running out, and you just don't know it.

You should be like the person described by Dr. Laura in this sentence: "There is an extraordinary quality of spirit that leads one to aspire to conquering rather than surviving. I hope you discover that spirit in yourself." (paraphrased)

HELPING OUR CHILDREN FIND THEMSELVES

I HAD BEEN STUDYING psychology again and had rediscovered a concept that has been lost during the past several decades. When many of us were in our late teens and early twenties, we were urged to discover the answers to some very important questions, especially two: "Who am I?" and "What is my purpose in life?"

As a young adult, I spent a lot of time making sure I knew exactly who I was in relation to family, to life itself, and to the God who created me. I also wanted to make sure that I knew my purpose in life. Those who have done at least that much self-analysis and soul searching spend little time in their adult lives wondering if they made the right choices in a spouse, a career, a place to live, and a relationship with God.

What happens to the adults and teens who never go through this process? First, most of them are consistently dissatisfied with their lives. They jump from job to job, spouse to spouse, place to place. It is hard for them to be really committed to one particular thing because they are not even committed to themselves. They have the idea that if they could just make more money and buy more things, they would be happy, never realizing that happiness comes from within and has nothing to do with possessions or position.

Secondly, they are usually untrustworthy. After all, they don't really trust themselves or their own life decisions, so it is difficult for them to trust others or to be trusted. This is also why it is hard for them to be truly committed to a marriage or even to the children they bring into the world.

Thirdly, most of the young adults and adults with this problem have a nagging feeling their lives are out of control, and, because of that, they are easily frustrated, easily angered, and they give up more readily on themselves and on what they are doing at the time. They are quite susceptible to gambling addiction, get-rich-quick schemes, day trading, or any method of getting money with no effort. They have little self-confidence and little hope that they can affect their lives for the better except for the delusions of *striking it rich*.

Another problem people have who do not know themselves is that they are often depressed. The unhappiness they feel, the inability to be able to commit to a particular person or decision, the financial obligations they incur from switching jobs and buying *things* all keep them in a state of turmoil. They may lean on alcohol or drugs or compulsions to relieve the depressions and/or the tension, but that only compounds the problem. The depression gives them a sense of being alone and vulnerable; it can facilitate poorly made choices, and it adds to the feeling of being out of control.

So, what does this have to do with parenting? Well, who DOES ask the teen or young adult to figure out who he is and what his purpose is in life?

I am aware of several young men in their twenties who are in this very dilemma. They have delusions of getting better jobs, but they are not willing to be committed to the job they have now so they can work up to a higher level; they floundered in college as most youth do who have no idea what they want in life and how they should go about it; some of them think a good time is to party, drink or do drugs, but they are unwilling to see what they are doing to their lives and futures; they may love the girl they are dating but can't bring themselves to marry her; their depression is exhibited in anger toward their parents, their girlfriends, or even a boss who has the audacity to tell him what to do (so they just quit—the "I'll show him!" mentality).

When your child has reached this age, you have few options, but I can suggest two. One, see if he will go for personal counseling—someone who can help him find himself. Second, suggest career counseling—the professionals who do this type of work can give a battery of tests to help determine his interests, aptitudes, abilities and personality and can direct him toward a career that fits who he is.

If your child is younger but has matured enough to do some soul-searching, ask him to write down who he is—not just as your child, but beyond that to a deeper meaning of "self". Then ask him the second question about his purpose here on Earth. Even if he doesn't want to share his findings with you, at least you have caused him to search himself and may have helped him to avoid some of the problems mentioned above.

"To every man there is a season and a purpose under God's Heaven." (Ecclesiastes 3:1 KJV) Part of our responsibility as parents is to help our young see their purpose so they can have happiness in life, and we can all breathe easier when they have found it.

Jan Knight

IMPORTANT INFORMATION ON ALCOHOLISM

WHETHER IT IS alcohol or pot or other substance, ingesting, shooting, or snorting a foreign substance, liquid or pill or tobacco that is known for its power to alter thinking, reaction, speech, habits or other life choices, can be destructive to ones' future, family and finances. I received some very good information on alcohol abuse from St. Dominic Hospital. Below are some interesting facts you may need to know.

Alcoholism is a disease characterized by a craving for drink. "An alcoholic will continue to drink despite serious family, health, or legal problems." It is chronic, which means that it can last a person's lifetime; it usually follows a predictable course which usually ends in the destruction of the family, loss of physical health, loss of self-worth.

Contributions to becoming an alcoholic include family history: (Is there is an alcoholic in your blood lines? Then there is an increased probability that you will have a drinking problem.), having friends who drink, availability of alcohol, not "seeing anything wrong with it", thinking it makes one cuter, smarter, funnier (a delusion—the humor is in how stupid you act).

Alcoholism can be treated, but it cannot be cured. "Most alcoholics need help to recover from their disease, and treatment programs use both counseling and medications to help a person stop drinking." There are also medications that can help one withdraw from alcohol dependency by reducing the craving or by making the person feel nauseated if alcohol is drunk. However, there is no med that will actually cure alcoholism. Research does show that the longer the alcoholic stays sober and refrains from drinking at all, the more likely he will overcome the addiction and remain sober. To guard against a relapse, an alcoholic must continue to avoid all alcoholic beverages.

So how drunk are you? "Simply defined; blood alcohol content (BAC) is the concentration of alcohol in one's blood, measured as a percentage." A BAC of 0.08 percent means 1 gram per 1,250 milliliters in a person's blood is alcohol. In most states, that constitutes legal intoxication whether a person has drunk 1.5 ounces of 80-proof liquor, 12 ounces of beer, four to five ounces of wine, or four ounces of liqueur. However, BAC is also dependent on individual as well as gender differentiation, on how much the person drank in a specific period of time, on whether the person has eaten recently, and on how much body fat the person has.

Alcohol affects virtually every nerve cell in the brain. It slows down information processing so it becomes tougher for the drinker to think clearly; it affects balance, making it difficult to walk a straight line. It alters levels of the brain chemicals called neurotransmitters, which relay signals controlling behavior, reaction time, thought and emotion.

The most destructive things a family can do to the alcoholic is to *cover up the problem:* You must stop making excuses and preventing him/ her from suffering the consequences of his addition or he will never know how he is affecting others and himself. Eventually, he must be confronted with the fact that his problem is damaging the people around him and that it may lead to his death or to the death of someone on the same road he is traveling. Until he faces his addiction, he will never seek help.

I fully support tougher laws on drunk driving. My sister-in-law was killed by a drunk under-aged driver. The killer has spent some time in jail, but will some day be free to live his life. My sister-in-law's grandchildren and children and friends will never be free of the pain of her loss. Until judges face life without a family member because of the choice of a person who has had too much to drink, they may remain too forgiving and too sympathetic, and, consequently, more people will die because of this terrible addiction.

Parents, if you have a drinking problem, try to stay sober enough to see what it is doing to your children. No person in the family is unaffected by the drinking of a parent, and the example you are setting may come back in years to haunt you. If one of your children has a drinking problem, don't hide your head in the sand; instead, get help for that child before you no longer have the right to seek professional help for him/her and he goes out into the world to destroy his life and possibly that of his family as well as that of an innocent person.

OVERCOMING A BAD CHILDHOOD TO BECOME A GOOD PARENT

THROUGH THE WORK that I did as a counselor, I saw many parents who made really bad and selfish choices that negatively influenced their families. Even though I didn't know anything about their childhoods, research indicates that many of those choices are the result of issues from their own childhood that have yet to be resolved, and that if they aren't settled, their childhood can do damage to their own children. Most of these adults are not aware of why they are living unproductive, poor-choice-ridden hours of every day.

One of the more devastating childhood issues is that of never having pleased the parent which creates a feeling of failure, of being inadequate and disappointing which outlives even that parent. Consequently, the adult consistently makes poor choices in people, in decisions, in attitudes because they are bearing the burden of never having been what the parent wanted. In addition, they often carry that same *displeased* attitude into their relationship with their children, who, unless they can break the cycle, carry it on into their parenting.

Another childhood issue that is difficult to handle in adulthood is that of being neglected or abandoned. The adult reaction can be to avoid trusting anyone, whether it is a spouse or even their children. That feeling and attitude of distrust is a lonely, sad way of living, and it cheats the family members of having a warm, loving, adult/parent in the home. On the other hand, some adults who were neglected in childhood keep looking for that "mother or father" figure who gives them security and love, and, therefore, they leap from one sorry relationship to another without finding it. The damage this reaction does to the children is evident: too many adults in their lives who don't really belong, who don't care for them, who are temporary. Thus they also experience neglect and abandonment and carry the problem into their adulthood as well.

Much of the same dynamic is true of the abused child who grows into adulthood thinking everyone is a predator and refuses to trust or to allow closeness, therefore losing a part of life that is rewarding and comforting. It is also often difficult for them to give warmth and comfort to their children.

There are many more issues that could be discussed here. However, it is best to begin to find a suitable solution to the adult problems brought on by a damaging childhood so that we don't, in turn, damage the childhoods of our own children.

On Dr. Schlessinger's radio show, many of her responders to this problem said that they realized that they were carrying emotional burdens that were negatively influencing their lives and their ability to parent successfully. However, rather than "wallow in their misery", they have chosen to take control of their emotions, their memories, their attitudes, and their goals and have made a conscious effort to refuse to allow the past to dominate their present or their futures. One said it this way, "I surrendered myself to the acceptance of my own responsibility for the conditions of my present life". They have also discovered that to hang on to the past is to stay there. It is only in letting go of the past and its ugliness that we can move on and forward. "What happened to me in my childhood was not my fault. How I handle it is my responsibility."

And does having overcome a difficult childhood make you a stronger person if you can move on? "When you come from a bad childhood, I think it makes you less sympathetic for anyone who uses it as a crutch for every poor decision they have made with their lives. I decided to make a good life for myself. I hung on that promise. I made it happen—and I don't look back". Does that take effort? Yes. Does it take fortitude? Yes. Is it worth it to you and to your children? Oh, my Yes!

RESEARCH REGARDING
ELECTRONIC USAGE FOR ALL OF US

W E SHARED A table with a nice, average family one night at a Japanese restaurant. The teenage son was appropriately bored and embarrassed that he was with his family, especially since there were two cute teenage girls at the next table. The dad had to answer his blackberry at least once. The mother was the perfect hostess as she tried to engage each member of her family. The teenage girl was oblivious to everything—from the exertion of the chef to engage her attention while he flipped shrimp, to the efforts of the mother, to the rest of the people around her. She was texting the entire time, or at least until her food was placed on her plate.

The next weekend we ate at a Mexican restaurant. I had watched the teenage couple come in. He was tall and awkward; she was small and short. They obviously had not been dating long and he was making every effort to be a good date. Sometime during their meal, she got a text, and rather than ignore it for the time, she sat and answered it while he sat and became more uncomfortable, looking around to see if others were watching them, staring at her, messing with his napkin—anything to try and make up for the fact that the text message was more important than being with him at the time.

These examples are just a few that show several negatives for the present "technological over-load", as the media is calling it. People today are becoming less and less social and less able to talk to others face to face because it is 1. Becoming less important to them, and 2. They are losing the practice it takes to be personally socially engaged. The loss of these elements of being a human will begin to have a serious impact on the young people of today because they will not be able to interview successfully for jobs; they will be less able to be a part of a business setting where many things are handled face to face; they will have difficulty conversing in a personal relationship, especially if their phone lets them know that they have a message or if they have Facebook where they can handle relationships without actually being with people.

Then there are the students who pride themselves on their skill at "multi-tasking", i.e. doing Facebook, using the internet, texting, talking, studying, attending classes, and so on who are actually not doing well academically. It is becoming apparent that they are doing too much and that since they cannot concentrate on just one thing, they are not doing any of it well. One college student I spoke with said that he was so obsessed with being in contact on Facebook that he could not concentrate on his classes and lectures and that his grades were suffering.

Then there are those who are so busy being technical that they are missing the important aspects of life, even their families. Sally Lee, the Editor-in-Chief of *LADIES' HOME JOURNAL*, said in her editorial in the March 2010 edition, "I have always considered myself the Queen of Multitasking. I can help my kids with their homework and make dinner at the same time. If I'm standing in line at the supermarket, I compose little to-do lists (now people are listing on their Blackberries or iPhones). Recently I managed to update my Facebook page while lying flat on my back at the doctor's office getting physical therapy. I congratulate myself for stuffing every single moment of every single day with important and productive tasks. But lately things have gotten a little crazy. The first thing I do when I wake up each morning is reach for my iPhone to check e-mail. I've started putting time limits on everything—even the fun stuff. When my daughter asked me to play a board game, I said 'Okay, you've got ten minutes". I rush through my 9-year-old's bedtime story, and lately I just can't afford the time to listen to my husband telling me about his day because I have so many things to do . . . . I'm so busy checking things off my lists that I'm barely present in my own life. Human contact, family time, fun—I've sacrificed them all to efficiency." She concludes that her real life (the one that really matters) consists of the little things her children do and the time with her husband and that they deserve her full attention.

Are you or your children living in the surreal world of electronics to the detriment of human contact and relationships? As an article in the same magazine says, "Technology is great for staying in touch with far-away loved ones. But for the near and dear who are physically near? Be with them when you can." Being on the internet can become addictive, and as a parent, you must never let anything be more important than your children or your spouse. In addition, it is your responsibility to limit the time your child spends on anything electronic. Take heed to the warnings being presented.

TEACH YOUR CHILDREN WELL,
PARENTS AND TEACHERS

SCHOOL USUALLY BEGINS in August or September each year and parents are justly concerned about the teachers their children will have. Will they be competent in the subject they teach? Will they be fair in their grading and evaluating? Will they be good moral examples for the students in their classrooms and on their teams?

We don't want our kids in the classroom with the history teacher who taught that the United States began World War II. We don't want to send our seniors on an outing with a teacher who ends up drunk and has to be taken home by the students. We don't want them exposed to an immoral lifestyle like the politicians who flaunt their sex lives in front of everyone in the nation and in the cities. We don't want a teacher like the mayor in a nearby city who is more concerned about his own self-importance than the people (students) who are supposed to trust him.

What we want, instead, are teachers who are, like us, good examples of what a responsible adult is like and how he conducts his life.

I found some quotes regarding how we as parents and the teachers who are in the schools should act:

"Be such a man, and live such a life, that if every man were such as you, and every life a life like yours, this earth would be God's Paradise" (Phillip Brooks) because our families and our students are watching.

"Example is the school of humankind, and they will learn at no other." (E. Burke)

"Human models are more vivid and more persuasive than explicit moral commandments." (Daniel J. Boorstin) In other words, our children can read the Ten Commandments in Exodus, but if they never see adults following them, they will never learn them or how to apply them to their lives.

"Not only should we teach values, but we should live them. A sermon is better lived than preached." (J.C. Watts) In that same vein, the next is a quote I memorized as a teen, "I'd rather see a sermon than hear one any day; I'd rather one should walk with me than merely show the way." (Edgar A. Guest)

"Nothing speaks louder or more powerfully than a life of integrity." (Charles Swindoll)

"Children have more need of models than critics". (Joseph Joubert)

What parent would dare to criticize a child who lies if his own life and his actions are a lie? What parent would criticize a student who is caught in immorality and yet would defend a politician who betrays his marriage vows, has children out of wedlock, is charged with driving under the influence, or other ridiculous actions that are embarrassing to most adults in society?

Instead, we should use the immorality of people in those situations, yes, even pop stars and movie stars, as a "teaching opportunity" to emphasize that their lifestyle will only bring them unhappiness and scrutiny and criticism that they could have avoided if they had made better decisions.

Warn your children that idolizing adults who are so-called "celebrities" will give them a *skewed* viewpoint of life because most of those people feel that they are above any law, especially the law of moral goodness. Let them know, that true happiness comes when a person lives a life that is a standard that can be followed by others and that will not lead them in the wrong direction.

However, it all comes down to how <u>you</u> are living in front of them at home. If they see you as moral and good and kind, they will eventually follow your lead rather than that of strangers. It is your *model* that should be above reproach. You cannot expect them to be so different from you if they see you live *badly* every day. As James Dobson says it: "It is desirable that children be kind, appreciative and pleasant. Those qualities should be taught and not hoped for." Teach your children well.

WHAT WILL THEY SNIFF NEXT?

W HEN I WAS a pre-teen living in Memphis, Tennessee, several other
kids and I were waiting for our parents to pick us up after a church
function. Two of the boys wanted to show us what fun it was to *sniff* the
exhaust coming out of the back of the car that was idling at the curb. One
boy, after sniffing, wandered away with glazed eyes and faltering steps
and lay down on the cold ground near the base of the church wall. The
other one took his turn and, after a few minutes, passed out in the gutter
behind the car. Frightened, we ran into the church for an adult who, after
examining him, called for an ambulance. Later, when I asked about him,
he was still in the hospital and was still unconscious.

Later in my life, my Mom was warned, when she bought airplane glue
for my brother's extensive hobby of constructing model airplanes, of the
potential danger of sniffing glue. Later, as a new teacher, we were told not
to allow our students to have access to the White Out or other such product
because the kids were sniffing the contents and achieving a high. Then
came paint thinner, magic markers, aerosol sprays, and on ad nauseam.

Of course, along with the high always came an excruciating headache,
often nausea, and the promise from the medical field that the *fun* could be
causing permanent brain damage. Parents were increasingly alarmed and
tried to keep the kids from purchasing the items that could do so much
harm, but, as has occurred throughout history, if the kids wanted to do
harm to themselves, they could find a way.

Naturally, their thought was that, if anyone was going to be damaged
by sniffing, it wouldn't harm them—couldn't be them—shouldn't be them.
Their illusion that what could cause harm to someone else but not them is
a typical non-reality that goes with the territory of being a kid, a teen, or a
foolish young adult, especially one who is determined to ingest some kind
of drug or alcohol no matter what they've been told or have read. Then,
when it is too late, the damage done is often irreversible, and they must live
with what they chose to do to themselves for the reminder of their lives.

Enter a new method of getting high—bath salts. I'm sure you have
seen the press and the warnings on TV news programs. I researched

some information on the internet about sniffing bath salts and learned three things: first, there are several places on the internet to order this hallucinogen; second, the most prevalent argument against the drug is that if the nation would legalize marijuana (pot), then kids would not have to use something like this to get a high (what stupidity); third, I learned what the effects are.

The principle effect is not necessarily a high, but it does cause dependency (addiction). One user said that he and his friends had stayed up for days on it (presumably without sleep). The most insidious effect is psychological depression. One newspaper headline said that a young man in St. Tammany Parish (Louisiana) had committed suicide after sustained use. Now, because of so many kids in that state who have been damaged by sniffing bath salts, the governor of Louisiana has requested that their Legislature declare the two main ingredients be made illegal. Those chemical ingredients are Mephadrone and methylenediozypyrovalerone or MDPV.

Other symptoms of sniffing bath salts, two names of which are *Dusted* and *Infinity* (there are more), are paranoia, delusions, high blood pressure, chest pain and hostility. In fact, research, though new at this time, is showing that long-term use can cause death from heart disease.

So, what can parents do to prevent bath-salt sniffing or sniffing of anything else that could cause such irreparable damage to their children?

First, of course, talk to your kids. They may already know more about it than you do, but at least you have the information given here to warn them about the dangers. Secondly, look for items in their rooms or even in their lockers that could be used to get a high. Don't hesitate to confront them, and don't ask them what the item is for—assume the worst. They are masters at masking the use or the symptoms or both. So forbid the item to be in their possession or there will be dire consequences. Third, talk to the parents of their friends to ascertain whether they are seeing any evidence of the items or the use. Even some of their "straight" friends may talk to you about the use if you ask them because they may also be concerned about your child. Fourth, be alert, be aware, be smart, and be informed. The life and future health of your child may depend on how much you know and how alert you are about their activities.

CHAPTER TEN

FINALLY,
PARENTING 101

AN ATTITUDE OF GRATITUDE

WE CELEBRATE THANKSGIVING as an American holiday which began when the Native Americans shared their bounty with the European settlers of this country. Since that time, we have set aside a day, not just to eat and be with family, but also to take the time to be grateful.

Some of you may find it very difficult to be grateful. Like the single mother who was talking to a man about God and finally ended the conversation by saying, "God has never done anything for me, so I don't want anything to do with Him". I wonder if she realizes how God really has blessed her despite some very poor choices she has made in her life. God, in turn, probably wonders why she never makes an attempt to be grateful for anything and why she can only find the negative in her circumstances.

Rather than *grumping* about what you don't have or complaining about your "lot in life", begin today to make a list of your blessings—however simple. In fact, some of the greatest blessings are those that probably cost you nothing. So, let's begin: each day for five days write down five things for which you are grateful. Then on Thanksgiving Day, read the list to yourself as you sit quietly or, if you feel like it, read it aloud to the people with whom you share that day.

To get you started, let me make a few suggestions of *gifts* we all have that costs us nothing or little at all: A sunrise—free on not-over-cast days for all who want to experience it; a sunset—free and available to all who take the time to notice; hugs—I get these mostly at church; family—parents, spouse if you have one, siblings if you still have that relationship and children even if they don't like your turkey and dressing. (This blessing does, in fact, cost you emotionally and financially, but it is worth it); the colors of fall leaves—free but you must slow down and spend some time taking notice of them; the devotion of a dog—free except for food, water, and yearly shots; freedom—hasn't cost me, but it has cost and is costing others who are fighting to maintain our American freedom; friendship—you are fortunate indeed, if there is one special friend in your life on whom you can depend.

Your problem with your list may be that you want to list all of the things you have bought or been given—the superficial things that add no intrinsic value to your life. If these make up your list, then you may have already noticed that your children are singularly ungrateful and whiney. Maybe they have learned it from you, and more than likely they are already living lives that are selfish, shallow, and unsatisfying. They see no value in being generous with their time or their money because they live for what they can have and can accumulate—just like you always have.

This could be the time when you become more aware of what you do have that is of lasting value and therefore become the example of living a life of gratitude for your children. For an assignment, write a note to a teacher, a pastor, a nurse, or someone who has been an inspiration in your life. This will take a few minutes of your time and possibly a stamp, but the feeling you will receive will be worth it—you will be giving a gift of gratitude.

God has been generous to all of us in this Country even if we are at present facing difficult economic times. Use the next few days to become a more grateful person—you are the one who will benefit.

AVOIDING THE PLAGUE OF GREED

H AVE YOU BEEN watching people as they shop lately? Except for those who may have lost their jobs, it appears that we actually are not in a time of economic stress and that money is vastly abundant and available. Rather than being less expensive, toys and clothes cost even more than they did the previous year and shoppers are paying for them without restraint.

It is obvious that we still have the financial mentality in this country that has been pervasive for too many years: "We are a nation that believes in having it all. In 1950, American families owned one car and saved for a second. In 2000, nearly 1 in 5 families owned three cars or more. Americans shell out more for garbage bags than 90 of the world's 210 countries spend for everything. Indeed, America has doubled the number of shopping malls compared to high schools." (Linda Kuhlman, "Our Consuming Interest," *U.S. News & World Report,* June 28-July 5, 2004. 59.) It is probably even worse now.

Max Lucado adds in *Cure for the Common Life,* "Our obsession with stuff carries a hefty price tag. The average American family devotes a full one-fourth of its spendable income to outstanding debts (Larry Burkett in *Cure*). We spend 110 percent of our disposable income trying to manage debt. We no longer measure ourselves against the Joneses but against the star on the screen." In fact, celebrities have become our guides in material excess, in moral standards, in religious values, in so many ways that American society is corrupting itself from within and spending itself into oblivion.

The root of all of this is a type of greed. "Greed comes in many forms", according to Lucado—(There is) "Greed for approval, Greed for applause, Greed for status, Greed for the best office, the fastest car, the (most opulence). Greed has a growling stomach." It is seldom satisfied—we always want more. So, not only are we teaching our children to be greedy, insatiable *grabbers* but also we will find that we are so much in debt that our lives will crumble and leave us devastated. Our marital arguments will consistently be fixed on money—the lack of it, the way one of us spends it, the way one of us wants to hold on to some of it. It is a never ending merry-go-round of greedy abuse, and, until we face what it is doing to us, it will never stop.

One the other hand, there are the parents who are trying to teach their children how to think for themselves and to value life more than material things. I met a mother who gave her two daughters a project (as a part of home schooling) of beginning a business of their own, including the bookkeeping, the purchasing, and the marketing. They sell a brand of coffee that they purchase in a small town in Mississippi and when I met them, they were selling at a Holiday Bazaar. What a valuable lesson for kids to know and experience!

We just hired three teenagers to paint a house we own. They are careful, work hard, clean up after their day, and are making plans to use the money to buy car insurance and other necessities their parents are leaving up to them rather than footing the bill for everything. They are learning to save for future purchases rather than having everything given to them.

During my years as a faculty member in high school, I watched kids work during the week, study when they could, and still make very good grades. Most of those went on to college. It was the ones who were allowed to become lazy and who spent their time playing video games and hanging out who principally didn't go to school and who were working menial jobs years later.

So what are you teaching your children by the way you are spending and saving? Do they expect *more and more* because you will *sacrifice* and make sure they have it? *Sacrifice* can include your marriage, your health, your mental stress, your fear of what you will owe when you get your credit card the next month. If that is true, what will you be like when it all comes crashing down? Can you have the patience and the concern for your children that they deserve while still worrying over the bills you owe?

If you are already doing it *wrong*, take something back. If you are making the effort to spend carefully, then good for you. Take the next week to bake something to replace something you were planning to buy; take a friend out for coffee rather than spending on something she may not want; give someone an IOU for babysitting one night. Do something creative rather than expensive. You will enjoy life more and in the coming months you will have much less stress which will give you a better chance of being a better parent—that should be what it is all about anyway.

THE DIFFERENCE BETWEEN *JOY* AND *HAPPINESS*

ONE SUNDAY AS I was teaching a Sunday school lesson, I made some comparisons between *happiness* and *joy*. Happiness has to do with transient things that seldom last or have lasting value.

If you receive something that you "have always wanted", receiving it gives happiness. I had "always wanted" a bicycle—a big-girl bike that could be ridden like the wind and would be mine alone. I could ride it around the block, be with my friends, and escape from my little brother—oh the freedom! I really did enjoy that bike and loved the feeling of the wind in my hair as I raced around on it. It made me *happy* to ride with speed and skill. That happiness lasted until I discovered that speed and wind in my hair could be achieved with—a horse! That would make me really happy. It took several years to get the horse, and even then, I had to break and train it myself. However, it gave me happiness to ride and to work with such a noble animal. Do I still have any of the horses I have owned? No. There comes a time in life when there are different interests and likes that make a person happy. Oh, sure, I have a convertible that whips my hair around as I drive, and it makes me happy, but it lasts for a while and then I have to park it.

See? Things can make us happy "for a season". Even people can make us happy for a while. We are happy when we are with a certain person and we feel that the giddy, happy feeling will last forever. Then we find that the person is, after all, human, and has failings and foibles that we didn't see at first. If we have based our happiness in life on that person and that relationship, then, when we find that he/she is not quite what we had assumed, we are unhappy, and there appears nothing that will alleviate the disappointment we feel.

Not even money can truly make us happy. Some of the unhappiest people I know have had the most money and all that it can buy. In fact, some of those people have found that they are miserable because their entire existence has been based on the acquiring of and spending of money. They have told me that there is still a huge void in their lives and that there is never enough money to satisfy them

Joy, on the other hand, comes from deep within us. It is the result of being content with who we are and what we have. I have seen it among the old and, yes, I have seen it among the young. It can be ours when we learn to sit quietly by ourselves without technological disruption or the need to have another person with us. It comes at the end of a day in which we have done work that we find fulfilling and satisfying because we took the time to prepare for it with education or other training and we have learned to work hard and smart. We find it in the smiles and laughter of our children and know that we are the reasons they are content and secure. We find it in the friends we have made and who are a vital part of our lives.

Notice that there was not the first material item in the previous list—no big-screen TV's, no new cars, no new iPods or other of the latest gadgets, nothing that costs.

The personal satisfaction and peace that you can have when you begin to wean yourself from the *things* in your life will make you a better person, a better parent, a better spouse.

Begin now to find that joy of life and leave the need for materialistic goods behind.

SPRING INSPIRES A NEWNESS IN ALL OF US

I SN'T SPRING WONDERFUL? Everyone I meet after winter is so thankful that the long cold spell is over and that spring has come with its beauty and its promise of newness, of rebirth, of hope. The first thing to bloom in my garden is the Lenten rose which begins to flower in February. Then the buttercups lift their pretty yellow heads; the forsythia blooms out in yellow; the saucer magnolia lends its lavender/purple beauty to the yard; and then the spirea begins to turn white against the greening lawn.

Even trees at the local hospital begin blooming—the Japanese magnolia and the cherries compete for attention, and off in the woods the white blooms of Bradford pears can be seen among the pines and the hardwoods.

If you are an outdoor-sort-of person, each day presents something new to see and enjoy, and even those of us who work in flower gardens and yards are excited about what we can contribute to that beauty.

This time of year is also when your grandmothers began spring cleaning: the rugs were taken out and hanged to beat out the dust, the bed linens were hung out to absorb the new spring-air freshness, the base boards were washed, the cabinets were cleaned, and the spiders had to find somewhere else to live for the time being. It is and has been the time for making things better, for giving a freshness to all that is around us.

So what about us? Do we need to look at our own lives and find something that should be made new? I don't mean that, like so many young married people, you should leave your spouse and children and find someone who makes you feel younger and more spring-like? (The feeling doesn't last forever, by the way. Winter eventually comes!).

What I do mean is that we may need to evaluate ourselves as spouses and parents and grandparents and see if there is a different way we could handle ourselves that would cause others to look forward to being with us and a way we could contribute to their lives.

I recently read an article about a lady who gave herself a challenge to be less caustic with the public and say something nice instead. She did it for seven days and was amazed at the positive result. People went out of their way to help her and to serve her. She, in return was surprised at the way she felt after she had gone out of her way to respond to people even if she had been treated badly by them and then had watched the responsive

313

smile. She didn't mention whether she had used the same experiment on members of her family, but I'm sure it works even better there.

Use the Spring time of the year and any other time to begin a newness in you. Let the beauty of each season permeate your being and refuse to allow yourself to respond negatively to immature teens, to demanding children, to an insensitive spouse. Rather than take them seriously, allow yourself to slow down and to measure your response to the situation. Recognize that the teen is irresponsible because of his immaturity and his lack of self-confidence. Don't allow him to be disrespectful, but use the situation as a learning time. Maybe he too would love to respond to others in a more positive way and could use your example as a stepping-stone to that end.

Children can get on your last nerve after you have worked all day (or night) when they demand attention and ask for things they don't need. However, just as you are grateful for the sunshine and warmth after a long winter, be grateful that you have children who are a part of your life and spend quality time with them no matter how tired or stressed you are.

Spouses are a different challenge. However, many times your response to them will make their reaction to you far more appealing. We choose how we react, not how someone treats us, and it is that reaction that can make life miserable or happy. We can avoid the *snowball affect* that happens to too many marriages. Decide today that this person you married can be treated well and appreciated and loved and that time together can be a blessing that can go on for many more years if we care enough about that person to be kind, thoughtful, and caring.

For some, there may be an empty place that was put there when you were created—a place that only a relationship with the Creator can fill. Is that why I love His creation so much, because I have personal contact with Him? He can make something new even after we have made a mess of things. I love His promise in Revelation 21:05, "Behold, I make everything new".

Yes!!!

TEACHING THE UNSELFISHNESS OF GIVING

I AM AMAZED AT the generosity of people , and I am concerned that we as parents are not teaching our children to be giving and generous.

I found this quote in the little Christmas book *The Christmas Promise* by Donna VanLiere: "From what we get, we can make a living; what we give, however, makes a life." (Arthur Ashe) I find that the people who handed me cash or provided food for the little family we had been helping at our school have a radiance that can only be attributed to the willingness to give and the joy giving brings.

One lady called me to ask if the need was "for real", and I understood her reticence. Too many people *use* the generosity of others to *milk the system*. So I too am careful where I give my time and effort. I want to know that there is a genuine need and that what I provide will be of real assistance to the family. The family we helped has that need and people are giving.

When I talked to one of the coordinators of the giving process, she said that a businessman in the area had given them a much-needed couch; her family had an extra twin bed and sheets and the oldest boy benefited from that gift; many had given so that a rental deposit on a house could be made; some of the money received would go for tires for the only car they have so the parent can be taken to chemo treatments; and the cans of food and other provisions will allow them to have meals for the rest of the month. Some church members are going to provide for them through Angel Food ministries for several months to come.

How are you teaching your children to have a generous, rather than a selfish, spirit? When you walk by the Salvation Army bucket, do you hand him a coin to put in it and then explain the work they do? Have you given goods to one of the many thrift stores so that they can continue to help neglected/abused children, abused women or disabled veterans? Have you given to the Ronald McDonald House or Target House after explaining to your child how they house the families of very ill children? Do you give your child money to give to missions in your church? Have you been to serve meals at one of the homeless missions in your area with your child? One lady even told me that she would rather her parent give to a worthy cause than to give her a gift. She will probably request that this year.

Did you know that there are scholarships based solely on what the student has contributed to his community? I once opened a scholarship offer that gives a generous amount to a senior who has begun a service to others that was his idea and his effort that got it started. Most scholarships have a place on the application for the community service the student has done, and that answer makes a difference in whether he will receive the monies or not.

I hate to use them as positive examples because their moral lives have and are contributing to decadence in our civilization, but even celebrities are beginning to show generous spirits and are being recognized for it.

The lesson of generosity will bless your child throughout his life, and he will miss it if you are too busy to teach it

PARENTING 101

PARENTING. Not for the "faint of heart". More than just conceiving a child. More than bringing a child home from the hospital. More than babysitting. More than dressing one up and taking him out to be seen by others.

Parenting should involve the planning and preparing for a baby. It should not be an "Oops!" but an "Oh, for joy, we're going to have a baby!!" By then there should be money saved for a nursery; insurance in place for the hospital; meals that strengthen the fetus; foods that increase the mental ability of the coming child. The mother has nine months of carrying the "bundle"; the father has the responsibility of taking care of her and of planning for the future of both of these people he loves.

After the birth, the first three years are crucial to the mental, physical, and social growth of the child. Every child should be read to from the time he can sit in your lap. Every child should be taught his A,B,C's and colors early so he is ready for his first days of education. Every child should have food that does not just add weight to his frame, but gives him strength, agility, and the right amount of growth for his years. Every child should have at least one or two social outlets—whether it is in church, in daycare, in having friends over for play time, in interacting with other siblings. Every child should be taught at an early age to share, to play fair, to ask politely, to respect others, and to obey authority.

In childhood, every child has a right to the attention of both parents as well as their instruction, their care, and their time. Parenting doesn't *go on hold* if both parents work, rather it just means that both parents spend a good amount of time in the morning and evening with the child to let him know that he is the most important thing in their lives, not the job, not friends, not any other obligation.

In pre-adolescence, as children branch out to include peers and friends, Parenting takes on a new level as you teach all-important lessons on social interaction, including the exclusion of bullying, both not to take part and not to be bullied. It includes showing respect to teachers, to grandparents, to people who work in the stores, to law enforcement officers.

In all of these previous years, children need the opportunity to play outside. They need the sunshine, the strength-inducing play like running, chasing, riding bikes, swinging, and any activity that stretches their limbs and tendons and muscles. Parenting does not include entertaining children because they can't "find anything to do". It does include, as one man put it "Sending me out the door after breakfast and Mom's saying she would see me at supper". (He stretched it a little, of course, she did fix lunch for him and his friends.) Parenting does include restrictions on the amount of TV time, internet time, and other time that prohibits physical exercise.

Parenting during the teen years includes setting rules and enforcing them. Being vigilant to problems that may crop up because of peer influence, scary internet access, too much texting, boy/girlfriend problems, self-esteem issues, academic progress or lack of it, teaching manners and other social situations for the future, encouraging an advanced education in college or a skill school, giving lessons on the control of money and giving the opportunity to save and have a checkbook, and multitudes more lessons that must be taught in these years.

Parenting in the after-high-school years includes letting go with reservations. If the child is still in the home, the rules are a little more lax but still there to maintain a good relationship between this now-graduated person and the rest of the family in the home. It includes being available for advice if requested and just being a presence in the young adult's life that is stable and secure. It includes helping him make plans for moving out when he has the money and the time is right but sometime before he is twenty-five.

Bottom line: PARENTING is a full-time effort that involves all of you—your time, your effort, your life lessons, your love. It is not to be entered lightly because there is a little life that depends on you, and that little life will still depend on you for the next eighteen to twenty-two years. You will have to be strong, patient, loving, and giving. There is no room for selfishness or self-indulgence in this important role.

So, if you are not ready for this type of obligation, don't have a child. There is too much at stake for you not to be fully engaged in this process. If you are ready, the world needs more good parents. Go for it!!

RECOMMENDED READING LIST

Blankenthorn, David. *Fatherless America*. New York: Basic Books, 1998.

Bryan, Mark. *The Prodigal Father: Reuniting Fathers and Their Children*. New York: Clarkson Potter, 1997.

Colbert, Don, M.D. *Deadly Emotions*. New York: Thomas Nelson, 2006.

Gurian, Michael. *A Fine Young Man: What Parents, Mentors and Educators Can Do to Shape Adolescent Boys*. New York: Tarcher, 1999.

Pausch, Randy. *The Last Lecture*. New York: Hyperion, 2007.

Pipher, Mary, Ph.d. *Reviving Ophelia: Saving the Selves of Adolescent Girls*. New York: Ballentine Books, 1994.

Slocumb, Paul D. *Hear Our Cry: Boys in Crisis*, Rev. ed. Highlands, TX: Aha! Process, Inc., 2004.

Stovall, Jim. *The Ultimate Gift*. Mechanicsburg. PA: Executive Books, 2000.

Winn, Marie. *Children Without Childhood: Growing Up Too Fast in the World of Sex and Drugs*. London: Penguin Books, 1984.